MW01253757

New Seeds of Profit

New Seeds of Profit

*Business Heroes, Corporate Villains,
and the Future of American Capitalism*

Mark S. Ferrara

LEXINGTON BOOKS
Lanham • Boulder • New York • London

Published by Lexington Books
An imprint of The Rowman & Littlefield Publishing Group, Inc.
4501 Forbes Boulevard, Suite 200, Lanham, Maryland 20706
www.rowman.com

6 Tinworth Street, London SE11 5AL

British Library Cataloguing in Publication Information Available

Library of Congress Cataloging-in-Publication Data

Names: Ferrara, Mark S., author.
Title: New seeds of profit : business heroes, corporate villains, and the future of American capitalism
/ Mark S. Ferrara.
Description: Lanham : Lexington Books, [2019] | Includes bibliographical references and index.
Identifiers: LCCN 2019009841| ISBN 9781498590228 (cloth : alk. paper) | ISBN 9781498590235
(electronic : alk. paper)
Subjects: LCSH: Capitalism—United States. | Equality—United States. | Income distribution—Unit-
ed States. | Entrepreneurship—United States.
Classification: LCC HB501 .F419 2019 | DDC 338.0973—dc23
LC record available at https://lccn.loc.gov/2019009841

∞™ The paper used in this publication meets the minimum requirements of American
National Standard for Information Sciences Permanence of Paper for Printed Library
Materials, ANSI/NISO Z39.48-1992.

For my brother Paul, reluctant corporate citizen

Contents

Acknowledgments

Perhaps no one deserves my gratitude more than Liangmei Bao, for her encouragement to finish this book in a timely manner meant enduring months with her husband hunched over a glowing laptop screen—even during holidays when most folks take a break from workaday life to visit family and friends. I always remember my teachers Walter Coppedge, Cliff Edwards, and Marcel Cornis-Pope at Virginia Commonwealth University and W. Scott Howard at the University of Denver for their continual support. I also owe a debt of appreciation to many friends and colleagues who reviewed sections of this work in draft form, or contributed to it through dialogue, especially Walter Coppedge, J. Jeremy Wisnewski, Wesley Graves, Arnaud Brichon, Geoffrey and Shirley O'Shea, Adam Spingler, Patricia Gourlay, Matthew Hendley, Tony Ferrara, and Kathleen Spivack (author and daughter of economist Peter Drucker).

How wonderful to have the encouragement of my mother Nicole Ann Jones, a retired nursing professional who knows firsthand the negative consequences of the corporatization of healthcare delivery. My father, gone from our red-dust world for eight years now, would have been proud of this study—though he might have disagreed with some of its assertions, particularly those concerning afflictive desire. My grandmother Rosalie Nitti passed away during the writing of this book, and while her life was tragic in many ways and profoundly hurtful to those closest to her, it was filled with moments of joy and good works that with the mercy of the Lord will lead her soul to the white light of peace.

The librarians and student-staff at Milne Library cheerfully assisted me in securing many of the books referenced herein through interlibrary loan. I also recall the robin who twice tried to nest under the small pagoda where the first draft of *New Seeds of Profit* was penned. She could not abide our proximity despite my best efforts to share that creative space. In addition to depriving her of a brood that year, a nearby hornet's nest had to come down after their air traffic became a hazard to the writer. During that busy summer, two cheeky chipmunks stashed away supplies of Virginia peanuts for the long New York winter, a baby bunny found a home under our deck, and the neighborhood three-legged doe miraculously survived another year—with fawns!

Introduction

Merchants in European Markets

Jamestown and Plymouth, two of the earliest European colonies in North America, were founded by joint-stock companies for the sake of profit. This curious feature of American history helps to explain a persistent valorization of commerce, trade, and industry, as well as the esteemed place that Americans reserve for their most successful business leaders (granting to them levels of celebrity normally allotted to acclaimed inventors, skillful diplomats, accomplished athletes, and superstar entertainers). As a consequence, more than any other nation, the United States developed a business culture—and its privileging of business and its leaders stands out in world history, where one frequently encounters perceptions of those plying the mercantile arts as conniving, manipulative, untrustworthy, and selfish—personality traits that excluded them from the upper echelons of society. The traditional Hindu social order, for example, relegated merchants to the third of four castes: they occupied the bottom rung in Tokugawa Japan (under samurai lords, artisans, and farmers), and in prerevolutionary France merchants were consigned to the Third Estate below the clergy and the nobility.

National cultures, composed of symbols and representations as well as institutions, may be conceived as discourses—ways of creating meaning that influence and organize our actions and our conceptions of ourselves.[1] National cultures construct identity by producing meaning about the nation through the telling and retelling of stories in literature, history, popular culture, and the media. All nations invent and reinvent stories to explain geographical borders, the origins of a people, and the idealization of a national character, and these reservoirs of narratives, images, and rituals—representing the shared sorrows, triumphs, and disasters of a nation—function as

1

principal sources of cultural identity.[2] In countries with ancient cultures (such as India and China), foundational narratives may stretch so far into the past that they become more mythic than historic.[3] By contrast, American founding myths, grounded firmly in sixteenth-century Calvinist doctrines prescribing hard work as the primary means to material prosperity, were uniquely infused with an openness to entrepreneurialism. These narratives emphasized diligence and productivity, turning a profit, and investing returns back into business enterprises.[4] Although early Americans traditionally measured business achievement "by counting the material rewards" (i.e., by the amount of money acquired), they simultaneously looked askance at lavish spending and riotous living, and instead valued the productive use of wealth through economic activity that integrated the land, labor, and capital in the production and exchange of goods.[5]

In pursuit of the origins of the American valorization of entrepreneurialism and its consequences in the twenty-first century, we reach back to the formation of markets and the rise of the merchant class in medieval Europe, for there we discover the capital accumulations that financed colonial enterprises in North America centuries later. The very earliest European business activities remain obscured in the mists of time, but it is highly unlikely that "markets and merchants were ever entirely absent from Western Europe."[6] Jewish merchants maintained trading networks until the ninth century (when they were destroyed by Norse invaders), and early monastics gathered the surpluses from their farms for exchange in local markets. When the German invasions of the fifth and sixth centuries left the cities of Italy and Gaul vulnerable to attack, aristocrats moved to their rural estates and surrounded themselves with agricultural dependents and military aids for defense. In the countryside, they sought economic self-sufficiency because decaying roads, highway brigandry, and the interruption of communications meant that commerce contracted, industry declined, and state revenues dwindled.[7]

To protect themselves from Saracen, Norse, and Magyar marauders during the eighth, ninth, and tenth centuries, European aristocrats coordinated defensive building projects and deployed military organizational models. Commoners prudently built their homes as close to a baronial castle or fortified monastery as possible, and in return for the protections offered by that proximity, they readily pledged allegiance to serve a lord (i.e., a law-ward) or a duke. Freemen requiring shelter and sustenance frequently contributed land or labor to survival efforts, and the feudalism that developed out of this arrangement codified the economic subjection and military alliance of a man to a superior, in return for economic organization and military protection.[8] Together with silver coined in new mints, fortified city walls offered the stability, market demand, and modicum of law and order needed to buoy manufacture and trade. In Italy, cities regained a measure of cultural continuity after the collapse of the western Roman Empire, though Flanders became the most densely urbanized region of Europe (with nearly every one of its cities established during the tenth and eleventh centuries). [9]

Cities, creations of law, offered their residents special rights of property holding, limited self-government, and jurisdiction granted by the sovereign in a foundation charter. The formal recognition of cities, frequently on the site of established market towns with sizable populations of merchants and artisans, created affluence and stirred demand for luxury goods among nobles. Peasants worked to supply a surplus, but merchants converted that surplus into money, purchased coveted luxury goods to sell to nobles, and thus profited from the role of the entrepreneur. In fact, the first great age of European business history was nothing more than a nearly infinite number of variations on this simple theme. [10] As markets arose in London and its surroundings, some of them (including those at Norwich, Winchester, and Lincoln) achieved regional importance by the Norman conquest of England in 1066. The main impetus for organizing markets, beyond local needs, came from religious customs associated with a cycle of festivals or fairs that brought people together, frequently on feast days commemorating local saints.

The medieval travelers who attended those celebrations provided merchants with customers, and gradually a cycle of fairs developed from the mid-eleventh to early twelfth centuries. Generally held between February and the beginning of November, and organized with two- to four-week intervals between events to allow for travel among locations, fairs lasted for up to thirty days. Champagne in north central France, situated on the most important overland routes connecting Flanders and England with the Mediterranean trading networks of the south, became a favored meeting place for northern and southern merchants and their merchandise. The fairs held in Champagne were the first truly international marketplaces in scope and significance and, enlivened by the increasing use of coinage, they reached an apex in the thirteenth century. [11]

While they depended on each other for survival, social relationships between lords, peasants, and merchants were driven by a combination of cooperation and compulsion, and therefore a stratified hereditary class system took shape based on birth, land, and localism that tied occupation and property to family units proudly conscious of their status over several generations. In feudal Europe, the lord (*dominus, seigneur, Herr*) was the manager of men. He protected his lands and the peasants living on them, organized agriculture and trade on his properties, and served his king in war. Lords founded markets (to sell the surfeit from their manors), exercised judicial and military powers over their domains, and unduly profited from fines levied in the manorial court. [12] Generally speaking, serfs retained customary rights to remain on the land, and they were prevented by custom from suffering confiscation of their surplusage. While social and economic realities varied significantly across Europe (villages were of many types, different crops were raised, and relations between lords and serfs took many forms), medieval peasants were largely unfree. Through relentless toil, however, they "fed themselves and their masters, their soldiers, clergy, and kings."[13]

Because medieval social hierarchies fixed people into the status and income into which they were born, the feudal or manorial social system was predisposed toward tradition and continuity, and highly resistant to change. Dominated by a nobility geared to the values of land, rank, family, arms, and honor as part of a chivalric code, the body of values it espoused was notably inhospitable to trade and the trader.[14] Since they viewed ownership and tillage of the land as sources of power, wealth, and prestige, the landed nobility regarded merchants as social inferiors—an attitude that persisted in northern Europe into the twentieth century. Manorialism or seigneurialism (the sum of man-made productive forces brought to bear in the forests, fields, and pastures of Europe) meant compelling peasants to the land, demanding various rents and payments from them, choosing the crops they grew, and requiring that their grain be milled at the lord's mills and bread baked in his ovens.[15] Medieval lords derived prodigious abundance from this model of organization, though they were too often indifferent to its social and economic consequences.

As their fortunes grew, the landed gentry developed a taste for the provisions of the "civilized" life, as peasants yearned only to secure survival for themselves and their families through unfettered use of the land.[16] Agriculture organized itself to meet those demands and laid the groundwork for the economic success of the High Middle Ages (around the eleventh, twelfth, and thirteenth centuries). Innovations such as the plow, water mill, and other technological breakthroughs saved labor in the fields that could be redeployed toward more specialized ends. Soon, the millwright produced the mill and the blacksmith the plow. Still, increases in output that resulted from specialization could not accommodate the needs of a growing population or satisfy aristocratic appetites for luxury goods. As a result, lords offered incentives for settling the hinterlands, and new communities were founded by chipping away at surrounding forests and putting more land under plow. From these circumstances peasants gained an increased share of crop production and the ability to move elsewhere—though many remained impoverished.[17]

The rise of self-employed members of the artisan class and masters of trade during the High Middle Ages, another important economic advancement, contributed to the formation of capitalism in later centuries. Many independent artisans and tradesmen worked out of the home, and the family became the basis of their business unit. The production of their wares might take place in the home, or in an adjacent outbuilding, but every member of the family contributed (in some way) to their completion. The apprenticeship system extended kinship relations and allowed masters to enter into contracts with the parents or guardians of minors to train, feed, clothe, and shelter them over several years in return for their labor.[18] After finishing a period of specialist training, apprentices might become wage laborers, journeymen (itinerant laborers), or even masters in their own right. The guild system also encouraged masters to form trade associations in the "industrial" crafts (including textile production, mining, construction, and transportation) that organized the production and distribution of many products. Although they tended toward monopoly, guild associations generally sought to regulate competition rather than eliminate it.[19] Theoretically, all guild masters were equal, but richer masters hired servants to complete less-skilled parts of production, or hired poorer masters and their shops outright, thus effectively reducing those masters to wage laborers and transforming themselves into capitalist entrepreneurs.[20]

As the merchant class grew with economic expansion, those belonging to it took on increasingly important social roles despite maintaining an uneasy relationship with a Church that looked disapprovingly upon mercantile minds and material pursuits. Catholic doctrine progressively modified an Augustinian view that business was inherently evil (because it turned people away from the quest for true rest in God).[21] Even after writers such as St. Thomas helped to reformulate Christian code to permit a wider array of capitalist activities, the Catholic Church never sanctified the economic practices of the merchant-entrepreneur, nor could it condone the entrepreneurial drive for worldly achievement in the same way that Calvinism later supplied a fortifying ethic for business activity.[22] Nevertheless, Catholic crusading marked an important stage in the growth of commercial exchange, since conducting foreign wars on such a large scale required transporting thousands of warriors and pilgrims to the edge of the then-known world and back again. The trading opportunities that resulted from those large-scale operations inspired some merchants to "hit the road" following routes popularized by knights, sailors, missionaries, and pilgrims. Lures of wealth, opened along with trade and religious tourism, proved irresistible to peasants, merchants, and lords alike. Active commerce began off the coasts of Syria and Egypt, for example, and tastes in food, clothing, and other consumer goods were forever altered as commodities from India came through Alexandria to Italy and spread across Europe.[23]

Many types of merchants plied their wares in growing market towns throughout northern Europe and the western Mediterranean during the thirteenth century. The wealth and social status of merchants depended on whether they were global traders, local dealers, artisans, or petty traders, as well as if these goods were regarded as "noble" or "base."[24] Global traders in luxury goods occupied the top rung of that mercantile order and itinerant peddlers the bottom. Successful merchants of the great Mediterranean trading ports enjoyed preeminence and formed the governing elite, but in inland Italy and Flanders the landed nobility remained contemptuous of trade and, like the Church, viewed the merchant class as inferior. Nevertheless, merchants provided the raw material and most of the capital for the production of trade goods, and they profited commensurately from the risks of their endeavors. Foreign trade, for instance, carried the promise of substantial rewards given the manifold opportunities for financial ruin (from shipwrecks to brigandry) inherent in such protracted engagements. As a class, merchants became progressively more prosperous in later centuries, and they were quick to convert their influence as capitalists, financiers, and moneylenders into political power on town boards. [25]

In Florence, in the late thirteenth century, merchant families became tax collectors for the papacy, and subsequently they opened banks in many European cities and profited from investments, loans, and exchanges of money. [26] Financial tools for managing risk (such as marine insurance), partnership contracts and shareholding, new accounting methods, letters of credit, and bills of exchange eliminated the need for transporting coinage across borders along with goods and encouraged the growth of long-distance trade. [27] Christian prohibitions against usury gave rise to various methods for their circumvention, including writing contracts for more than sums lent, awarding "gifts" to lenders, or assessing fees for "damages." [28] As the administrator of Western Europe's largest single enterprise, the Church slowly learned to appreciate the social contributions of business, to understand the economy, and to engage in commerce itself. Religious tourism made up nearly all leisure travel in medieval Europe, and pilgrimages to holy sites (far and near) depended upon networks of monasteries and hostels for food and boarding along trading routes. That increased movement fomented a brisk trade in relics too. Geoffrey Chaucer's pilgrims provide modern readers with an enchanting window onto medieval pilgrimages to Canterbury, and his bawdy Merchant's Tale features a humorous depiction of a self-interested misogynist who turns marriage into a business transaction and views his wife as a commodity (who brings ease to his later years).

While many merchant and monetary societies existed around the world, they did not develop the "new form of capitalism, endowed with such great creative and destructive capabilities" as that which took shape in Western Europe by the sixteenth century. [29] It emerged within Europe because as part of "Western Christian civilization," European nations shared a common worldview, "a similar frame of rational-legal forms, and the basic institutional requisites of capitalist development (transferability of resources, free labor, et cetera)," which gave the entrepreneur a role of special significance. [30] Where once the beliefs and values of the medieval world preserved a hierarchical social structure with values "notably inhospitable to trade and the trader," and medieval European lay society remained openly contemptuous of the "aggressive commercial behavior functionally inherent to an expanding capitalism," those attitudes transmuted as the merchant class displaced the aristocracy as repositories of prodigious wealth in later centuries.[31] Across Western Europe, commercial capitalism and bourgeois institutions ruptured feudalism, and as those forces began to prevail, they brought the rationalism and secularism that cut deeply into traditional values, symbols, and relationships.

In the fifteenth century, urban merchants in Italy, Germany, and the Netherlands developed new business techniques that included various forms of contracts, some of them temporary partnerships and others more permanent arrangements, called in Italian *compagnie* (the root of the English word "company"), which organized land and sea expeditions in search of better routes, sources of supply, and markets.[32] Venture-oriented merchant banks, monarchical greed, systematized pillage, organized traffic in slaves, and forced vagabondage helped to create the capital that made colonial settlements, including those in North America, possible. That villainous hunt for wealth via trade and plunder began in earnest as Bartolomeu Dias led an expedition around the Cape of Good Hope in 1487, Christopher Columbus made landfall in the Americas in 1492, and Vasco da Gama arrived on the shores of India in 1497. Companies representing business interests and speculations financed similar expeditions, and soon "capital, more abundant merchandise, sailing ships, and weapons" fostered the expansion of commerce and conquest.[33]

Investors in Francis Drake's circumnavigation of the globe (1577–1580), for instance, received a return on their investment of a staggering 4,700 percent.[34] Massive returns of that sort resulted from an influx of gold and silver bullion from the New World. Consider that a single site mined by the Spanish crown (Cerro de Potosí in present-day Bolivia) accounted for an astonishing 60 percent of the world's silver production in the sixteenth and seventeenth centuries.[35] The pious pretext of converting indigenous populations may have sanctified these enterprises, but unadorned greed drove colonial activities in the Americas. For example, the conquistadores hauled away 1.3 million ounces of gold in a single load after the plunder of the Incas in 1534, and official figures (likely underestimating the spoils of conquest) show that *18,000 tons of silver and 200 tons of gold* were transferred from the Americas to Spain between 1521 and 1660.[36] Although global trade did not get fully under way until the seventeenth century, the business schemes of these explorers heralded the beginning of a "continuous and lasting maritime connection among the earth's large landmasses" over which the exchange of products became continuous enough, and sufficient in quantity and value, to fundamentally influence all trading partners involved.[37] As that nexus of trade became stronger and more intense in later centuries, silver and gold wrested from the Americas provided capital for mercantile exchanges, as well as for more labor-intensive endeavors such as plantation agriculture.

The production of sugarcane, the trade in slaves, and the extraction of precious metals and ores from the earth—these were the means by which European adventurers, nobles, and merchants built their fortunes. For the native inhabitants of the New World, their first encounters with the avaricious Europeans were portentous: they were slain in war, sent to Europe as slaves, or consumed in the mines. Between 1495 and 1503, over 3 million people simply disappeared from the islands of the New World, and in little more than a century, the indigenous population of Mexico fell from 25 million to just 1.5 million, and in Peru it declined by 95 percent.[38] With the conversion into capital of peasant surpluses from previous centuries, combined with returns from the pillage of the Americas, the economy in many parts of Europe was quite different after 1600 from that of just two centuries before. In places like northern Italy, the Netherlands, London, and Paris, wealth increasingly derived not from land, but from trade and production. Investment in machinery needed to process metal and cloth goods grew, and governments at all levels began bestowing tax exemptions and issuing licenses to trade. Accumulated state capital took the form of royal manufacturers, ports, and highways, while bourgeois capital was concentrated in real estate, private fortunes, and precious metals.[39] In this manner, capitalism put into place the future developments of nation-states by means of conquest and domination; a banking and merchant bourgeoisie with immense fortunes and financial networks; and (most crucially to all these projects) a conception of the world that valued wealth and enrichment.

Although the corporate charters of the twelfth and thirteenth centuries provided a prototype for incorporation, they were more frequently created to formalize a borough or municipality (with a mayor and aldermen forming the corporation), rather than a business as we know it. A corporation assumed that the chartering authority (usually a king) would delegate the creation of a body politic and employ political power to ends specified in the instrument that created it.[40] By the seventeenth century, incorporated commercial companies, superimposed over the guild structure of association, sought to maintain harmony between members and emphasize their mutual economic interests. Factors of the Levant and East India Companies, for instance, "shared a camaraderie abroad and they acted dutifully as executors for each other after returning to England."[41] Most importantly, the corporate structure helped to guarantee perpetual succession and continuity of management, to protect sea lanes, and to maintain forts and factories established on foreign territory. A single institution with fixed assets could coordinate shipping, regulate the flow of goods, purchase in advance and sell in bulk, avoid wasteful duplication of services, and lobby for diplomatic, military, and naval support.

In addition, regulated companies provided a compromise between individual and group organization, and they became the preferred choice of merchants because they provided an institutional framework for their business activities while leaving members free to exercise their own initiative and employ their own capital. Joint-stock companies, by contrast, traded on borrowed capital through the issuance of bonds, and many of them were rather small, informal concerns with unlimited liability and a short life.[42] The classic case is the East India Company, which initially did not have imperial ambitions, and suffered from inertia and indecision, compromises and delays, and slow communications that made directors leery of acting based on information most likely already overtaken by events. What made the East India Company profitable, at least for its employees (if not passive shareholders), was corruption and the private trade, for senior officers responsible for enforcing company policy were themselves dishonest. That private trade could not be eliminated altogether either, since it was necessary to maintaining the flow of goods. Early joint-stock companies, in other words, succeeded not because they were legal-rational entities that followed universal rules, but rather due to "a coalition of individual merchants who identified for their own personal gain the areas of greatest profit."[43]

On the other hand, some entrepreneurs in seventeenth-century England ignored obvious possibilities for profit, failed to distinguish bold possibilities from lunatic ideas, overresponded to market stimulus, and were either overconfident or too undisciplined to prosper. Several ruined their associations, but they were usually indifferent to the harm inflicted on others, while success tended to breed complacency as "innovators of one generation became the conservatives of the next."[44] Those failures notwithstanding, entrepreneurial behavior (directed toward diverse ends) filled growing demand for manufactured and imported goods, a call that began in the late fourteenth century and led to a substantial consumer boom in the seventeenth century. That dynamism in the English economy produced a plethora of creative entrepreneurs who responded aggressively to events, who committed to change oriented towards growth, who chose to invest in new concepts and techniques, and who inspired others to learn from their failures.

The historical timing of the establishment of American colonial settlements resulted in a highly selective social and cultural transfer of European heritage that privileged an entrepreneurship conducive to private capitalist development. That selective inheritance included Puritanism, Lockean individualism, Newtonian automatic harmonies, and the late Enlightenment's faith in reason and individual effort as a means of human progress. Given new lands and opportunities, "American society fused these elements into a new faith, into a new vision of the promise of American life. Oriented toward building an ever-expanding future spelled out in terms of increasing material welfare, confident of the inevitable progress of man therefrom, glorifying economic achievement, mobility, competition, change, boldness, bigness, it was a creed designed to fortify creative and aggressive entrepreneurship."[45] Still, the earliest colonies in North America were tiny and underfunded affairs, and so colonial inhabitants frequently depended on the generosity of indigenous people to survive. The first ventures proved so precarious that half failed due to conquest by another colonial power, disease, abandonment, economic or environmental collapse, or indigenous opposition.

By the 1660s, a second wave of North American colonies took hold, many of them founded by England, a rising power whose forces occupied New Netherland (and the settlement at New Amsterdam) and renamed it "New York."[46] English colonies in South Carolina and Georgia established in 1670 created a buffer between Virginia and the Spanish territories in Florida, and they provided an opportunity for the introduction of profitable subtropical crops, including indigo, tobacco, and rice. Georgia also became a penal colony for the transportation of debtors, vagrants, and criminals.[47] In light of the intensive demands of large-scale cultivation of sugarcane, tobacco, and cotton in the American and Caribbean colonies, Europe could never have supplied enough laborers, due to its limited population. To locate workers and reduce operational costs, Europeans originally enslaved Native Americans, but many of those luckless human beings perished as a consequence of excessive labor, poor diet, and torturous treatment. Colonizers looked next to indentured poor whites and put convicts into service, before turning to Africa for a supply of forced slave labor.[48] The first English slave-trading expedition took place in 1562, and those captured were sold to Spaniards and bound for the West Indies. That trade remained desultory and perfunctory until the establishment of British colonies in the Caribbean and the rise of the sugar industry.[49]

The Company of Royal Adventurers, a monopolistic enterprise, was granted control of the slave trade in 1663 for a period of 1,000 years. Failing within ten, it was followed by the Royal African Company in 1672, whose monopoly was broken in 1698 when the free trade in slaves was recognized as a natural right of Englishmen. The Royal African Company went bankrupt shortly thereafter, but corporate business had turned human beings into commodities to be bought and sold in international markets. As many as 2 million people were enslaved throughout the British colonies between 1680 and 1786. Where once the Royal African Company conveyed about 5,000 slaves per year, following the introduction of free trade, ships sailed with a total capacity of 36,000 slaves in 1760—a figure that rose to 47,000 by 1771.[50] One reason for that expansion was slave gangs made more profitable use of the land than small farmers could alone. On the flipside, plantation slavery quickly depleted the soil, and constant expansion became necessary to colonial slave societies (such as those in the South, which gradually moved westward).[51] In time, the plantation slavery model would also revolutionize the cotton industry, an important base for modern capitalism.

The commencement of the consumerism that now defines the cultures of the West (and others around the world) can be located in the increased appetites of seventeenth-century Europeans, who devoured ever-greater quantities of tobacco, caffeine drinks, and sugar products—passions stoked by the lobbying efforts of trading companies, merchants, and planters (in the belief that the supply of these commodities would come under better control through the expansion of trade).[52] As the public clamored for tropical goods such as pepper, spices, textiles, and cacao, merchants grasped the means by which to accumulate capital, while governments grew their revenues by granting monopolies and charging import duties and excise taxes.[53] In nearly every case, the sites chosen for European colonies reflected consumer calls for tropical "luxury" goods (many of which later became staple household products). Demand was also considerable for low-quality metalwares and lightweight textiles, two of the manufactured goods in which industrialization first manifested itself.[54]

In the early seventeenth century, London was home to wealthy merchants with capital available to invest in large ventures like those waiting on the other side of the Atlantic, only they understood from the sixteenth-century failure of the "lost colony" at Roanoke Island (found abandoned and its inhabitants disappeared) that the colonization of the continent would not be an individual endeavor. Together, urban capitalists and aristocratic landed politicians made focused attempts at permanent colonial settlements, but instead of providing protective military posts, royal administrators, and state-financed exploration and mapping, "the crown turned the job of colony building over to the corporate entrepreneurs."[55] The colonies that would later make up the United States became businesses as soon as prominent men such as Walter Raleigh, Thomas Smith, and John Popham sought the aid of substantial merchants anxious to exploit the New World through the device of the chartered stock company.[56] This decision by the crown gave settlers the initiative that they needed to profit from their labor and investments, and it contributed to the individualism and mercantile orientation that still characterize the United States. The nation's earliest settlers brought with them a hierarchical social system that accepted high degrees of inequality in terms of wealth, power, and position. Even so, the realities of colony founding demanded communal relationships and mutual cooperation—a feature of American society that stands in contrast to the "impersonality, universalism, individualism, and conscious rationality characteristic of a wide range of capitalist institutions" that emerged in Europe after 1500.[57]

Conspicuously present over 400 years of American history, commerce remains as "important as any social institution other than the family and its social or religious rituals."[58] Positive American business values encourage material well-being, an optimistic confidence in the effectiveness of individual effort and self-help, and a conviction in hard work as the primary means to success. The tendency for Americans to make cultural heroes out of self-made entrepreneurs, tycoons, and inventors—from Benjamin Franklin and Cornelius Vanderbilt to Andrew Carnegie and Henry Ford—is explored in chapter 1. That overview helps to account for the admiration and esteem in which many Americans continue to hold their business leaders—as well as the unexpected rise of a narcissistic business mogul and reality television star with no political experience to the highest elected office in the land in 2016.

Americans have historically bestowed social prestige and political power upon successful merchants and entrepreneurs in the belief that society as a whole benefited from their commercial activities. Chapter 2 challenges that heroic view of capital by illustrating the ends to which American business leaders and their companies have gone to exploit human and natural resources in the name of profit. As one of the most powerful sectors in society, American business controls the flow of resources (from food to oil) and has a disproportionate voice in how the country is run—and by whom.[59] Since highly effective corporate advertising campaigns encourage consumption-driven lifestyles that intensify our material appetites but fail to make us happier, chapter 3 features religious and literary warnings against afflictive desire, as it outlines the contours of the mercantile mind and explores the high rate of psychopathy among leaders of modern corporations.

The final two sections retain the thematic opposition between heroes and villains of American business. Chapter 4 interrogates the supposition that business and science (handmaidens in our New Gilded Age) make our lives more affluent, comfortable, and exciting by letting market forces direct production and consumption—and it scrutinizes the effects of downsizing and outsourcing, of eliminating employee pensions and cutting healthcare benefits, and of maximizing profits and shareholder returns at any cost. The conclusion, by contrast, posits the emergence of a new business hero who puts people before profit, models good stewardship of the earth, and yet grows rich. It highlights the added value of environmentally conscientious business planning, the benefits of corporate social responsibility, and the importance of providing self-actualizing just work. The new seeds of profit are being sown every day—and the enlightened business leaders featured in the conclusion suggest the potential for enterprise to drive healthful social transformation. As renowned consultant and author Peter Drucker reminds us, if the leaders and managers of our major institutions, "and especially of business, do not take responsibility for the common good, no one else can or will."[60]

NOTES

1. Stuart Hall, "The Question of Cultural Identity," in *Modernity and Its Futures: Understanding Modern Societies*, ed. Stuart Hall, David Held, and Tony McGrew (Cambridge: Polity Press, 2003), 292.

2. Hall, "The Question of Cultural Identity," 293.

3. Hall, "The Question of Cultural Identity," 294–95.

4. James Oliver Robertson, *American Myth, American Reality* (New York: Hill & Wang, 1980), 194.

5. Herman E. Krooss and Charles Gilbert, *American Business History* (New York: Prentice-Hall, 1972), 6.

6. Edwin S. Hunt and James Murray, *A History of Business in Medieval Europe, 1200–1550* (Cambridge: Cambridge University Press, 1999), 24

7. Will Durant, *The Age of Faith: A History of Medieval Civilization—Christian, Islamic, and Judaic—from Constantine to Dante: A.D. 325–1300* (New York: Simon and Schuster, 1950), 552.

8. Durant, *The Age of Faith*, 553.

9. Hunt and Murray, *A History of Business in Medieval Europe*, 27.

10. Hunt and Murray, *A History of Business in Medieval Europe*, 28.

11. Hunt and Murray, *A History of Business in Medieval Europe*, 25–27.

12. Durant, *The Age of Faith*, 560.

13. Durant, *The Age of Faith*, 552, 558.

14. John E. Sawyer, "Entrepreneur and Social Order," in *Men in Business: Essays in the History of Entrepreneurship*, edited by William Miller (Cambridge: Harvard University Press, 1952), 11.

15. Hunt and Murray, *A History of Business in Medieval Europe*, 18.

16. Hunt and Murray, *A History of Business in Medieval Europe*, 15.

17. Hunt and Murray, *A History of Business in Medieval Europe*, 19–20.

18. Hunt and Murray, *A History of Business in Medieval Europe*, 32–34.

19. Hunt and Murray, *A History of Business in Medieval Europe*, 34–35.

20. Merry E. Wiesner-Hanks, *Early Modern Europe, 1450–1789* (Cambridge: Cambridge University Press, 2006), 208–09.

21. Hunt and Murray, *A History of Business in Medieval Europe*, 11.

22. Sawyer, "Entrepreneur and Social Order," 12.

23. Hunt and Murray, *A History of Business in Medieval Europe*, 32.

24. Hunt and Murray, *A History of Business in Medieval Europe*, 52.

25. Hunt and Murray, *A History of Business in Medieval Europe*, 54–55.

26. Wiesner-Hanks, *Early Modern Europe,* 37.

27. Hunt and Murray, *A History of Business in Medieval Europe*, 64–65.

28. Hunt and Murray, *A History of Business in Medieval Europe*, 72–73.

29. Michel Beaud, *A History of Capitalism: 1500–2000* (New York: Monthly Review Press), 9–11.

30. Sawyer, "Entrepreneur and Social Order," 10.

31. Sawyer, "Entrepreneur and Social Order," 11.

32. Wiesner-Hanks, *Early Modern Europe*, 16.

33. Beaud, *A History of Capitalism*, 14.

34. Arturo Giraldez, *The Age of Trade: The Manila Galleons and the Dawn of the Global Economy* (Lanham, MD: Rowman & Littlefield, 2015), 30.

35. Giraldez, *The Age of Trade*, 30.

36. Beaud, *A History of Capitalism*, 15.

37. Giraldez, *The Age of Trade*, 29.

38. Beaud, *A History of Capitalism*, 15.

39. Beaud, *A History of Capitalism*, 21.

40. Oscar Handlin, "The Development of the Corporation," in *The Corporation: A Theological Inquiry*, edited by Michael Novak and John W. Cooper (Washington: AEI Press, 1981), 1–16.

41. Richard Grassby, *The Business Community of Seventeenth-Century England* (Cambridge: Cambridge University Press, 1995), 365.

42. Grassby, *The Business Community of Seventeenth-Century England*, 404–05.

43. Grassby, *The Business Community of Seventeenth-Century England*, 406–407.

44. Grassby, *The Business Community of Seventeenth-Century England*, 411.

45. Sawyer, "Entrepreneur and Social Order," 20–21.

46. Wiesner-Hanks, *Early Modern Europe*, 459–61.

47. Wiesner-Hanks, *Early Modern Europe*, 461.

48. Eric Williams, *Capitalism and Slavery* (Chapel Hill: University of North Carolina Press, 1994), 6–7.

49. Williams, *Capitalism and Slavery*, 30–31.

50. Williams, *Capitalism and Slavery*, 31–32.

51. Williams, *Capitalism and Slavery*, 7.

52. Carole Shammas, "The Revolutionary Impact of European Demand for Tropical Goods," in *The Early Modern Atlantic Economy*, edited by John J. McCusker and Kenneth Morgan (Cambridge: Cambridge University Press, 2001), 171.

53. Shammas, "The Revolutionary Impact of European Demand for Tropical Goods," 172.

54. Shammas, "The Revolutionary Impact of European Demand for Tropical Goods," 179.

55. Thomas C. Cochran, *Business in American Life: A History* (New York: McGraw-Hill, 1972), 9.

56. Cochran, *Business in American Life: A History*, 9.

57. John E. Sawyer, "Entrepreneur and Social Order," in *Men in Business: Essays in the History of Entrepreneurship*, edited by William Miller (Cambridge: Harvard University Press, 1952), 11.

58. Cochran, *Business in American Life*, 1.

59. Mihaly Csikszentmihalyi, *Good Business: Leadership, Flow, and the Making of Meaning* (New York: Viking, 2003), 189.

60. Allan Ornstein, *Class Counts: Education, Inequality, and the Shrinking Middle Class* (Lanham, MD: Rowman & Littlefield, 2006), 195.

Chapter One

Titans, Tycoons, and Captains of Industry

Feudal lords successfully encouraged peasant laborers to clear the hinterlands and put them under tillage during the late Middle Ages in Europe. The expansion of the guild system and the early stirrings of industrialization made natural resources and cultivatable land increasingly scarce, and the prospects of upward mobility and financial improvement narrowed. Hence, the New World became an attractive option for those seeking new opportunities. Jamestown, the first permanent English settlement in North America, was chartered by the London Company (a joint-stock enterprise) and established with clear commercial and mercantile objectives. The funds raised by the London Company, which by charter controlled land and resources, outfitted the Jamestown expedition with supplies for the settlers who worked on its behalf. Investors in that enterprise hoped to generate wealth by converting an abundance of natural resources, such as timber for building and ship making, into capital—and they stood to profit in accordance with the size of their investments.

The first English settlers to arrive in North America were intrepid souls who undertook the perilous voyage from Europe in search of profit, as much as for God or political freedom. In December 1606, John Smith sct sail with the Virginia-bound expedition comprising three ships, 155 settlers, and fifty-five crewmen; those aboard endured a miserable six weeks at sea off the English coast amid storms and contrary winds, which delayed their entry into Chesapeake Bay until late April 1607.[1] Had they more quickly agreed upon a settlement site, they might not have missed the spring planting season, much to their peril. The location eventually chosen possessed virtues, such as being high enough for the largest ships to tie directly to shore, but it was situated in a low-lying swampland, surrounded by marshes and tar bogs, and it could easily be cut off by Native Americans. The settlers built a desultory fortification of sorts (named James Fort), but no houses. Instead, gentlemen stayed in crude tents, and commoners slept on the ground. When the scorching heat and thick humidity of summer hit, their water supply grew foul, and a combination of improper diet and pestilence resulted in an onslaught of disease (including scurvy, dysentery, and typhoid). By September, forty-eight people had died, and the winter brought influenza and pneumonia, so that by January 1608, twenty-eight more perished.[2]

Although the situation remained dire, the arrival of the first supplies later in the year and the assistance of Native Americans (some of whom would live to regret helping the Europeans) somewhat stabilized the settlement. Captain Smith, an unlikely and controversial early leader of the Virginia Colony (also charged with mutiny on the voyage from England), managed to bring some semblance of order to the floundering venture and to survey the upper Chesapeake Bay along with the Potomac, Susquehanna, and Rappahannock rivers. Those missions provided valuable geographical data, but after two years, the London Company managed to secure only a small beachhead in Virginia—and their stockholders received no dividends. Even the "gilded dirte" that hopeful settlers sent home turned out to be fool's gold (iron pyrite).[3] As new settlers streamed in, lured by untold promises, they added to difficulties the leadership experienced providing sustenance to those already there. During the bleak winter of 1609—10, known as the Starving Time, as many as 430 of 500 settlers died. After five brutal years and the arrival of 1,600 colonists (two-thirds of whom perished), the Plantation of Virginia in America was firmly settled.[4] Although the gold and silver anticipated by investors never materialized, Jamestown was the earliest English colony to survive, and it became a template for those that followed.

Smith returned to England in 1609 to nurse a terrible leg injury, but in 1614 he sailed again, this time for the coasts of Massachusetts and Maine, christening the region "New England." The son of a yeoman and landholder, Smith raised himself from relatively humble origins to attain a good measure of prominence in the world as an author and explorer. In striving to overcome the obstacles that he encountered in life, he made himself into one of the first entrepreneur heroes in American history. His romanticized account of seeking food from the Powhatan people for his starving comrades, and his rescue from imminent execution by a daughter of the chief of the Powhatan Confederacy (Pocahontas) raise legitimate questions about Smith's credibility. Through his pen and his adventures, Smith nevertheless became an effective advocate for the mercantile settlement of the New World.[5] In *A Description of New England* (1616), a prospectus for investors and settlers, Smith extoled the profits that industry and hard work would bring to those willing to settle the territories that he charted. Some of those who took up his challenge yearned for religious freedom along with the wealth that for them signified

God's grace, and indeed the Puritans and Pilgrims brought English society, and its entrepreneurial spirit, with them to North America in a more comprehensive way than the original (mostly male) settlers of Jamestown.[6]

More than one hundred Pilgrims, a radical faction of the religious reform movement Puritanism (so called for its desire to purify the Church of England) left Europe behind in 1620 to establish a colony at Plymouth. After little more than two months at sea, the *Mayflower* landed on the shores of Cape Cod in present-day Massachusetts. Following a disastrous first winter, in which half of their company perished due to lack of proper housing and infection with scurvy and other maladies from the voyage, the comparative success of Plymouth Colony is attributable to a careful study of Jamestown's record and a learning of its lessons.[7] Histories written by seventeenth-century English Puritans indicate that they saw themselves as establishing a City of God, after St. Augustine. Accordingly, they celebrated the stalwart dedication of the first generation of founders (including William Bradford, John Winthrop, and Edward Johnson) together with members of the third generation (contemporaries of Cotton Mather). In this way, the Puritans took up the important task of self-definition and myth creation.[8] In his *Magnalia Christi Americana*, Mather encouraged "a grand history of the New Israel" in which New England's uniqueness and potential role in the transformation of a vast wilderness into an ideal commonwealth had already "become worthy of merit in the eyes of God."[9] Puritan narratives became elemental to national mythologies of the United States, and by the end of the Puritan era in the late seventeenth century, an ideal American character took shape around competing conceptions of the New World adventurer willing to risk resettlement in a dangerous non-Christian land for the sake of profit—and the seeker after a new social order, a spiritual realm founded and maintained by the practice of virtue, religiosity, and self-sacrifice.

The orthodox theology of Puritanism was Calvinistic, and despite differences of doctrinal interpretation among assemblies, they believed that no mediator should come between the individual soul and God—a belief attacking the Catholic Church, which insisted on spiritual intercession. Initially inspired by Martin Luther, John Calvin formulated a radical theory of predestination in which the minutest details of the universe were shaped through God's will. Calvin taught that after expulsion from the Garden of Eden, Adam and Eve, along with a few elect souls, were granted grace, while the rest of humankind was destined for eternal damnation.[10] No number of good works could earn one a place in heaven, and to believe otherwise represented a blasphemous exaltation of human will, of hubris, of pride. Nonetheless, Calvinists did seek a means by which they might know if they were among the elect, and they found it in work and prosperity. Although good works could never earn salvation, the harder they worked and prospered, the more pious Calvinists saw evidence of their own election.[11]

Still, according to the Protestant ethic, the accumulation of personal wealth could only be justified by the good accomplished with it, an injunction that informs a long-standing American tradition of business philanthropy. Benjamin Franklin, among others, secularized that work ethic, which transmuted into a cult of self-help during the nineteenth century under the guidance of notable clergymen such as Henry Ward Beecher and Lyman Abbott and the popular novelist Horatio Alger. The full impact of that secularization defies easy measure, but consider that early in the twentieth century 90 percent of leading American businessmen were Protestant.[12] In fact, the Calvinists produced more prominent self-help publicists than any other denomination in the Congregationalist Church, a family of denominations that practiced an independent form of governance whereby every local church retained ecclesiastical sovereignty. That system allowed for the independence of local congregations, and it remained an important framework for a community of autonomous churches offering "mutual care in taking thought for one another's welfare."[13] Protecting the autonomy of local churches remained a priority, but Congregationalism meant belonging to a community (of autonomous churches).

Because the chartered companies that first settled Virginia and New England vastly underestimated the hazards and costs of early development, the crown encouraged private enterprise in North America by granting large tracts of land, including Maine and New Jersey, to individuals or small groups of proprietors who held the right to govern, exploit the land, and sell parcels to new settlers. Most early proprietors made no profit on their landholdings, because they remained unwilling or unable to invest the substantial capital necessary to begin new settlements that would not prove lucrative for generations.[14] Nevertheless, they became important members in a new society whose leaders were driven by expansionist aspirations and a desire for ever-greater material prosperity. The great majority of settlers to the New World went not for the glory of God, nor for the British Empire, but to benefit themselves economically, and most migrants quickly adopted pragmatic businesslike values as a consequence of the hardships of early colonial life that included illness, famine, and hostility from Native Americans. An initial lack of local historical traditions, a hereditary aristocracy (and similar feudal artifacts), and other privileged orders removed some of the most powerful obstacles to economic and social change in the colonies.[15] That openness created significant possibilities for upward social mobility, particularly for industrious individuals, and a high rate of migration helped to create a distinct American culture more favorable to the needs of business than those of older Western nations.

Early colonial markets were small and constraining affairs for those with grander aspirations, but English and European markets were too large for American entrepreneurs to enter, except by furnishing raw materials to be fashioned elsewhere into goods of every sort. Early colonies lacked the trained laborers, capital for investment, and machines necessary for industrial production. Enticing poor people to the New World as indentured migrant farmers and artisans offered one solution to the labor shortage. Generally young, ambitious, and eager for betterment, the audacious people who indentured themselves for money or land intended to improve their lot in life through such a move.[16] Of course, voluntary migration also indicates a certain degree of discontentment with the familiar environment and enough vigor and imagination to seek a way out of it. In the handful of substantial American colonies that existed before the Revolutionary War, merchants conducting foreign trade acquired moderate wealth, prestige, and influence, while other businesspeople (including shipbuilders, distillers, iron masters, and craftsmen operating large shops) became important citizens, as well.

Landownership and small business ownership often went together as settlements grew into the thirteen colonies, but nowhere more so than in New England, where the free distribution of land basically ended by the mid-eighteenth century. Despite its plentitude, money could still be made on land since it frequently went through the hands of several speculators before coming into the possession of dirt farmers, and the constant influx of new migrants into the colonies meant a good deal of land was traded as value increased. A tendency to reinvest in land, sometimes by holding back country acreage for future sale, meant that many farms provided homes for planters and became a source of capital stock that could secure the credit that "over the course of American history, financed industry and transportation."[17] A plantation economy developed on the southern seaboard of the colonies that produced crops such as tobacco and rice using large capital investments in slave labor. Southern farm operators aspired to be regarded as landed aristocrats and held "attitudes similar to their English counterparts," whereas in the North farm operators wanted to be thought of as good businesspeople.[18] These divergent identities and business orientations hardened over the next century (and culminated in the American Civil War). During the colonial era, however, southern planters like George Washington purchased western lands in violation of British prohibitions on settlement beyond the Appalachian Mountains. Washington, a land surveyor in his youth, warned his friends that if they did not seize that investment opportunity straightaway, they would never regain it. Washington was correct, and the greatest colonial estates were built by purchasing "the rich backlands" at low cost.[19]

Given those vast lands, abundant resources, and endless opportunities for self-betterment, a uniquely American vision of life took shape around a glorification of economic achievement, a belief in progress, and a celebration of social mobility, competition, individualism, change, bigness and boldness, risk taking, and innovation.[20] All of these factors fostered creative entrepreneurialism in the country and embedded business into the culture. Printer, publisher, writer, and statesmen Benjamin Franklin exemplifies the rise of the successful nonmercantile urban businessmen in the colonies. While many scholars today eschew a notion of national character, Franklin is a prototype for the self-made man, and his life is a classic American success story.[21] In the opening pages of his autobiography, Franklin gives thanks to "Providence" that from "the poverty and obscurity in which I was born and in which I passed my earliest years, I have raised myself to a state of affluence and some degree of celebrity in the world."[22] Born in the Massachusetts Bay Colony in 1706, Franklin was one of seventeen children. After only two years of formal schooling, his father apprenticed Franklin as a candle and soap maker, but because the young man was so miserable in that trade, his father agreed that printing might better suit his bookish inclinations. Later a versatile and successful printer, Franklin enjoyed doing business, and he believed that the wealth he acquired from his chosen occupation purchased independence and shielded him from the temptations that poverty brought.

As a businessperson, Franklin valued his reputation as a form of capital that could secure influence. He claimed to pursue self-improvement and cultivate the curiosity that led him to important inventions such as his famous stove, which he refused to patent. Franklin reasoned, "As we enjoy great advantages from the inventions of others, we should be glad of an opportunity to serve others by any invention of ours, and this we should do freely and generously."[23] In his quest to become a writer of repute, he read voraciously, including titles like John Bunyan's *Pilgrim's Progress* and Plutarch's *Lives*. He promoted a notion of gentility not grounded in birth and parentage (as in the Old World), or in good manners or taste, but in industriousness and frugality. Without condemning the dissipation of the wealthy or the idleness of the poor, Franklin charted a path for the shopkeepers, traders, clerks, and businessmen of the new middle class in the nineteenth century.[24] A polymath, Franklin made substantial contributions to society as a statesman, diplomat, scientist, and revolutionary. The full story of his genius, his foibles, and his extraordinary life would take a volume to fill, but the fabulization of the Franklin story provided American businessmen with favorable historical narratives (including that of the independent farmer and the Leatherstocking frontiersman).

Rugged pioneers who, cut off from civilization, battled the forces of nature alone, became celebrated figures as the colonies expanded. They embodied a frontier spirit equated with freedom, equality, progress, and natural rights.[25] Born to a family of Pennsylvania Quakers in 1734, the folk hero pioneer, merchant, and land speculator Daniel Boone was the sixth of eleven children. As a boy, Boone led the family cattle into wooded pastures during the day and brought them home for milking in the evening. Fond of the woods, he became a capable marksman after his father gave him a rifle at thirteen.[26] He never attended school for a meaningful length of time, but he put his skilled marksmanship to good use collecting pelts on a frontier that during his long game hunter's life was pushed ever westward. In pursuit of the coinage that furs brought on the market, Boone and other white rifle-bearing hunters contributed to the destruction of wild game, as did Native Americans who skinned deer in quantities that rivaled the white hunters. The decrease in deer populations that resulted portended a crash in the market for commercially viable wild animals, as the farming, fencing, and pasturing of domestic cattle (a consequence of increasing human settlement) transformed the environment in ways not conducive to the flourishing of wild game.[27] His contribution to the loss of sustainable game hunting notwithstanding, in seeking profits in the wilderness, Boone helped to open virgin hunting grounds in Kentucky, and he went on to serve as a captain in the Virginia militia and to establish the village of Boonesborough—an early settlement west of the Appalachian mountain range.[28] Boone suffered many setbacks in his other business ventures, most notably as an operator of a trading post and land speculator, but through romanticized literary and journalistic accounts of his life, he became an early American folk hero. In the symbolic narratives that took shape around figures such as Franklin and Boone, American business leaders reaped positive rewards for success, and they could feel part of a national epic aimed at improving the world "by producing goods and wealth on an ever-expanding scale."[29]

The general merchandise store remained the most characteristic retail outlet on every frontier during the colonial period. Often little more than small wooden structures fitted with rough wooden counters and shelves, or an outbuilding or alcove piled with barrels and boxes, frontier storekeepers nevertheless supplied nearly all required goods not made by local artisans, and in return for credit they took items such as furs, venison, hides, beef, pork, dairy products, grain, lumber, hoop poles and staves for barrels, and firewood from local producers.[30] As the colonial economy developed, general stores grew into vast emporiums that stocked a variety of foods, liquors, dress goods, hardware, and finished clothing items. Because many merchants who achieved success in shipping and foreign trade started as shopkeepers (including first families of New England and New York), the proprietors of general stores became citizens of eminent importance in society.[31] Itinerant peddlers were also essential contributors to colonial enterprise, since they brought the selection of the general store to the farm family and the dealer to the countryside, and they remained part of the American commercial landscape for centuries. Small business enterprises were the norm before about 1880, when thousands of small firms handled the production and distribution of goods and services in the national economy.[32]

In terms of colonial manufacturing, artisans sold a wide range of hand-made items (farming tools, clothing for the family, candles, and soap), fabricated often out of necessity, and they plied their trades in communities and outlying farms as blacksmiths, carpenters, coopers, curriers, tanners, and bricklayers. A system of apprenticeship helped to expand production and ensure the passage of important skills sets to the next generation. Colonial mills (gristmills, flour mills, sawmills) generally operated on a toll system in which farmers forfeited a share of their grain or flour as a milling fee. Mill owners, often farmers themselves, became trader-agents, who helped cultivators sell their surplusage to merchants in nearby cities, and they developed into diversified entrepreneurs who operated farms, mills, and stores, and probably engaged in land speculation too.[33] Shipbuilding, glassmaking, ironworks, and textile manufacturing became important colonial industries, and colonial businesses were so successful that long before the American Revolution the colonies surpassed Britain in number of ironworks and volume of iron produced.[34]

The British government and the colonies competed with each other to bend American manufacturing to their respective ends. The British attempted to restrict the manufacture of goods that competed with their own and tried to encourage the production of raw materials that only the colonies could produce (including lumber, tar, turpentine, and hemp) by offering bounties and tariff reductions on desired commodities.[35] For their part, the colonies encouraged all manufacturing, and domestic mercantile policies throughout the seventeenth and eighteenth centuries intended to increase the value of exports while decreasing those of imports, in order to strengthen the economic power of the state. Colonial governments commonly granted bounties to promote manufacturing of flax, woolen cloth, and hemp, and as inducements they offered public land grants, limited monopolies, direct contributions to manufacturers, and sometimes even loans to prospective businessmen.[36] Because the colonies could not locally produce every desired commodity, petty merchants (often captains of small ships or shopkeepers) provided import and export services, and some of them prospered mightily and became major businessmen of their day.

Found in every major port city, prosperous colonial merchants acquired unparalleled social and economic influence. These ship owners and freight operators ran their own warehouses and imported goods in bulk that could be sold wholesale (although many were also retailers). As merchant-capitalists, they supervised coastal or international operations from their counting houses, and they served as "commission agents and brokers, insurers of marine cargoes, money lenders, dealers in foreign exchange and bills of exchange, and agents for other merchants both foreign and domestic."[37] Some of these entrepreneurs diversified their business enterprises by dabbling in shipbuilding, iron smelting, distilling, and candle making on the side. Their multiple undertakings, and the keen intelligences that supported them, reinforce the notion that the nation's "best talent went into business, whereas in other nations it went into the land, the government, the military, or the church."[38] As persons knowledgeable about world events in a singular way, these merchant-capitalists were looked to for guidance in public and business politics. Like bankers in later decades, colonial merchants of a certain stature were expected to cultivate a grave and dignified bearing, to demonstrate honesty beyond reproach, and to possess personalities that inspired confidence.

Postal roads ran from Maine to South Carolina by 1750, and mercantile travel from Boston to New York and Philadelphia was faster by land than water. Intermarriage connected leading merchant families in cities of commerce as never before, and those kinship ties established "some of the community of interest achieved by corporate devices in later centuries."[39] The ease of entry into small business further distinguished the colonies from Europe, as did the fact that business in America was strongly associated with top levels of social prestige. Thus, the role of the entrepreneur and business leader was fundamentally different in American society, and rapidly expanding colonial markets and economies made finding entrepreneurial success more likely. Although businesspeople in the colonies ranged in status from itinerant peddlers to landed merchants, money was the primary reward for (and symbol of) achievement. Unlike in Europe, wealth and property, regardless of its origin, qualified families for membership in the elite class of American society.[40] Moreover, since the influence of landlords and accumulated wealth were less important to finding prosperity in the New World than in the Old, with a few years of work, some "new arrivals were able to close the initial gap between themselves and their wealthier predecessors" more rapidly than back home.[41]

While cheap land and a lack of capital created an economic rationale for the democratic spirit that endured before, during, and after the Revolution, many of the reasons that the colonies demanded independence from Britain were economic: chronic shortages of labor and high wages that resulted in constrained growth, and colonists feared that the taxes and regulations enacted by Parliament after 1763 threatened their economic prosperity and high degree of political autonomy. The British imperial system also kept American merchants in a subordinate position by preventing the formation of banks in the colonies. In the mid-1760s, a group of young artisans, shopkeepers, journeymen, and apprentices in New York and Boston, known as the Sons of Liberty, engineered tea party protests against the economic tyranny that the Stamp Act of 1765 represented. Soon thereafter, appeals to nationalism, home rule, democracy, and no taxation without representation emerged in northern cities and quickly spread.[42] Their revolutionary activities severed some important mercantile ties with Britain but they facilitated the rise of banking and chartered corporations in the fledgling nation. The business functions and social standing of merchants did not dramatically change im-

mediately following the success of the American Revolution, though a bur-
geoning trade with China from 1790 to 1807 further enriched New England
merchants.[43] After that lucrative exchange fizzled out, business interests
shifted toward domestic capital investment in transportation, manufacturing,
banking, and the acquisition of western lands.

The flowering of American commercial capitalism and bourgeois culture
from the late eighteenth century to around 1840 produced celebrated entrepreneurs like George Washington, Benjamin Franklin, and Alexander Hamilton—along with lesser known figures such as Robert Morris, William Duer,
and Robert Livingston. These were creative, cultivated, acquisitive gentlemen who traversed international, social, and business borders with ease.
They were often part businessman, lawyer, politician, and moral philosopher
who dabbled in the science and invention that drove the Industrial Revolution.[44] Shrewd, aggressive, venturesome, and ingenious, these men moved
adroitly between multiple enterprises. As for women, colonial law assumed
that they were dependent on men for economic support. Laws governing
dower rights, for instance, reinforced that inequality (even as they attempted
to protect women from improvident husbands).[45] Common law, however,
permitted married or single women to make contracts, to buy and sell, and to
control any business enterprise.

Because credit was difficult to obtain, many businesswomen sold to
neighbors, friends, and acquaintances using a barter system of exchange.
They produced goods, provided services, and profited as "middlewomen"
through trade, barter, wholesale and retail merchandizing.[46] In New York,
Boston, and Philadelphia between 1740 and 1775, more than 400 women
engaged in commerce, and although import-export businesses were dominated by men, during the eighteenth century, women ran small shops every-
where in North America. Most of them, including the imaginatively named
Benedicta Netmaker, sold dry goods or catered to women customers.[47] A few
women plied traditionally male trades (such as cobbling, tinsmithing, and
coach making) although usually as widows, wives, and daughters contributing to the household economy. More often found in less physically demanding skilled trades such as printing, colonial women frequently took over
family businesses when exigency demanded it. Anne Franklin, the widow of
Benjamin Franklin's older brother, continued to run the family print shop
after her Loyalist husband left the colonies during the Revolution, and Abigail Adams invested in federal and state bonds while her husband was focused on land.[48]

Almost immediately after the adoption of the American Constitution,
impassioned arguments between Alexander Hamilton and Thomas Jefferson
(and their respective followers) erupted, not over the industrial capitalism
that seemed a remote possibility for such an underdeveloped country, but
regarding the nature of progress itself. Hamilton "envisioned a vigorous

commercial civilization, urban-centered, absorbing the latest scientific and technological discoveries, resting on an extensive division of labor and expansive international trade, steered by private/public elites of merchant princes and statesmen who were deferred to by ordinary workaday folk."[49] By contrast, Jefferson desired a stable, egalitarian, and democratic society, and he imagined an agrarian republic composed of smallholding farmers and artisans, not too much engaged in international trade, but whose integrated economies ensured some measure of economic independence due to their proprietary self-sufficiency.[50] Hamilton's vision prevailed, but these competing conceptions of American society fueled passionate arguments about the meaning of progress until the Gilded Age.

Specialized stock brokerage houses appeared with the establishment of exchanges in the last decade of the eighteenth century, but before the 1820s, stock exchanges (where mostly government bonds were traded) had not yet become important business institutions. New transportation enterprises were much in vogue, and wealthy people subscribed to shares in turnpike, bridge, and canal companies out of a sense of community obligation. George Washington and his friends led the way with the establishment of the Potomac River Company in 1784 to canalize that river.[51] Large infrastructure projects like that one, and the early nineteenth-century expansion in the private building of hard-surfaced toll roads that followed, required bank support. By 1800, there were twenty-eight American banks in operation, a number that rose to eighty-eight in 1811, and four years later reached 208, more than in any European nation. By mid-century, approximately 800 chartered banks, along with many smaller private ones, employed young men from good families who were "probably better informed regarding business and political trends, both at home and abroad, than similarly situated men in industry, transportation, or wholesale trade."[52]

While the Napoleonic Wars raged on the continent, the new nation maintained its neutrality and in a singular way laid the groundwork for an unprecedented transformation from an underdeveloped republic into an industrial powerhouse over a few generations. Commercial banks, trust companies, and private banks supplied the capital funds once provisioned by merchant-financiers. Bankers in private institutions tended to be less tradition bound and more aggressive than their merchant-capitalist forbearers, too. The earliest American private investment banks expanded along with mercantile shipping, merchandizing, and foreign exchange, and the advent of railroads gave financial institutions a new avenue for capital expenditures. To appreciate the impact that such innovations exerted on business activity, consider that stock market transactions were absurdly low before 1830. Daily trading averaged just one hundred shares in 1827 but grew to 6,000 shares per day by 1835. In the boom of the 1850s, transactions *over one four-week period* totaled almost 1 million shares, and by then $1.5 billion in securities were listed on the exchanges.[53]

Given that women's involvement in business usually involved addressing the needs of their families, rather than seeking to gain personal autonomy or individual satisfaction (though those may have followed), the nineteenth-century liberal model of entrepreneurship as individualized endeavor did not fit the preindustrial role for American women, which was "based on either a communal or familial model."[54] In the highly decentralized preindustrial economy, local and regional markets were vital, and women operated in a variety of business roles (as artisans, shopkeepers, farmers, landlords), roles that would radically change, or disappear altogether, after 1830. Rebecca Pennock Lukens helped to chart a new path for women through her leadership of what would become the Lukens Steel Company from 1825 to 1847. Lukens transformed the debt-ridden enterprise that her deceased husband left behind into a financially stable business that gained regional prominence. Along the way, she adeptly engaged in legal battles over water rights and navigated her company through the treacherous shoals of the Jacksonian marketplace (as market capitalism began to permeate all aspects of American society).[55]

The onset of the American Civil War in 1861 created an urgent need for rail, arms, steel, and war supplies, but it also had the grizzly consequence of reducing population growth. By the time that ruinous conflict was over in 1865, a businesslike culture took root in the North that influenced later generations. It idealized an American way of life fostered by a high degree of internal migration and economic activity and created "a culture that differed significantly from that found in any of the nations of Western Europe or their overseas colonies."[56] The builders of business empires during the late nineteenth century were individualists with enormous self-confidence, and they envisioned the social and economic lives of humans as being dominated by a Darwinian notion of "survival of the fittest," a process of natural selection through which competition for resources ensured that the ablest of a species survived. The transition from the petty capitalism of small businessmen to industrial capitalism created the social conditions for the emergence of American tycoons such as Cornelius Vanderbilt, Andrew Carnegie, Henry Ford, and Hetty Green—enormously wealthy forerunners of the celebrity CEOs and business magnates of the 1980s to 2010s.

The fabled life of Cornelius Vanderbilt reflects an American penchant for heroicizing successful businessmen and businesswomen through a reservoir of stories and images depicting the shared experiences that lend meaning to the nation. As industrialization gathered steam, land and water routes increasingly unified the country and facilitated communication and exchange of goods and services. The natural resources that provided the foundation of early capital accumulations in the colonies seemed endless as the youthful nation stretched westward. Americans wanted to move farther and faster, and their drive for material prosperity and faith in social mobility led them to venerate the self-made individuals who exemplified their ideal of self-reliance, competition, hard work, and affluence. Born on Staten Island in 1794 to a family whose Dutch farming ancestors emigrated in the middle part of the seventeenth century, Cornelius Vanderbilt was an energetic lad. Though he loathed school, and quit at the age of eleven, five years later he launched his own ferry service in New York using a single two-masted flat-bottomed periauger, perhaps belonging to his father (already established in that line of work) and a $100 loan from his mother.

Although he came to regret his illiteracy, he excelled on the harbor, sailing even in the roughest weather and always making the best time. Whenever possible, he spied odd freighting opportunities on the side that might prove lucrative. The young man seemed "driven by a Calvinistic urge, derived from his mother, to make every possible profit at the expense of personal comfort and even safety."[57] Scrappy, competitive, highly individualistic, and known to live by a set of strict self-imposed rules (such as spending less every week than he earned), Vanderbilt ran his boat on a schedule, instead of waiting for a full load before departing.[58] His eagerness to ferry passengers and freight around New York Harbor earned him the playful epithet "Commodore," an appellation that remained with him the rest of his life. With his profits, Vanderbilt purchased a schooner to expand his operations, and while maintaining that business, he went to work for Thomas Gibbons as a permanent captain. Gibbons observed that the enterprising man stood in stark contrast to the "worthless fellows" who operated so many of the harbor's boats.[59] The War of 1812 provided Vanderbilt with another chance to distinguish himself as a fearless sailor who could get the job done when others could not. However, as ship technology advanced, Vanderbilt found his sailing vessels being overtaken by steamships. He initially derided the noisy machines, but it soon became apparent to him that steam, not sail, was the future.

Vanderbilt returned to work for Gibbons after the war, operating a steamship called the *Mouse* between New Brunswick and the Battery in New York City—in violation of a monopoly. Vanderbilt left Gibbon in his mid-thirties to establish his own steamboat line, and in the California gold rush of 1849 he struck it rich, not by digging for gold, but by transporting prospectors on steamships from New York to San Francisco via Nicaragua. Vanderbilt's reputation as an aggressive and able businessman was so firmly established by the next decade that members of the American Party desired to connect his name "with the high office of President of the United States." He replied to such adoration appreciatively, conceding that the office was "unquestionably the most distinguished of the high places of the earth," but added: "I can assure you that I am not now, and that I have never been at any time, in any

degree desirous of political or personal distinctions, and that I am so consti-
tuted that I cannot well appreciate the pleasures which allure those who make
the attainment of places of honor the object of their exertions."[60]

A patriot nonetheless, Vanderbilt put his vessels into government service
during the Civil War, and unlike most of his associates, who exploited the
critical need for shipping, the Commodore emerged with a pretty decent
record of putting the war effort—not his own business interests—first. For
example, when in March 1862 Secretary of War Edwin Stanton asked what
sum Vanderbilt would require to sink or destroy the Confederate navy's
ironclad *Merrimac*, Cornelius traveled to the White House to meet with
President Abraham Lincoln. Estimating "nine chances out of ten" of dis-
patching the Confederate vessel, Vanderbilt refused to take any money for
his services, and he donated his great steamship the *Vanderbilt* to the war
effort.[61] Although the *Merrimac* was destroyed before Vanderbilt's confidence could be tested, two years later the Commodore received a gold medal
from Congress for making that sizable gift to the nation. Vanderbilt could
afford to make such a liberal donation to the war effort because he had
accumulated a fortune during the 1840s and 1850s from investments in railroads worth more than $20 million.

One contemporary summarized Vanderbilt's railroad investment technique in this way: buy a line, stop the theft that went on under the previous
ownership, improve it as much as possible by way of reasonable expenditures, consolidate lines for efficiency, then water the stock and make it pay a
large dividend.[62] Whether or not one accepts that description, Vanderbilt
unquestionably worked in the interests of his stockholders, and he once remi-
nisced that making $2 million on the Harlem railroad (the one rail line that
entered New York City) paled in comparison "to that bright May morning
sixty years before when I stepped into my own periauger, hoisted my own
sail, and put my hand on my own tiller."[63] The future course of his life
indicates that he discovered a higher calling than making money. Following
his failure to seize control of the Erie Railroad and the death of his wife,
Sophia, Cornelius remarried a much younger woman, directed his attentions
to spiritualism, worked on philanthropic endeavors, endowed what would
become Vanderbilt University with a million dollars, and donated generously
to a variety of churches.

Another great industrialist would fill the demand for steel created by
escalating industry, and in his later years he would work full-time *to give his
fortune away*, a daunting task when you are Andrew Carnegie. As a handloom weaver of fine damasks in Dunfermline, an ancient Scottish capital just
beginning to experience the Industrial Revolution, Carnegie's father plied a
trade common in Scotland and Britain in the early nineteenth century. The
invention of weaving machines increased efficiency and reduced the preparation time needed to run new designs, and the output of textile manufacturers

ramped up significantly. Although the delicacy of designs crafted by Dunfermline weavers protected them for a longer time than the textiles of cotton or wool workers, the Panic of 1837 in the United States negatively impacted imports from Scotland. When the weavers went on strike, journeymen took their work at reduced rates, thus further exacerbating the downward pressure on the wages of people like his father. As a child, Andrew attended Swedenborgian services at the Church of New Jerusalem, took lessons in a one-room schoolhouse, and fetched water every day for household use from the town reservoir (where he developed a reputation as an "awfu' laddie" for not obeying a queuing system devised by the "old wives" of the town).[64]

As once-elite handloom weavers fell to the status of the lowest class of laborer, the poverty experienced by Carnegie's nuclear family bit harder. After the starving times of 1847 to 1848, his family managed to raise funds for the long voyage to the United States. Once arrived in New York Harbor, the four Carnegies headed for Allegheny City, a manufacturing city near Pittsburgh with a reputation for soot and grime. Even with relatives ensconced in the city, Andrew's father peddled tablecloths of his own manufacture to make ends meet, and his mother repaired shoes for $4 a week. At the age of thirteen, Andrew, an undersized and unskilled boy with a heavy Scottish accent, was sent to work. As a bobbin boy at Anchor Mills, Andrew spent twelve-hour days "running up and down the aisles exchanging fresh bobbins for used ones."[65] Before long, he was offered double his wages for soaking bobbins in oil, firing the boiler, and occasionally doing some bookkeeping. He gained a measure of local celebrity when the *Pittsburgh Daily Gazette* called him "an honest little fellow" after he returned a lost draft for $500.[66] Carnegie landed a position as a telegraph boy when that nascent technological innovation was driving a communications revolution, and before the age of sixteen, he learned Morse code.

A year later Carnegie moved to the Pennsylvania Railroad, where he worked as a secretary and telegraph operator. Once established, he "ingratiated himself with superiors, learned as much about the industry as possible, and did more than was expected."[67] Lacking the time and money to attend school, Andrew educated himself by reading voraciously, writing for Swedenborgian journals, and finding other ways to hone his writing and sharpen his critical thinking skills. The outbreak of the Civil War fired in him a strong anti-slavery sentiment, and Carnegie helped to supervise the transportation of arms, armaments, and troops along the Pennsylvania Railroad. Afterwards, the indefatigable young man invested in oil, a natural resource recently made refinable to burn more efficiently than whale, lard, or coal oil. Instead of spending, he reinvested profits in more oil ventures, and before long he became well-to-do. To announce that newfound affluence, he returned opulently to Dunfermline with his mother, who always regretted the poverty and hardship that drove the family from her homeland.

By the time he was thirty-five years old, Carnegie's estimated worth exceeded $1 million, and yet this tenacious five-foot three-inch Scot was just beginning to acquire his fortune. In 1872, he traveled to Sheffield to tour Henry Bessemer's steel plant where new furnaces were forging a "malleable iron" known as steel. Thereafter, Carnegie directed his many talents, and growing capital, toward making steel, a move that made him one of the wealthiest men in American history. Later in life, Carnegie advised young people eager to acquire their own fortunes that unceasing hard work was the necessary prerequisite for business success. He demonstrated that virtue by devoting more of his time to self-education after 1878, as well as to literary and cultural pursuits.[68] Philanthropy consumed his later life, so much so that the *New York Times* referred to Andrew Carnegie as a "millionaire socialist" on account of the radical views articulated in his "Gospel of Wealth" essays. Once asked by a *New York Times* reporter if he was a socialist, Carnegie retorted: "I believe socialism is the grandest theory ever presented, and I am sure some day it will rule the world."[69] In books and articles, some of which included pro-union sentiments, Carnegie assailed those who left great fortunes to their children instead of to posterity. He unabashedly asserted: "He who dies rich dies disgraced."[70]

From 1881 onward, Carnegie dedicated his remaining years to giving away his massive fortune, a task requiring a full-time occupation, but Carnegie believed that the pursuit of money could only be ennobled by laboring to advance the common good. Putting his beliefs into action, he gave away an estimated $350 million through the Carnegie Corporation in New York, the Carnegie Institution in Washington, DC, the Carnegie Institute of Technology in Pittsburgh, Carnegie Mellon University, Carnegie Scottish Universities Trust, and other foundations. His legacy also includes some 3,000 libraries worldwide (not all of them still in existence), a large body of writing, and a commitment to nonmercantile pursuits such as securing world peace. An immigrant who uniquely embodied the positive ideals of the self-made tycoon turned philanthropist, Andrew Carnegie epitomized the conviction that hard work paves the road to success. He also gave definition to notions about charity enshrined in the nation's early religious history, and his story attests to aspirations enshrined in the myth of the American Dream.

The decades following the Civil War, marked by prodigious invention, bore witness to the power of machine technology to transform the nature of work—and American society along with it. Even as a youngster Henry Ford yearned to join the ranks of the great inventors who gave us the cotton gin, steamboat, steel plow, and telephone. A rural mechanic from Springfield Township in Michigan, Ford received no formal education beyond the fifth grade, but he was an inveterate tinkerer who came of age at a moment when "many of America's most durable heroes were bold individualists whose careers had melded science with commerce."[71] Like many farm boys who rose from obscurity to social prominence, Ford despised the chores required of him, and whenever possible he repaired farm equipment instead. Even so, he subscribed to a doctrine of work, an ideological consequence of a strict Scots-Irish upbringing, and at times the fires of John Calvin's hell seemed to inspire him, although otherwise Ford had little use for religion. Above his fireplace hung a pragmatic reminder from Benjamin Franklin: "Chop your own wood and it will warm you twice."[72]

Henry's natural gift for mechanics included a visionary experience in his early teens during which he "saw" a self-propelled steam boiler on wheels "with a water tank and coal cart trailing behind" and a chain connecting the boiler to the wheels.[73] From that moment forward, he dedicated his life to building machines that moved. At sixteen, Henry moved to Detroit and apprenticed at local machine shops before taking a position at the Edison Company (where he rose to chief engineer).[74] Never one for academic pursuits, he held a disdain for "city slickers," whom he found perfectly useless in a machine shop, research laboratory, or manufacturing plant.[75] Because of his reputation, in 1885 Ford was summoned to repair an Otto engine from England, though he had never worked on one. He learned enough from that experience to begin building his own gasoline-powered engines, and he soon improved on them with a double-cylinder design.[76] Ford's hero, Thomas Edison, observed that Henry was not only a natural mechanic and businessman—but the rarest of types, "a combination of the two."[77]

Ford brought his childhood vision of a self-propelled vehicle to life in 1896 with the Quadracycle, a crude buggy-like vehicle mounted on wire bicycle wheels with rubber tires. Although Ford did not invent the automobile, he was among its pioneers. Still in its infancy, the American automobile industry nevertheless contained many competitors eagerly trying to get ahead through invention and innovation. Ford drew attention to himself by racing his vehicles—a necessary activity that he found terrifying, and for which he later hired professional drivers. Ford did not limit his genius to designing better vehicles and putting them through the rigors of racing; he also revolutionized how automobiles were manufactured. Populist to the core due to his humble origins, Ford determined to produce vehicles that were affordable to the masses. Following the failures of the Detroit Automobile Company and the Henry Ford Company, the Ford Motor Company was successfully established in 1903. At his Mack Avenue facility, Ford began assembling Model As, body to motor, all in one place—a method of manufacturing that initially limited production to fifteen vehicles a day.[78]

The Model N, an entry-level vehicle introduced in 1906, sold for just $500. It was followed by a host of other models, but it was the Model T (in production from 1908 and 1927) that put America on wheels. A sturdy vehicle well equipped to handle the rutted unpaved roads with an inventive three-point suspension system, it was also the first left-hand drive car. Due to its

agility and durability, the Model T transformed the farmwork that Ford detested. Not only could the Model T be used for hauling, but one of its rear
wheels could be removed and a belt attached to its drive assembly to allow
the vehicle to power farm equipment (including pumps and generators). He
tirelessly strove to reduce the price of the Model T over its long production
run without lowering its quality. His billboards promised: "Even You Can
Afford a Ford."[79] Henry delivered on his guarantee of lowering prices without sacrificing quality by adapting the assembly line method of production,
an idea inspired by Philip Armour's meatpacking warehouse in Illinois, to
the production of automobiles. By moving a chassis through a conveyor
system in which a single task was accomplished at a variety of points along
the way, production at Ford Motor Company nearly doubled *every year for a
decade* after 1913, as the price of the Model T fell by two-thirds.[80] Henry left
it to the Dodge brothers (Horace and John) to build cars for the wealthy. Ford
was looking out for ordinary folk.

When the drudgery of the repetitive tasks associated with assembly line
work threatened the stability of his labor force with incessant turnover, Ford
announced the $5 Day wage. Economist Peter Drucker believed this innova-
tion "established the American workingman as fundamentally middle-
class."[81] While rival corporate leaders assailed him for raising wages across
the automotive industry, Ford stood his ground because he recognized that a
fair wage not only secured a more loyal workforce, but provided the means
by which his workers could purchase Ford vehicles—thereby creating a virtuous circle of growth. As his company grew, Ford retained his "Midwest
values" and signaled his dislike for conspicuous consumption and social
climbing by remaining in a rented row house until 1905. Even after he
purchased a more sumptuous abode, he managed to live without much pre-
tention, given his great wealth. Then again, like many business geniuses,
money was never a primary motivator for Ford. One story that made its way
around the factory floor had it that once the boss absently unfolded a crum-
pled piece of paper he found in his pocket and it turned out to be a check for
$68,000, or hundreds of millions in today's money.[82]

For focusing on making affordable automobiles, for paying a living wage,
and for his simple lifestyle, Henry Ford was to many Americans a farm boy
millionaire and populist hero who remained close to the soil, safeguarded his
independence, and practiced self-reliance and the creed of hard work. The
social impact of the $5 Day aligned the entrepreneur with a reformist and
progressivist spirit in the air, and indeed he once declared that his company
would outlive its "usefulness as a money-making concern," unless some
good could be done with the money: "I do not believe in charity, but I do
believe in the regenerating power of work," he quipped, and he gave expression to a desire to see his "whole organization dominated by a just, generous,
and humane policy."[83] Whether or not he achieved that goal is the subject of

ongoing debate, but Henry Ford was a real-life Horatio Alger: he was full of energy and determination, and his luck rarely seemed to run out.

While not a populist celebrity, like Henry Ford, Hetty Green became the richest woman in the United States during the Gilded Age. Green's personality and attitude towards money stood out among the superrich of her day, as it does in our own time of overconsumption and wealth inequality. Most Americans, who associated great wealth with the opulence of the Rockefellers, were perplexed by the somberness of Green's clothing, the plainness of her diet, the austerity of her home, and her reputation for parsimony. Born to a Massachusetts family of Quakers, a dissenting Protestant tradition that broke from the Church of England, everyone in Hetty's hometown of New Bedford during the 1830s, "white or black, worldly or Quaker, had an interest in whaling," due to the town's proximity to the Atlantic Ocean. In the Protestant tradition, members of the New Bedford community made material prosperity synonymous with virtue, and the great wealth of the Howland and Robinson families (who owned the ships and banking institutions that made whaling possible) was interpreted as a "visible sign of election by God."[84]

The Religious Society of Friends (or Quakers) regarded everyone as equal in the eyes of the Lord. Quaker women occupied important roles in the religious and business affairs of the community, and many of them were independent and outspoken citizens who conducted their own meetings, made their own decisions, and frequently managed their own businesses. Hetty Green's father, obsessed with bettering the material life of his family, made moneymaking the "great object" of his life.[85] He longed for a son to mentor as a future entrepreneur, and therefore the birth of Hetty, his first child, disappointed him. When his second born, a son, died less than two years later, Hetty was banished to her grandfather's home, an unwanted child. Shipped off to a strict Quaker boarding school at the age of ten, Green read three chapters from the Bible every day, learned her lessons by rote, and gradually grew accustomed to the school's tasteless food. When her father's eyesight started to fail, she left to read aloud to him from the evening paper. After demonstrating an interest in investment, she pleaded with her father to teach her the "meaning of stocks and bonds, bulls and bears, commodities and market fluctuations."[86] Although she stood to inherit significant sums from well-heeled relatives, Hetty worked for her money and kept accurate accounts of her spending. She married Edward Green, but allowed him no claim on her future inheritance. When he betrayed her, by using her money without permission and risking it for his own financial gain, she bade him farewell. The couple remained married, but thereafter they maintained separate residences.[87]

Often disheveled and dressed in shabby clothes, Green had a quick temper and foul tongue, but her financial acumen became readily apparent during the Civil War when she repeatedly moved opposite the market—and prospered. When that bloody conflict ended, most people sold their "green-back" notes printed by the government during the war. She bought them up as others rushed to gold, invested the yield from her investments (and inheritances) in U.S. bonds and railroad bonds, and her portfolio doubled, tripled, and quadrupled. The most that Green ever made in a single day, she confessed, was $200,000. With such wealth at her fingertips, she became "a de facto bank."[88] In the financial panic of 1873, Hetty wanted to keep trading. "I believe in getting in at the bottom and out at the top," she often said, acknowledging that when she saw "a good thing going cheap" because nobody wanted it, she would buy plenty and "tuck it away."[89] At the turn of the twentieth century, business consolidation and merger became all the rage, and hundreds of small business enterprises were folded into huge conglomerates. The age of big business had arrived, and the United States was the world's foremost supplier of copper, cotton, corn, coal, steel, iron, and oil by 1901. An abundance of easy money ran up stock prices, and seemingly everyone was buying, except for Hetty, who held fast to her strategy, hunted out bargains, and never purchased with borrowed money.[90]

Her courage in moving against the crowd was extraordinary, but Green's frugality meant that she skimped when it came to her own spending, and an eager press spread stories of her that highlighted that miserliness—for instance, that she bought sacks of broken graham crackers to save money, asked the butcher for free bones for her dog, and bargained over the price of a peck of potatoes.[91] These accounts are likely exaggerated, as are those concerning her unwillingness to pay for medical treatment of her son Ned's broken leg, but there is little question of her thrift. Irrespective of her reputation for stinginess and her own repeated denials, reports suggest that she donated $500,000 to the Nurses Home in New York and $50,000 to their settlement house, though the majority of her philanthropy seems to have taken the form of loans to public institutions and assistance in finding people jobs.[92] In her will, she left most of her fortune to her children (who directed some of her assets to charitable causes), remembered friends, left monies to several universities and private schools, and sponsored the construction of a new hospital at Bellows Falls and a library in New Bedford.[93] On her deathbed, she remarked, in the Quaker spirit: "I do not know what the next world is, but I do know that a kindly light is leading me, and that I shall be happy after I leave here."[94] Like Cornelius Vanderbilt, Andrew Carnegie, and Henry Ford, Hetty Green mapped her own route through the world of business, even though it meant enduring charges of self-interest and suffering villainous portrayals in the media.

Between the American Revolution and the start of the Civil War, merchant capitalism gave way to the industrialization that held sway until the Great Depression. During the Progressive Era from 1890 to 1920, public attention focused on solving political and social problems, using regulation to ease competition, creating efficient and effective government, and improving public education and welfare. The professionalization of vocation, another consequence of those social and economic transformations, opened some occupations once inaccessible, but it blocked others through a process of gendering whereby women were encouraged to enter fields such as teaching and nursing.[95] Sarah Breedlove (Madam C. J. Walker) found a middle path between that openness and gendering in the professions, and her establishment of a beauty aids company, and decision to market her products to black women, made her one of the first women in the United States to become a millionaire through her own efforts.[96]

Her path to fortune defies belief, as she was born into abject poverty, suffered the loss of her parents at an early age, and endured physical abuse at the hands of her brother-in-law. Married at just fourteen and widowed at sixteen, she was left with two children to raise. In St. Louis, she eked out a living washing laundry, and her life seemed to hit a dead end—until she started designing products for a different type of hair. In 1904, she dreamed of a recipe for a new hair preparation. Due to her shrewd entrepreneurship, Madam Walker's business expanded rapidly, and by 1910 she employed over 5,000 African American women to sell her products on commission; nine years later, that number reached 25,000.[97] She founded beauty schools, developed a real estate complex in Indianapolis, built a mansion on the Hudson, and contributed to numerous philanthropic charities that benefited black colleges, orphan homes, churches, and other institutions assisting African Americans.[98] Like many progressive people of her day, Walker saw business entrepreneurship as a means for economic well-being, as well as racial advancement.

By in the late 1920s, American business was changing rapidly. Corporations became too large and unwieldy for a model of governance based on the leadership of single individuals (sometimes assisted by partners or family members). The managerial capitalism that took shape in response represented a significant break with the past in terms of labor relations. To achieve organizational stability, planning was coordinated; command was effected through management hierarchies; and evaluation (assessment) became a means of exercising control over programs and people. Improvements in transportation and communication infrastructure coincided with a final wave of exploitation of the country's natural resources (particularly in the West) and with a rise in immigration that increased the availability of low-cost labor.[99] As growth in output from streamlined production continued, newer models of organization divvied up various corporate functions—such as marketing, manufacturing, research and development, and human resources—so that managers soon oversaw but a single part of the production process.

The reputation of American business morphed along with changing notions of social justice. In the wake of the Great Depression, once heroic

"Captains of Industry," cultural icons whose biographies reflected key aspects of an American way of life, suddenly became "robber barons," greedy villains who caused the stock market crash of 1929. Many members of the business elite retained their wealth as their social standing diminished, but ordinary people endured the loss of work, stood in soup lines, and felt abandoned by business, government, charities (like the Red Cross), their fellow men, and even by God. President Herbert Hoover's slow response to the devastation of economic collapse and to dust bowl conditions in the Midwest exacerbated the cumulative effects of economic depression. A landslide victory for Franklin Delano Roosevelt in the 1932 presidential election signaled a determined rejection of industrial capitalism, by which a small percentage of people grew wealthy beyond measure while ordinary people barely got by. To Americans disillusioned with the economy and with big business, Roosevelt's "New Deal" marked a significant departure from the ideology of less government intervention and regulation. This new ethos guaranteed an important social role for government, one that persisted until the 1980s when other business heroes emerged in American culture, exulting in acquisition and pursuing self-interest.

Although New Deal programs do not constitute a single body of thought, they grew out of universally acknowledged principles (such as the Golden Rule) and aimed at social betterment during a time of economic crisis. Roosevelt claimed that the legislation reflected a "recognition of the old and permanently important manifestation of the American spirit of the pioneer," and he argued for passage of key components as the surest way to secure enduring economic recovery.[100] The Agricultural Adjustment Act of 1933 (and its replacement in 1938) helped to establish parity prices on basic commodities by reducing supply to check overproduction and restore prices, and the Works Progress Administration attempted to address persistent unemployment by putting millions of people to work in labor-intensive projects. The Farm Tenancy Act created a program of land conservation and utilization that addressed soil erosion, reforestation, and preservation of natural resources, and it provided credit to farmers to buy land. Consequently, the Farm Tenancy Act reflected a Jeffersonian ideal of property and enterprise. These and other acts also retained a high-minded vision of broad opportunity and moral responsibility fundamental to the American mind.[101]

Entrepreneurs "dominated and largely shaped the American physical and social environment" in the one hundred years before 1929, whereas from the Great Depression onward, they were forced to adjust to changing political and social conditions.[102] New technologies, which increased productivity, needed to be balanced against employee rights and welfare. Large unions became a positive feature of the labor landscape, and more emphasis was put on controlling the pollution of the environment in the 1930s. The net effect of these and other changes in social attitudes and perceptions was the rebirth of the business hero, but in a different mold from the Vanderbilts, Carnegies, Fords, and Greens of the previous generation. The heroic entrepreneur of the postdepression era resisted greed and self-interest for the well-being of workers and the sake of the common good. Company pensions became a part of worker remuneration to provide financial security in old age, corporate sponsorship of the arts and education surged, and tax rates increased on the wealthy. Many companies also set up nonprofit institutions to augment that newfound charitable impulse (e.g., the Ford Foundation in 1936).

At General Motors, the professional management philosophy of Alfred Sloan became an important model for American corporations from the late 1920s to the late 1970s. Sloan emphasized letting headquarters set policy for each division and then evaluating their performance based on the internal rate of return for each one. Direct control by an owner such as Henry Ford was replaced "by symbolic leadership and by top managers overseeing other managers."[103] Planning cycles, performance objectives, subordination of workers, and evaluations based on overall company goals typified this period of American business history. In addition, a revolutionary recognition took hold that a certain amount of social accounting made good sense for business when used alongside traditional market calculus.[104] Business philanthropy suddenly became de rigueur, and it helped reinstill overall positive impressions of business among the general public. With the onset of World War II, members of the urban middle class in the United States "acquired the attitudes that were to characterize twentieth-century managerial society."[105]

Successful New Deal programs ended quietly as business and government joined forces to defeat fascism and fight the Cold War. Reluctant to enter another world war on the continent, but facing the real prospect of a Nazified Europe, Franklin Roosevelt allowed the Washington Naval Treaty, which limited the growth of that branch of the military in the name of arms control, to expire in 1936. He ordered a major shipbuilding program, and two years later the Army Air Corps received the largest authorization for airplane purchases in history.[106] As Europe went to war in 1939, American defense spending reached a billion dollars for the first time since 1918, and the armed forces grew to 334,000 members. Still, the nation could not mount a proper defense in the event of a German landing anywhere on the coast.[107] In a bid to build munitions quickly, Roosevelt commissioned Bill Knudsen, an executive at General Motors, as a general to lead the war production effort.

An immigrant from Denmark, Knudsen started his working life in the shipyards, learned to box, and moved on to locomotive repair before going to work for Henry Ford making steel for the Model T. A pivotal figure in the introduction of the assembly line at Ford Motor Company, when this wizard of production announced his resignation (much to Ford's dismay), Knudsen was offered a position by Sloan at the ailing Chevrolet division at General Motors. Chevrolet, the company that lost $8.6 million as Knudsen stepped in, soon showed an income of $11.2 million, and under Knudsen's leadership sales of cars and trucks grew from just over 70,000 to almost a quarter million.[108] As president of General Motors, Knudsen contributed significantly to the war effort. Based on his previous work with Chrysler and Packard, it occurred to him that the entire automotive industry could help solve military production problems.

On the Tuesday following the Japanese attack on Pearl Harbor in 1941, Roosevelt summoned Knudsen to the White House and explained to him that the nation required 30,000 planes in 1942 and 75,000 tanks in 1943.[109] Knudsen accepted a three-star generalship—the only civilian in history to earn such a high-level appointment—and he went right to work.[110] His efforts were so successful that on D-Day in June 1944, General Motors made 10 percent of everything that America produced during World War II, including thousands of aircraft engines, hundreds of different parts for Boeing, Martin, and North American, and entire airplanes for Grumman. Knudsen called it an "arsenal of democracy."[111] After the surrender of Japan, Knudsen resigned his commission and returned to Detroit, where the mayor gave him a key to the city. During the war years, total economic production in the United States doubled and wages rose by 70 percent.[112] Thus the tragedy of war became a foundation of sustained prosperity for millions of American people—a shared prosperity, as many people see it, until the advent of the Reagan era.

Following the cessation of hostilities in 1945, the American economy proved unable to accommodate an influx of returning soldiers, and so the Servicemen's Readjustment Act of 1944 (better known as the G.I. Bill) eased the transition to civilian life for millions of men and women by providing tuition and living expenses to veterans. The government funding of higher education made possible an era of unprecedented economic expansion between World War II and 1980, as federal monies to encourage economic competitiveness combined with state support to transfigure the United States into a superpower.[113] With more money in their pockets, Americans began to spend more on consumer goods, such as cars, houses, and later television sets, and it was not long before the effects of the postwar "baby boom" reverberated across the nation. The suburbanization of America began when Levitt and Sons built the first of four housing developments (in New York, Pennsylvania, New Jersey, and Puerto Rico), which "gave middle-class families the option of inexpensive, single unit housing outside of urban neighborhoods."[114] These planned communities included churches, schools, swimming pools, and shopping centers—though the Levitts too often pushed the cost of building urban infrastructure (such as wells and roads) onto the budgets of local governments and allowed parks and sidewalks to go unmaintained.[115]

Levittown in New York grew to include 82,000 residents living in 17,400 separate houses, and most of them included a living room and fireplace, two bedrooms, one bath, and an attic that could be finished later. Cape Cods initially started at $6,000 (and rose to $8,000) while more spacious ranches sold for $9,500. There were no closing costs, no down payments, and no "hidden costs." It was, in short, a spectacular deal made possible by Federal Housing Administration and Veterans Administration production advances.[116] These prosperous partnerships among business, government, and higher education persisted through the early decades of the Cold War and contributed to unparalleled national prosperity. During the 1950s, 1 million people entered the middle class every year.[117] In the face of that shared affluence, new voices were calling on business to abandon stakeholder logic and to recapture the spirit of profit and acquisitiveness that preceded the New Deal. Among them, Milton Friedman correctly predicted a renewed focus on markets and bottom-line profitability. The University of Chicago economics professor and Nobel Laureate believed that governments should help to set the rules of the game, but otherwise they should get out of the way of business. The list of activities that Friedman thought governments should avoid was extensive and included rent control; legal minimum wage rates; detailed regulation of industry; social security programs particularly for the aged that in effect compelled people to buy a retirement annuity; forced conscription into the military; the establishment and maintenance of national parks; and publically owned and operated toll roads.[118]

In *Capitalism and Freedom*, Friedman attempted to relocate a sense of liberalism and liberty that he thought lost after the New Deal. In its opening pages, Friedman responded to President John F. Kennedy's inaugural address of the preceding year, declaring that the "free man will ask neither what his country can do for him nor what he can do for his country."[119] Friedman rejected government paternalism, insisting the question was not one's service to the country, as Kennedy claimed, but how to keep the government that "we create from becoming a Frankenstein that will destroy the very freedom we establish it to protect."[120] Friedman argued that the scope of government must be limited to protecting laws and enforcing private contracts, and that any other power the government possesses should be dispersed between local, state, and federal entities. In his view, private enterprise should check the power of government because the "great advances of civilization, whether in architecture or painting, in science or literature, in industry or agriculture, have never come from centralized government."[121] For Friedman, private enterprise operating in a free market (competitive capitalism) was a necessary condition for political freedom.

Recognizing that a stable and democratic society required a minimum of literacy and knowledge on the part of its citizens, Friedman nonetheless found it "highly desirable" to impose the costs of schooling "directly on the parents."[122] In regard to corporate social responsibility, an ideal that re-emerged after the Great Depression, Friedman adamantly insisted on "only one social responsibility of business—to use its resources and engage in activities designed to increase its profits so long as it stays within the rules of the game, which is to say, engages in open and free competition, without deception or fraud."[123] Although they did not always adhere to the rules, a new generation of American business heroes emerged in the 1980s who drank deeply from this wellspring. Friedman, now a Nobel Laureate, taught an economic philosophy increasingly advanced in business schools around the nation. Jack Welch, known as "Neutron Jack" for his legendary temper, embraced Milton Friedman's creed of profit for shareholders and rode it to prominence after streamlining General Electric. Welch grew up in Salem, Massachusetts, where his father worked as a railroad conductor. Afflicted with a stutter from an early age, he went on to study science at University of Massachusetts and to earn a doctorate from the University of Illinois.

Welch joined GE as an engineer in 1960, and he worked his way up the corporate ladder. As the youngest chairman and CEO in General Electric history, he transformed the company from a manufacturing enterprise into a multibillion-dollar conglomerate in less than two decades. In 1990, *Fortune* magazine named him "manager of the century" citing not only the multiplication of GE's market capitalization from $14 billion to more than $400 billion by the turn of the twentieth century, but also his elimination of entire layers of management. He also launched a workout process whereby employees at all levels gathered for "town meetings" with their supervisors to make suggestions or inquiries—the majority of which were answered immediately.[124] Incredibly well paid for his leadership, Welch helped to establish a trend of high executive salaries that continues today. In 1996, for example, he took $6.3 million in salary, $15.1 million from a long-term incentive program, and $6.2 million by exercising options on GE stock for a total package of $28.2 million. *Businessweek* estimated that Welch held an additional $107 million in stock options. His wage alone, "complained the unions, was 148 times that paid to the average GE worker."[125] Nonetheless, it seemed to many stockholders that he was worth every penny.

An American business hero conspicuous for his humility and modest lifestyle in a time of freewheeling acquisitiveness, Warren Buffett's acumen for the financial markets earned him the nickname "Oracle of Omaha" for the sage investment advice that he continues to offer the public. Like many great business minds, Buffett demonstrated a proclivity for numbers from a young age. A native of Nebraska, where he still resides, Buffett could complete complex mathematical calculations in his head as a boy. At eight years of age, he began reading his father's books on the stock market, and by eleven he was marking the board in the brokerage house where his father worked.[126] After attending business school at University of Nebraska and earning a master's degree in economics from Columbia University, he started a limited investment partnership at twenty-five with $100 of his own money and capital raised from family and friends—and over the next thirteen years, "Buffett compounded money at an annual rate of 29.5 percent."[127] When he acquired Berkshire Hathaway in 1962, it was an ailing textile company with a net worth of $22 million; forty years later he grew its value to $69 billion.[128]

One key to success as an investor, Buffett argues, is thoroughly understanding the investments one holds and that means gaining familiarity with each company's revenues, expenses, cash flow, labor relations, pricing flexibility, and capital allocation. He calls the acquisition of this knowledge a "circle of competence," since in the absence of that comprehensive understanding, "it is impossible to accurately interpret developments and therefore impossible to make wise decisions."[129] Examples of Buffett's expertise abound: his investments in Coca-Cola and Gillette paid handsome dividends, as did his purchase of $98 million in Amazon.com bonds in 2002 (which he found "extraordinarily cheap" given his faith that the company would thrive under CEO Jeff Bezos, who accurately accounted for stock options as an expense).[130] Americans marvel at the success of Buffett's formula, and for his ability to correctly identify bubbles in the markets (including the speculative Dot.com bubble of the late 1990s), but we admire his humble integrity and simplicity in tandem with his fiscal insight. Buffett continues to live in the five-bedroom home that he purchased in 1958 for $31,500, and he plans to leave most of his fortune to charity or to a foundation. In 2014, Buffett donated $2.8 billion in Berkshire stock to a variety of family charities, including the Bill and Melinda Gates Foundation, as part of a plan to give away nearly all of his wealth.[131] He helps shareholders and stakeholders to become better investors through his Berkshire annual reports (often sixty to seventy dense pages in length). The busy chairman and CEO of Berkshire Hathaway also writes about business—and for a time he even taught adult continuing education and undergraduate courses.

Like Ford with his Model T automobile, Bill Gates envisioned the mass appeal of his personal computer. Gates did not aspire to build computers (as Ford did vehicles). Rather, Bill wanted to create software that would make hardware hum. Gates displayed a talent for what would become his vocation at a young age; he learned the BASIC computer language by the eighth grade, and in the eleventh he wrote a program that handled class scheduling for his high school in Seattle. He famously attended Harvard University for two years before dropping out to launch Microsoft. Not long after Gates and his business partner Paul Allen moved Microsoft, a forty-person company, to Washington State around 1980, IBM requested that Microsoft develop languages and an operating system for their first personal computer. Gates and Allen designed a disk operating system known as MS-DOS for short. In a shrewd business move, Gates pressured IBM to grant Microsoft sole rights to license it, because, as he explained, "it didn't take a rocket scientist to figure out that eventually we license DOS to others."[132] Today, Gates is the richest man in the world with a net worth in excess of $75 billion. In fact, by the age of forty-three, Gates was already a billionaire eighty times over.[133]

That level of business accomplishment demands a certain set of personality traits, which though unique to each person, are nevertheless generalizable. Gates possessed an iron will as a child. His mother, known for her strong determination, once took her truculent son to a psychologist. After one year, the good doctor told her: "You're going to lose. You had better just adjust to it because there's no use trying to beat him." His father recounts that she "came around to accepting that it was futile trying to compete with him."[134] Gates was a genius, and he knew it from a young age. He could be quite arrogant, and as a schoolboy, he did not hesitate to insult the intelligence of his teachers or throw tantrums when angry. All the same, his persistence, industriousness, dedication to work (studying sometimes thirty-five hours at a stretch in college),[135] desire to succeed, and willingness to take risks were, in the end, a winning combination. An aggressive entrepreneur, at the helm of Microsoft, Gates eliminated or co-opted competition to his operating system, understood and developed brand, and kept his employees from leaving for other software companies by offering them stock options. Friends and colleagues noted his impressive ability to "parallel process," his "unlimited bandwidth," and his aptitude for "multitasking."[136] Some complained about Gates's contentious style and his focus on flattening competitors rather than creating excellence. A friend and competitor called him "one part Albert Einstein, one part John McEnroe, and one part General Patton."[137] In 2000, Gates passed the leadership of Microsoft Corporation on to others so that he might dedicate more time to his family's charitable foundation, which focuses on education, health, and poverty.

One who did compete with Microsoft, one who captured the American imagination with sleek, elegant hardware designs and innovative software while at the helm of Apple, Inc. was Steve Jobs. Jobs, a skinny adolescent full of energy, sporadically attended Reed College in his twenties and went on a pilgrimage to India seeking spiritual enlightenment in 1974. As a technician at Atari (a pioneer in the video game industry), Jobs sometimes wore a saffron robe and went barefoot. Known for being prickly and demeaning about other people's work, somehow he also managed to be compelling and inspiring, as well.[138] A partnership with inventor and engineer Steve Wozniak in 1976 led to the development of the Apple I computer (in a hobbyist context), but their Apple II became the first simply and fully integrated computer—hardware to software.[139] A newer machine followed shortly after Jobs "borrowed" technology, which he saw on display at Xerox (a graphic interface, which he improved upon and integrated into his own designs).[140] When Jobs debuted the Macintosh machine in 1984 at an Apple shareholder event, it set in motion a computing revolution. The Macintosh played the song "Chariots of Fire," ran through a dazzling presentation of its applications, and then spoke to the audience. The standing ovation that followed lasted for five minutes. Steve Jobs would amaze Americans, and millions of others around the globe, over the next three decades with technologies that changed how we live and work (iPhone, iMac, iPod, and iTunes among them).

The searingly intense personality of Steve Jobs, Walter Isaacson explains, was that of a "creative entrepreneur whose passion for perfection and ferocious drive revolutionized six industries: personal computers, animated movies, music, phones, tablet computing, and digital publishing," and he became "the ultimate icon of inventiveness, imagination, and sustained innovation" in late twentieth-century American culture.[141] A long-standing meditation practice and interest in Buddhism contributed to his ability to focus, to tune out distraction, and to design elegant streamlined devices (with a Zen aesthetic). Jobs could be cruelly honest too, and he knew how to cajole and sometimes hurt colleagues, friends, and family. He was an intuitive inventor; his passion and perfectionism (along with his demons, desires, artistry, devilry, and obsession for control) "were integrally connected to his approach to business and the products that resulted."[142] It took a complex personality to launch a startup in his parent's garage and to build it into one of the world's most valuable companies.[143] Summing up his own legacy, Jobs contended: "My passion has been to build an enduring company where people were motivated to make great products. Everything else was secondary. Sure, it was great to make a profit, because that was what allowed you to make great products. But the products, not the profits, were the motivation." He detested people who called themselves "entrepreneurs" but were "unwilling to do the work it takes to build a real company, which is the hardest work in business."[144]

During the mid-twentieth century, women such as Estée Lauder (cofounder of Estée Lauder Companies) and Fanny Goldberg Stahl (founder of Stahl's Knishes) created business opportunities in sex-typed industries and built successful enterprises, though in some ways their efforts did not mark a radical departure from the gendering of professions noted earlier. From the 1950s to the 1990s, however, women business leaders came to the fore to challenge the status quo by making inroads in fields of endeavor previously regarded as the province of men. Women increased their representation in many industries as executives, managers, and entrepreneurs, and MBA programs became a primary vehicle for that advancement. In 1977, women earned 6 percent of all MBA degrees, but they made up 31 percent of degree takers by 1986. Similarly, women went from constituting 5 percent of executives, administrators, and managers in 1974 to 12.4 percent in 1994, and they made significant gains in the construction, transportation, communication, and other industries.[145] In 1996, for example, Kim Polese was appointed CEO of Marimba (later acquired by BMC Software), a company developing management solutions software. Those advances notwithstanding, most women-owned and women-chaired businesses remained in the personal service sector, their longtime business niche, during the 1990s. The top fifty women-owned or -operated businesses in 1996 (among them TLC Beatrice, Warnaco Group, Jockey International, and Tootsie Roll Industries) were concentrated in food, personal service, nondurable goods manufacturing, and clothing. Oprah Winfrey's Harpo Entertainment Group, one of the largest African American-owned firms during the mid-1990s, became an industry powerhouse with sales revenues of $150 million and about 140 employees in 1994.[146] A civically minded person with an interest in spirituality and social amelioration, Winfrey creates humanistic work environments, supports a variety of charities, and speaks out for children's rights.

In positively glossing the lives of so many successful American merchants, entrepreneurs, inventors, and innovators in this chapter, we traced the contours of a powerful archetype of the merchant-entrepreneur-executive as hero in American culture. Beginning with the early colonial period permitted us to ponder the implications of founding a nation for the sake of profit, and to consider how that unique feature of American history informed cultural attitudes about business for over four centuries. We saw that the first European settlers to the colonies sold natural resources from the Americas to Europe before developing their own manufacturing base and accumulating their own capital resources out of which sprang the Industrial Revolution, which gave us some of our most enduring business icons. We have admired their belief in hard work, marveled at their business triumphs, and respected their many philanthropies and social contributions. The time has come to examine a competing national narrative, the entrepreneur as rascal and rogue, before moving on to the psychology of desire.

NOTES

1. Frank Grizzard and D. Boyd Smith, *Jamestown Colony: A Political, Social, and Cultural History* (Santa Barbara: ABC-CLIO, 2007), xxiv.
2. Grizzard and Smith, *Jamestown Colony*, xxvi–xxv.
3. Grizzard and Smith, *Jamestown Colony*, xxxi.
4. Grizzard and Smith, *Jamestown Colony*, xxxv–xxxvii.
5. Russell M. Lawson, *The Sea Mark: Captain John Smith's Voyage to New England* (Hanover, MA: University Press of New England, 2005), 4
6. Grizzard and Smith, *Jamestown Colony*, xxvii.
7. Karen Ordahl Kupperman, *The Jamestown Project* (Cambridge, MA: Belknap, 2007), 3.
8. Francis J. Bremer and Tom Webster, *Puritans and Puritanism in Europe and America, Volume One* (Santa Barbara, CA: ABC-CLIO, 2005), 505.
9. Bremer and Webster, *Puritans and Puritanism in Europe and America*, 508.
10. Floyd Stovall, *American Idealism* (New York: Kennikat, 1943), 7–8.

11. Irvin G. Wyllie, *The Self-Made Man in America: The Myth of Rags to Riches* (New Brunswick, NJ: Rutgers University Press, 1954), 87.

12. Wyllie, *The Self-Made Man in America*, 56–57.

13. Andrea Greenwood and Mark W. Harris, *An Introduction to the Unitarian and Universalist Traditions* (Cambridge: Cambridge University Press, 2011), 128.

14. Cochran, *Business in American Life*, 10.

15. Cochran, *Business in American Life*, 10–11.

16. Cochran, *Business in American Life*, 12–13.

17. Cochran, *Business in American Life*, 16–17.

18. Cochran, *Business in American Life*, 16.

19. Cochran, *Business in American Life*, 17.

20. Sawyer, "Entrepreneur and Social Order," 21.

21. Gordon S. Wood, *The Americanization of Benjamin Franklin* (New York: Penguin, 2005), 2.

22. Benjamin Franklin, *The Autobiography and Other Writings* (New York: New American Library, 1961), 16.

23. Franklin, *The Autobiography and Other Writings*, 92.

24. Wood, *The Americanization of Benjamin*, 19 & 42.

25. Stovall, *American Idealism*, 18–19.

26. Meredith Mason Brown, *Frontiersman: Daniel Boone and the Making of America* (Baton Rouge: University of Louisiana Press, 2008), 6.

27. Brown, *Frontiersman*, 37–38.

28. Brown, *Frontiersman*, 65.

29. Sawyer, "Entrepreneur and Social Order," 22.

30. Krooss and Gilbert, *American Business History*, 29.

31. Krooss and Gilbert, *American Business History*, 31.

32. Mansel G. Blackford, *A History of Small Business in America* (Chapel Hill, NC: University of North Carolina Press, 2003), 3.

33. Krooss and Gilbert, *American Business History*, 39.

34. Krooss and Gilbert, *American Business History*, 41.

35. Krooss and Gilbert, *American Business History*, 44–45.

36. Krooss and Gilbert, *American Business History*, 46.

37. Krooss and Gilbert, *American Business History*, 51.

38. Krooss and Gilbert, *American Business History*, 7.

39. Cochran, *Business in American Life*, 25.

40. Cochran, *Business in American Life,* 26–27.

41. Thomas Piketty, *Capital in the Twenty-First Century* (Cambridge, MA: Belknap, 2014), 152.

42. Cochran, *Business in American Life*, 51–52.

43. Cochran, *Business in American Life*, 62.

44. Dorothy Gregg, "John Stevens: General Entrepreneur," in *Men in Business: Essays in the History of Entrepreneurship*, edited by William Miller (Cambridge: Harvard University Press, 1952), 120–21.

45. Angel Kwolek-Folland, *Incorporating Women: A History of Women and Business in the United States* (New York: Palgrave Macmillan, 2002), 23.

46. Kwolek-Folland, *Incorporating Women*, 28–30.

47. Kwolek-Folland, *Incorporating Women*, 33–34.

48. Woody Holton, *Abigail Adams: A Life* (New York: Atria, 2010), 26–27.

49. Steve Fraser, *The Age of Acquiescence: The Life and Death of American Resistance to Organized Wealth and Power* (New York: Little, Brown, and Company, 2015), 21.

50. Fraser, *The Age of Acquiescence*, 21.

51. Cochran, *Business in American Life*, 62–63.

52. Cochran, *Business in American Life*, 64–65.

53. Krooss and Gilbert, *American Business History*, 119.

54. Kwolek-Folland, *Incorporating Women*, 45.

55. Kwolek-Folland, *Incorporating Women*, 47–48.

56. Cochran, *Business in American Life*, 138.

57. Wheaton J. Lane, *Vanderbilt: An Epic of the Steam Age* (New York: Alfred Knopf, 1942), 16–17.

58. T. J. Stiles, *The First Tycoon: The Epic Life of Cornelius Vanderbilt* (New York: Alfred A. Knopf, 2009), 25.

59. Stiles, *The First Tycoon*, 46.

60. Lane, *Commodore Vanderbilt*, 160–61.

61. Lane, *Commodore Vanderbilt*, 174–77.

62. Lane, *Commodore Vanderbilt*, 227.

63. Lane, *Commodore Vanderbilt*, 14.

64. David Nasaw, *Andrew Carnegie* (New York; Penguin, 2006), 4–5.

65. Nasaw, *Andrew Carnegie*, 33–34.

66. Nasaw, *Andrew Carnegie*, 38–39.

67. Nasaw, *Andrew Carnegie*, 57.

68. Nasaw, *Andrew Carnegie*, 184–85.

69. Nasaw, *Andrew Carnegie*, 257.

70. Andrew Carnegie, *The Gospel of Wealth and Other Timely Essays* (Eastford, CT: Martino Fine Books, 2010), 43.

71. Douglas Brinkley, *Wheels for the World: Henry Ford, His Company, and a Century of Progress* (New York: Viking, 2003), xvii.

72. Marshall William Fishwick, *The Hero, American Style* (New York: D. McKay Co., 1969), 101.

73. Brinkley, *Wheels for the World*, 11.

74. Fishwick, *The Hero: American Style*, 93.

75. Brinkley, *Wheels for the World*, xvii.

76. Steven Watts, *The People's Tycoon: Henry Ford and the American Century* (New York: Knopf, 2005), 29.

77. Watts, *The People's Tycoon*, 33.

78. Watts, *The People's Tycoon*, 87–88.

79. Brinkley, *Wheels for the World*, 115.

80. Brinkley, *Wheels for the World*, 155.

81. Brinkley, *Wheels for the World*, 162.

82. Brinkley, *Wheels for the World*, 105.

83. Watts, *The People's Tycoon*, 207–08.

84. Janet Wallach, *The Richest Woman in America: Hetty Green in the Gilded Age* (New York: Doubleday, 2012), 7–8.

85. Wallach, *The Richest Woman in America*, 9–10.

86. Wallach, *The Richest Woman in America*, 18.

87. Wallach, *The Richest Woman in America*, 118.

88. Charles Slack, *Hetty: The Genius and Madness of America's First Female Tycoon* (New York: Harper Perennial, 2005), 73.

89. Wallach, *The Richest Woman in America*, 94.

90. Wallach, *The Richest Woman in America*, 191–92.

91. Wallach, *The Richest Woman in America*, 99–100.

92. Wallach, *The Richest Woman in America*, 196.

93. Slack, *Hetty*, 226.

94. Wallach, *The Richest Woman in America*, 225.

95. Kwolek-Folland, *Incorporating Women*, 87.

96. Kwolek-Folland, *Incorporating Women*, 117.

97. Kwolek-Folland, *Incorporating Women*, 118.

98. Kwolek-Folland, *Incorporating Women*, 118.

99. Paul Olk, "Lessons from U.S. History for the 21st Century Corporation: The Changing Structure of Organizations and Role of Managers," in *Good Business: Exercising Effective and Ethical Leadership*, ed. James O'Toole and Don Mayer (New York: Routledge, 2010), 76.

100. Gordon Lloyd, *The Two Faces of Liberalism: How the Hoover-Roosevelt Debate Shapes the Twenty-First Century* (New York: M&M Scrivener, 2006), 163–164.

101. Paul Conkin, *The New Deal* (Arlington Heights, IL: Harlan Davidson, 1975), 53.

102. Cochran, *Business in American Life*, 245.

103. Olk, "Lessons from U.S. History," 79.

104. Cochran, *Business in American Life*, 159.

105. Cochran, *Business in American Life*, 190.

106. Arthur Herman, *Freedom's Forge: How American Business Produced Victory in World War II* (New York: Random House, 2012), 6–7.

107. Herman, *Freedom's Forge*, 9–10.

108. Herman, *Freedom's Forge*, 31–32.

109. Herman, *Freedom's Forge*, 157.

110. Herman, *Freedom's Forge*, 166.

111. Herman, *Freedom's Forge*, 115.

112. Herman, *Freedom's Forge*, 337.

113. Mark S. Ferrara, *Palace of Ashes: China and the Decline of American Higher Education* (Baltimore: Johns Hopkins University Press, 2015), 165.

114. Richard G. Wagner and Amy Duckett Wagner, *Levittown* (Charleston, SC: Arcadia, 2010), 7.

115. Carroll Pursell, *Technology in Postwar America: A History* (Cambridge: Cambridge University Press, 2007), 28.

116. Kenneth T. Jackson, *Crabgrass Frontier: The Suburbanization of the United States* (Oxford: Oxford University Press, 1985), 236.

117. Lawrence R. Samuel, *The American Middle Class: A Cultural History* (New York: Routledge, 2014), 30.

118. Milton Friedman, *Capitalism and Freedom* (Chicago: University of Chicago Press, 1962), 35–36.

119. Friedman, *Capitalism and Freedom*, 2.

120. Friedman, *Capitalism and Freedom*, 2.

121. Friedman, *Capitalism and Freedom*, 3.

122. Friedman, *Capitalism and Freedom*, 86.

123. Friedman, *Capitalism and Freedom*, 133.

124. Geoffrey Colvin, "The Ultimate Manager," *Fortune*, November 22, 1999, http://archive.fortune.com/magazines/fortune/fortune_archive/1999/11/22/269126/index.htm

125. Janet Lowe, *Jack Welch Speaks: Wit and Wisdom from the World's Greatest Business Leader* (Hoboken, NJ: John Wiley & Sons, 2006), 222.

126. Robert G. Hagstrom, *The Warren Buffett Way* (Hoboken: John Wiley & Sons, 2005), 2.

127. Hagstrom, *The Warren Buffett Way*, 3.

128. Hagstrom, *The Warren Buffett Way*, 4.

129. Hagstrom, *The Warren Buffett Way*, 63.

130. Hagstrom, *The Warren Buffett Way*, 149.

131. Jonathan Stempel, "Buffett Donates $2.8 Billion to Gates, Family Charities," *Reuters*, July 15, 2014, http://www.reuters.com/article/us-buffett-charities-idUSKBN0FK2D920140715

132. Howard Means, *Money and Power: The History of Business* (New York: John Wiley & Sons, 2001), 238.

133. Means, *Money and Power*, 237–40.

134. Walter Isaacson, *The Innovators: How a Group of Hackers, Geniuses, and Geeks Created the Digital Revolution* (New York: Simon & Schuster, 2014), 314–15.

135. Isaacson, *The Innovators*, 328.

136. Means, *Money and Power*, 231–32.

137. Means, *Money and Power*, 235–36.

138. Isaacson, *The Innovators*, 346–47.

139. Isaacson, *The Innovators*, 352–53.

140. Isaacson, *The Innovators*, 365.

141. Walter Isaacson, *Steve Jobs* (New York: Simon & Schuster, 2011), xx–xxi.

142. Isaacson, *Steve Jobs*, 560–61.

143. Isaacson, *Steve Jobs*, 564–65.

144. Isaacson, *Steve Jobs*, 567–69.

145. Kwolek-Folland, *Incorporating Women*, 171.
146. Kwolek-Folland, *Incorporating Women*, 197–98.

Chapter Two

Rascals, Scoundrels, and Corporate Villains

The self-made entrepreneur who builds capital through hard work and introduces advanced labor-saving tools or techniques that increase production along with productivity, and thereby improves the economic lives of ordinary people, along with his own, is an important iteration of the American business hero. Faith in a doctrine of work and a gospel of wealth stand firmly at the heart of the American Dream—a mythic vision grounded in liberty but retaining strong materialistic appeals, since its attainment implied a level of financial success that "bought" some measure of independence. Yet, for all of its virtues, that affirmative portrayal of the American business hero omits unethical business activities and their adverse impact on society, and masks certain realities about the creation of wealth. This chapter balances that asymmetry by following a counternarrative present in American culture that frames business leaders not as heroic entrepreneurs who drive economic expansion, but as exploiters of labor and reckless pillagers of natural resources. Mercantilism may be fundamental to a prosperous society, but profit-oriented exchange driven by avarice, deception, and selfishness cannot be reconciled with notions of social justice and communal harmony.

In Western Europe, overt hankering for profit raised suspicions about the morality of those plying the mercantile arts. One thirteenth-century French Dominican lamented the quarrels, drinking, fraud, perfidy, and injustice that permeated medieval marketplaces, and contemporaneous literary portrayals of medieval markets reveal social spaces teeming with variety and opportunity, but also "insidious, deceitful, and harmful" environments where people and traders competed with each other for material goods, driven by their own venality, cupidity, and gluttony.[1] Our notion of the "huckster" as a deceitful seller comes from the medieval bazaar where the term denoted retailers of small batches of goods, often women, at the bottom of marketing hierarchies. Hucksters were watched closely by authorities, lest they usurp the privileges of more permanent retailers, sell substandard foodstuffs, or engage in unacceptable regrating, forestalling, or other price-raising activities.[2] Another negative term associated with shoddy retail practice is "trumpery," a term dating from the fifteenth century.

As medieval European feudalism transitioned to capitalism, trade expanded and new markets developed, spurred on by the civil turmoil resulting from fluctuating property relations. Capitalism, a system of exchange relations and profit accumulation driven by entrepreneurial activity and the rise of the market ethic from the twelfth and thirteenth centuries onward, challenged moral and economic ideals associated with the agrarian society championed by the Church (which viewed profit making for its own sake as a temptation toward avarice).[3] To combat flagrant fraud in the marketplace, systems of law, morality, and sociability were established with the intention of eliminating dishonesty and creating the mutual trust and confidence required of virtuous economic relationships.[4] Medieval literature and art frequently touched upon figures of vice in the marketplace, and accusations were leveled against traders for selling unwholesome victuals at excessive prices, for using false measures and weights, and for outright deceit potentially harmful to the common good.[5] The stock character of the untrustworthy, rapacious, and unrepentant retailer remained popular into the sixteenth and seventeenth centuries, as European mercantile activities in the New World brought into sharp relief the incompatibility of religious ethics and marketplace values—of salvation and profit, a discord that dominated much of European and American business history.

On October 11, 1492, as his ships approached shore after more than a month at sea, Christopher Columbus spotted a faint light off in the distance, possibly a handheld torch of some sort, indicating land. The indigenous inhabitants of the Caribbean island, in the present-day Bahamas, were friendly and generous, and lived communally. Little did they realize how radically murderous would be the arrival of these strangers from the West who would alter the landscape of the Americas and impact indigenous societies. In his diary, transcribed by Bartolomé de Las Casas, Columbus describes the worthless red caps and bric-a-brac that they presented to the Arawak people as gifts, as well as the "parrots and cotton thread in balls and javelins and many other things" that the islanders traded "to us for other things which we gave them, such as small glass beads and bells."[6] Columbus found them "very poor in everything," since they went "around as naked as their mother bore them," but he conceded that they were "all very well formed, with handsome bodies and good faces."[7] Unlike the Europeans, they did not carry arms, made no iron, and were so ignorant of steel that they cut themselves on edges of swords shown to them. For these reasons, Columbus concluded, they would make "good and intelligent servants" and "would become Christians very easily, for it seemed to me that they had no religion."[8] He brought six guileless Native Americans, ignorant of the value of gold and silver and content with their "poor" lives, back to Europe for the edification and amusement of his royal Spanish sponsors.

Although the conversion of indigenous populations to Christianity made a good pretext for exploiting them and despoiling their lands, Columbus drew up a contract with King Ferdinand and Queen Isabella of Spain before his first voyage that entitled him to keep one-tenth of "all and every kind of merchandise, whether pearls, precious stones, gold, silver, spices, and other objects and merchandise whatsoever, of whatever kind, name and sort, which may be bought, bartered, discovered, acquired and obtained" by him in the New World.[9] Columbus continued to quest for capital on subsequent voyages, and in pursuit of it, he enslaved and brutalized many indigenous inhabitants. For example, growing resistance to Columbus on the island of Hispaniola, and his demands for a soft yellow metal, created a cycle of violence and reprisal. In one extreme case, Columbus tortured and murdered those who refused to adhere to a tribute system that he put in place. Rather than submit to his tyranny, 50,000 native islanders destroyed their food reserves and committed mass suicide. Shockingly, by 1548, only 500 indigenous inhabitants remained out of an original population of many hundreds of thousands.[10] In the mercantile mind lurks a profit pathology that Spanish explorer Hernán Cortés mistakenly believed could be allayed with more loot. When an ambassador to the Aztec ruler Moctezuma II asked the conquistador why Europeans hunted so feverishly for gold, Cortés answered, "I and my companions suffer from a disease of the heart which can only be cured by gold."[11] That malady damaged the hearts—and distorted the minds—of many European colonizers.

The ravenous looting of the New World by European adventurers vindicated lingering fears held by the Church (and many literary luminaries) regarding the moral hazards of the mercantile impulse, but profit-driven enterprise aggregated capital from the conquest of the Americas that, together with the advent of joint-stock companies, made possible the establishment of colonies around the globe. King James I of England and Scotland chartered London Company and Plymouth Company in 1606 (about the time that the French reached the West Indies, the Dutch explored New Amsterdam, and Spanish missionaries settled Santa Fe). The London and Plymouth charters carefully balanced corporate ends with national interests. For instance, the London Company held a trading monopoly, but only so long as trade was conducted in English ships and through English ports.[12] English (and Dutch) joint-stock companies effectively raised enormous sums for business ventures involving transatlantic voyages and the establishment of colonies by limiting each investor's loss to the amount of his share. Dividing up risk among shareholders promoted the financing of long-distance trade to Asia and other parts of the world as well, since many people, with limited liability, could join together in pursuit of profits derived from the exploration and colonization of far-flung lands. A direct ancestor of the modern corporation, the joint-stock company (together with the nation-state) was the most important organizational invention of the European Renaissance. Without it, the modern world could not have come into being—and the history of the United States might have taken a different course all together. [13]

The joint-stock companies that founded Jamestown, the Plymouth Colony, and the Massachusetts Bay Colony permitted self-government (a privilege subsequently passed onto the colonies) although their aim was to turn a profit—not to encourage independence. "Planters" traveled to the New World and donated their labor to the colonial enterprise, while "adventurers" (from which the phrase "venture capitalist" derives) contributed financial resources but remained in England. An acute shortage of labor in the early colonies meant that many planters who stayed were rewarded with land allocations and inclusion in the founding of colonial towns. Some of them sold their land allocations or rented them out, and thus became precursors to modern real-estate developers. One especially enterprising fellow, Joshua Fisher, arrived in Massachusetts as an indentured servant, but ended his life with thirty parcels of land in four towns, largely due to his membership in the General Court (which granted permission to establish new towns). Such corruptions, however, were "strictly business as usual" in the New World. [14] Town founders were not always scrupulous either. James Fitch enticed settlers onto more than 1 million acres in eastern Connecticut titled from indigenous peoples, and in an early American "bait and switch" scheme he kept the best land for himself, and left some of those whom he lured with false promises and "pore rockey hills." [15]

The Puritan town-founding system, a capital-intensive process funded using a joint-stock model to encourage permanent settlement, proved highly effective, and southern and coastal New England were settled with astonishing speed. That feat owed much to individuals known later as "entrepreneurs," people such as Joseph Parsons who turned his knowledge of the fur trade, native languages, and the process of land acquisition for settlements into a sizable fortune in just fifty years. [16] Other colonists made money harvesting natural resources, expanding trade, and generating new manufacturing operations, as well as selling urban land for immediate income while holding backcountry acreage for future appreciation. While there existed a desire among some colonists to build a shining city on a hill, most settlers aimed to make a little money while it was being constructed. [17]

Supplying commodities to other colonial enterprises in the Americas, such as those in the Caribbean, was another way to profit. For example, the sugarcane that Columbus brought to the islands on his second voyage re-

quired large-scale planting operations to make cultivation feasible and production profitable. Because few Europeans were willing to undertake the
backbreaking toil that sugar farming demanded (including wielding machetes
and hauling cane), Spanish settlers were given rights to compel the *enco-
mienda* system.[18] Many indigenous forced laborers fled that miserable plight;
those who could not escape died of excessive work and torturous treatment.
Diseases such as measles, mumps, bubonic plague, influenza, and smallpox,
unwittingly brought by Europeans and for which native populations had no
immunity, killed more than 90 percent of local populations in Central and
South America and in the Caribbean.[19] Rapid depopulation allowed colonial
powers to set up trading posts and survey new territories more easily, but it
deprived them of cheap forced labor. Consequently, profiteering colonizers
began importing slaves from Africa.

By the 1480s, "workers in many sugar plantations, especially those on the
Atlantic islands off the coast of Africa, were all black African slaves."[20]
Growing consumer demand in Europe for luxury goods, including sugar,
accelerated the exploitation of forced labor. In fact, in the 350 years after
Columbus's second voyage, mercantile slave operations conveyed more
Africans across the Atlantic than Europeans.[21] Any sea voyage to the New
World was harrowing, but African slaves endured imprisonment in pens
before being boarded onto ships, where they were crowded into filthy cargo
spaces below deck sometimes without enough room to sit down. These luckless souls suffered regular beatings at the hands of crew members, and with
food and water scarce, as many as half of the captives, often grabbed from
their houses and fields, died in route during early slave voyages. Societies
around the world permitted slavery in 1500, but plantation slavery was a
particularly repugnant form of that institution. It prevailed because European
Christians and Arabic Muslims regarded black Africans as inferior primitive
peoples, and that racism sufficiently justified their capture and enslavement.[22] Colonial plantation owners (often absentee merchants or investors)
and their operators came to view their black slaves as machines that lasted
about seven years before needing replacement. Catholic, and later Protestant,
churches officially acknowledged slavery—and some church leaders even
praised the reprehensible practice. They reasoned that although enslavement
thoroughly debased the lives of the captives, "it gave them the opportunity of
getting into heaven by becoming Christian, so in the long run they were
better off."[23] Such claims passed as rational for centuries, and the plantation
model expanded to include the planting and harvesting of commodities such
as indigo, cotton, coffee, and eventually tobacco.

In the Providence Island colony, established in 1630 off the coast of
Nicaragua by a small joint-stock company composed of the most prominent
lay Puritans in England, investors and planters overcame their misgivings
about the risks forced labor posed to their godly enterprise. The islanders

created a plantation economy, with tobacco as its principal product, bolstered by slavery and privateering (legalized piracy of Spanish ships). They enslaved so many Africans that the latter became "a larger percentage of the total population than in any other English colony for decades to come."[24] Many Puritan investors in the Providence Island Company were seasoned veterans in organizing and running other colonial settlements (in Virginia, Bermuda, Massachusetts, Connecticut, and Maine), and they saw these efforts as part of an integrated plan "for the creation of a godly English society in America."[25] Although they expected Providence Island to be more profitable than Plymouth Colony in the cold, rocky north—and regarded it as a more promising location for trade, the Spanish captured Providence Island in 1641 to stop the piracy of its ships and expelled the English.

Mercantile outposts and colonial settlements tended to measure their success by the economic bottom line (profits generated for owners and stockholders), and commercial companies operating in the rugged American West shared "in common an agenda of exploiting available resources (land, animal, mineral, and people) for greater profits."[26] From the 1500s to early 1800s, a lucrative fur trade encouraged extensive harvesting of terrestrial and marine mammals (including sea otters and fur seals) from Alaska to Southern California, but particularly beavers whose fur-wool was used in the manufacture of hats. British companies (such as Hudson's Bay and North West) and American enterprises (including the American Fur Company and Pacific Fur Company) hunted and trapped on diverse lands in the late eighteen and early nineteenth centuries. Staffing mercantile outposts presented significant challenges, and frontier shopkeepers hired Native Americans as porters and manual laborers and generally exploited them as cheap labor. By 1700, a process of social segregation reinforced by discriminatory provincial laws and statutes allowing slavery gradually arose across the colonies. A rural society based on plantation slavery and cotton was established in the South by 1770. The plantation economy that developed along the southern seaboard required large capital investments in slave labor, so that the black population was 40 percent of the total from Maryland on south.[27]

Southern planters wanted to preserve the manners and pretensions of the landed gentry in Europe, but as slavery became their main business, that feature of society hardened distinctions between North and South, distinctions that ultimately simmered into civil war. In the South, blacks were used as field hands, trained for skilled work (including carpentry or masonry), and sold for higher prices amid the rising demand for slaves. Most owners limited their plantations to a size that one white overseer could manage, and therefore expansion involved establishing new sites, often noncontiguous to existing ones.[28] Merchants in eastern coastal colonies thrived supplying commodities vital to sugar planters and their slave laborers in the Caribbean. Prior to the Revolutionary War, a considerable share of continental exports (of dried fish, oats, corn, beans, flour, butter, cheese, rice, onions, soap, candles, sheep, hogs, poultry, and slaves) made their way to the West Indies. In exchange for these commodities, mainland colonists bought rum, sugar, and molasses from the West Indies. The wealth that accumulated from this lucrative trade arrangement assured the prosperity of New England and the middle colonies.[29] Although it declined after the American Revolution, trade continued between the two regions, and sugar produced in the West Indies remained an important commodity well into the nineteenth century.

The Declaration of Independence famously insisted that "all men are created equal," but that noble ideal did not apply to African Americans. The Three-Fifths Compromise reached by the Constitutional Convention in 1787 saved the new nation from collapse, due to a weak federal government created by the Articles of the Confederation, but at the price of the continuance of slavery. A black slave counted as three-fifths of a person when determining the legislative representation of southern states in the House of Representatives.[30] The brutality of slavery increased with legal recognition and conferred upon enslaved and freed blacks a subordinate social status, but the compromise gave southern states more political power in the national government than if slaves were not counted. Generally speaking, the American slave trade was "in the hands of small entrepreneurs, operating with $10,000 to $20,000 in capital," and, like horse-trading, "the business was rife with misrepresentations of the age, health, and the ability of the slaves."[31] Extensive human smuggling from abroad, theft of slaves from plantations, and kidnapping free blacks persisted alongside the legal slave trade. The congressional prohibition of the importation of slaves in 1807 only raised the value of slaves and made breeding programs lucrative.[32] Slave narratives penned by victims such as John Jea, Harriet Jacobs, Moses Roper, and Frederick Douglass illustrate the cruelty of American slavery in stark terms. Jacobs describes the psychological effects of slavery on women repeatedly stalked and sexually abused by their white masters. Roper recounts being tortured with a cotton screw (for packing and pressing cotton) and having his nails pulled off, the fingers of his left hand crushed, and his feet beaten after trying to escape a torturous master.[33]

The highly exploitative nature of slavery made that institution insanely profitable for slaveholders. From 1770 to 1800, the number of slaves grew from 400,000 to 1 million, and the 1860 census counted more than 4 million slaves—meaning that slavery was still growing before the Civil War broke out. Of course, not all southern whites owned slaves, and only a tiny number of them held as many as Thomas Jefferson (over 600), but the "fortunes based on slavery were the most concentrated of all."[34] Between 1770 and 1865, the total market value for slaves represented nearly a year and a half of the national income, a figure roughly equal to the total value of farmland. If slaves were included along with other components of prosperity, then total

American wealth stood at around four and a half years of national income (or about the same as the present day).[35] Breaking those figures down by region, we see that the combined value of enslaved individuals and land exceeded four years of national income in the American South, meaning that southern slave owners in the New World controlled more wealth than the landlords of old Europe.[36] In the North, by contrast, where there were almost no slaves, total wealth stood at about half of that in the South or Europe. Northern states became more egalitarian because capital in the north was not worth very much; land was abundant and becoming a landowner remained relatively cheap.[37] The North also mechanized first, which gave it a significant advantage during the Civil War. South of the Mason-Dixon line, the inequities of ownership took the most violent and extreme form possible—since one half of the population owned the other half.[38]

When the North emerged victorious from the Civil War, big business and industrial capital were just getting under way, but the term "entrepreneur" had already acquired positive connotations. It was a curious semantic transition. The French word *entreprise* designated war actions, and *entreprendre* meant "to attack a person or a castle for pillage or to take prisoners for ransom."[39] Traditionally, the entrepreneur "took risks, devoted himself to calculation and trickery, and had no respect for established conventions," and his transgression of guild norms substantiated the suspicion in which he was regarded well after the French Revolution.[40] To determine the most characteristic forms of behavior by those engaged in business, the scholars Michel Villette and Catherine Vuillermot collected and classified commentary by social philosophers, economists, and sociologists from 1707 to 2000. Their subjects generally pursued their own egotistical interests, practiced risky behaviors, and speculated on uncertainty, and they were contemptuous of the law and might easily skirt the dictates of the political, social, and moral order (thus leaving them open to accusation and prosecution). They derived wealth from exclusive information and control over secrets, and the methodical exploitation of labor often augmented their accumulated capital.[41] The entrepreneurs from whom Villette and Vuillermot derived commentary sought ways around the rules of the market and used every means at their disposal— most notably political control of the state—to restrain free trade when disadvantageous to their business interests, or to secure monopoly positions when beneficial (often by taking advantage of political disequilibria).

From the late eighteenth century to the late nineteenth century, the logic of capitalism profoundly reorganized American society by emphasizing the production of goods and the retention of surplus worth realized by "adding value" to a product. That approach to capital accumulation extended to clothing and textiles, machines, tools and metal utensils, railroads, and armaments during the first wave of industrialization—and in a single century, capitalism spread, became concentrated, and asserted itself through new production techniques and industries that expanded to include the entire world by feeding imperialism and providing a new means of dominion over the worker.[42] With massive capital accumulations, big business occupied an increasingly prominent position in American society as the move away from agriculture to industry accelerated. To this day, it remains an unexamined axiom that American businesses are engines of economic growth and social progress, when in reality the heads of enterprise generally make decisions that maximize corporate growth and profitability, attract investors, compete with rival companies, and accumulate resources. In choosing how to carry out their decisions, they select from all possible forms of organization for labor and the production of goods and services, and they pick those forms that provide the highest return on invested capital.[43] From 1780 to 1880, capitalism acquired an unprecedented transformative power that impacted every aspect of society, including productive systems, producing classes, mentalities and values, transportation and communication channels, and ways of living and consuming.[44]

Moreover, to the extent that capitalism obliges the rich to make the poor work harder and longer, the fortunes of the wealthy increase and those of the poor deteriorate.[45] In England, the bourgeoisie (who owned the means of production) chained the proletariat to factories, mines, and industrial farms so completely that preteenage children accounted for 13 percent of cotton industry labor in 1834. Many workers in textile mills writhed under severe regulations, fines, wage reductions, and dismissals, and they somberly bore unwholesome work spaces, harsh jobs, long days, illness, and workplace accidents, which were then part and parcel of the exploitation of human beings for the sake of profit.[46] No wonder eighteenth-century poet-painter William Blake called such places "dark Satanic Mills" and yearned for the restoration of "Englands mountains green" upon which the "Countenance Divine" once shone.[47] In the United States, the deskilling of artisanal production (by breaking down production to its most elemental parts) widened the gap between rich and poor and helped to lay the groundwork for market crashes in 1819 and 1837. When social inequality exploded during the Gilded Age, it engendered a brutal confrontation between wealthy business magnates and their miserable workers, between cultivated comfort and unrefined anguish, between absolute power and utter destitution, between tycoon robber barons and workaday folk looking for a "square deal." Cornelius Vanderbilt and Andrew Carnegie remained heroic figures to some, but to others they were villainous opportunists.

The life of J. D. Rockefeller, the son of a real rascal, typifies that moment in American history when a small group of powerful business moguls reaped colossal gains. Rockefeller's ancestors settled on a farm in New Jersey around 1723 where they flourished and acquired large landholdings.[48] Rockefeller's paternal grandmother Lucy Avery, a "rawboned and confi-

dent" enterprising former schoolteacher, endured the checkered successes of
her husband Godfrey's business ventures, which caused them to live a no-
madic existence between New York and Massachusetts.[49] In 1839, the Rockefellers moved to Richford, New York, southeast of Ithaca and northwest of
Binghamton, where Lucy managed family and farm and developed an interest in herbal medicines.[50] John D.'s father, William Avery Rockefeller, a
sworn foe to conventional morality, lived a vagabond existence. Throughout
his life "he expended considerable energy on tricks and schemes to avoid
plain hard work."[51] A confidence man who sometimes posed as a deaf-mute
to sell cheap novelties, he presented false claims about himself and his wares
and cleverly worked a large territory to elude the law.[52] J.D.'s mother Eliza
came from a Baptist family of Scotch-Irish descent, but that religious upbringing did not prevent her from falling for "Big Bill" Rockefeller, who
may have been after her family fortune.

Far from reforming his ways after their marriage, Big Bill brought his
girlfriend, Nancy Brown, to live with them as a "housekeeper."[53] Big Bill's
antics, all told, would take pages to fill, but on their account John's childhood
was passed in relative squalor and his adolescence in threadbare fashion.
Sometime around 1843, Bill put down a thousand dollars for a ninety-two-
acre parcel in the hinterlands of upstate New York that sloped down gently to
Owasco Lake, and there he built a two-story clapboard house replete with
cracks large enough to let through winter squalls.[54] John attended Sunday
school a short distance from their hilltop house, and he grew up on a steady
diet of the proverbial wisdom of evangelical Protestantism, which led him to
acquire puritanical attitudes of work, frugality, and charity that remained
throughout his life.[55] By the time the family relocated to Cleveland, his
father's clandestine bigamous marriage prevented John from attending university. Instead, he completed a short course of study at a commercial college
and at sixteen years of age took a position with the commission merchants
and produce shippers Hewitt and Tuttle as a bookkeeper, collector of rents,
letter writer, and bill payer—duties that exposed Rockefeller to a broad commercial universe at a young age.[56] With the help of a loan of $1,000 from his
wayward father at 10 percent interest, he became a partner in the commission
house Clark and Rockefeller at the age of eighteen and went on to become
the richest man in the world (though not without exhibiting some of the
unsavory attitudes and behaviors indicative of Gilded Age business and the
mercantile mind).

Wealth was a sign of God's favor, according to the celebrated Congregationalist preacher Henry Ward Beecher, who called poverty the fault of the
poor. In a like manner, J. D. Rockefeller never wavered in the belief that his
career was divinely favored, once asserting flatly, "God gave me my money."[57] The Gilded Age was the most fertile period in American history "for
schemers and dreamers, sharp-elbowed men and fast-talking hucksters, char-

latans and swindlers."[58] As the South rebuilt and the North grew its industrial might, a mania for patents and invention, along with a contagion of greed, swept the nation. Perhaps a depletion of altruism resulting from the high drama of saving the union and emancipating the slaves left behind a residuum of cupidity, but many people in the North took shortcuts to success in that postwar era of unrestrained growth. Their "universal race for riches threatened to overthrow existing moral systems and to subvert the authority of church and state" that for centuries acted to check business avarice.[59] Rockefeller entered the oil-refining business with his brother William originally to supply kerosene for lamps (replaced by electric lights), but later to fuel the nascent automobile industry. In an incessant effort to drive down costs, Rockefeller pitted suppliers against each other, and because of the large scale of his operations, he obtained discounted railroad and shipping rates that shut out small business owners (much in the same way that Walmart has leveraged the vast scale of its operations in our time). Although they insured uniform shipments of crude and refined oil in massive quantities, Ida Tarbell, Rockefeller's staunchest critic, called his early deals with the Lake Shore Railroad the original sin from which all the others sprang. Tarbell rightly perceived that this position gave Standard Oil a special power to compel railroad-freight concessions (or rebates), a controversial practice that unfairly drove competitors out of business.[60]

When over-capacity in refining tumbled oil prices, the entire industry teetered on the brink of ruin. His massive fortune put in jeopardy by the actions of competitors beyond his control, Rockefeller envisioned a giant cartel to reduce capacity, stabilize prices, and streamline the industry by long-term planning and strategic alliances. In establishing the joint-stock firm Standard Oil in 1870, Rockefeller avoided the pitfalls of speculative drilling, and instead invested in delivery and storage, thus cutting out middlemen to create permanent corporate institutions, and to develop the world's first multinational company. His success owes much to a pact with the South Improvement Company (SIC), which reduced rates even further and allowed "drawbacks," instruments of unparalleled competitive cruelty. For instance, drawbacks meant that on oil shipments from western Pennsylvania to Cleveland, Ohio, "Standard Oil would receive a forty-cent rebate on every barrel it shipped, plus another forty cents for every barrel shipped to Cleveland by competitors!" Biographer Ron Chernow calls it an "astonishing piece of knavery, grand scale collusion such as American industry had never witnessed."[61] It paid off, though, and at a time when most Americans earned $2 per day, Rockefeller made $2 a second—or $50 million per year.[62] When the Supreme Court declared Standard Oil a monopoly in 1911, and broke it up into thirty-four different companies, Rockefeller shrewdly retained control over them all—to his great financial advantage.

Rockefeller's reputation as a businessman declined steeply following the 1914 Ludlow Massacre. The tragedy occurred when Rockefeller's private security forces joined with members of the Colorado National Guard, opened machine-gun fire on striking workers at Colorado Fuel and Iron, and set fire to their tent colony. Rockefeller purchased that Colorado company in 1902, and under his command the working conditions grew so onerous that after a dozen years more than 11,000 workers went on strike to demand union representation, better wages, humane hours, and improved housing. The fact that their appeals were met with murderous rage led one Cleveland paper to assert that the "charred bodies of two dozen women and children show that *Rockefeller knows how to win.*" Author Helen Keller called Mr. Rockefeller "a monster of capitalism" who "gives charity and in the same breath he permits the helpless workmen, their wives and children to be shot down."[63] John D. Rockefeller, Jr. was shaken by the massacre and the public outcry that followed, but his father kept his cool, perhaps because his net worth had reached an apex a year earlier, when his fortune was estimated at $900 million or 2.5 percent of the nation's gross national product.[64]

Industrialists such as Andrew Carnegie and Henry Ford also struggled against labor and at times exhibited unsavory business behaviors. Despite his experience as a bobbin boy, boiler attendant, and soaker of bobbins in vats of oil during his early teens, Carnegie's relationship with his workers remained strained throughout his career, as evidenced by his purchase of a steel plant in Homestead, Pennsylvania, in 1883 with a "history of labor militancy, a union contract, several well-organized Amalgamated lodges, and a rail mill that competed with his own at Edgar Thomson."[65] With the workers' collective bargaining agreement set to expire in June of 1892, Carnegie and Henry Clay Frick (who oversaw company operations) intended to break the union, reorganize, and introduce a sliding wage scale. When Amalgamated rank-and-file voters rejected Carnegie's final contract offer, they were locked out for three days. On June 25, payday at Homestead, notices were posted throughout the plant and adjoining town stating that the union rejected management's proposals. New construction put the mill behind eleven-foot fences topped with barbwire and searchlights and fitted with portholes for guns.[66] The workers referred to it as "Fort Frick."

Homestead strikers would not give up without fighting Carnegie's effort to cut costs at their expense. Determined to keep his plant closed, the workers defied lockout notices, and with military efficiency they set up patrols of the river that ran alongside the plant. They scoured the area for newcomers possibly linked to management. It was a shrewd maneuver, for during the earlier morning hours of July 6, 1892, 300 private security forces (arranged by Frick in advance) attempted to infiltrate plant property. Bringing in the Pinkerton agents under cover of night, Frick hoped to escape detection by worker-scouts, but his barges were intercepted by foresighted strikers. An alarm sounded around 3 a.m. that brought townspeople, workers, women, and children to the scene, some of them armed with rifles and old Civil War weaponry. They surged toward the riverbank to prevent the troops from landing. When the Pinkertons attempted to come ashore and secure company property, shots rang out, and Billy Foy and Captain Heinde of the Pinkerton force were killed. Over the next two hours, three steelworkers lost their lives and dozens more were injured.[67] By 5 a.m., news of the battle, telegraphed to Pittsburgh, brought hundreds of working men to the fray, along with reporters and illustrators. Troops attempting to disembark were repulsed again by gunfire at 8 a.m., and with few options left, they surrendered at around 5 p.m. that evening. Furious at the mercenaries, members of the crowd formed a 600-yard gauntlet and pummeled them with fists, stones, and wooden clubs. Some surrendering soldiers of fortune were beaten over the head with the butt end of rifles and had clothes torn off their backs, but no lives were lost in that gruesome procession.[68] On July 10, Governor Pattison mobilized the Pennsylvania National Guard, which took possession of the plant two days later, but the damage to Carnegie's reputation was severe. American and British newspapers condemned the savagery of American business practices, and they made clear that the massacre of laborers at Homestead was only one example of the atrocities committed by capitalist tycoons.

Robber barons like Rockefeller and Carnegie had few fiercer critics than the economist and social scientist Thorstein Veblen. The child of Norwegian immigrants who settled in Wisconsin, Veblen learned English, attended Carleton College, and completed a doctorate at Yale University before embarking on a career as a writer, educator, and acerbic social commentator. Perhaps due to his humble origins, and the difficulty that he encountered establishing an academic career, Veblen took aim at academe in *The Higher Learning in America* (1918), a spirited defense of the disinterested pursuit of knowledge in which he advocated for enhanced faculty representation as a ballast against the unchecked power of university presidents and business-minded governing boards. He recognized that "the intrusion of business principles in the universities goes to weaken and retard the pursuit of learning, and therefore to defeat the ends for which a university is maintained," and he found the same pattern of corporate influence in American culture more generally.[69] Veblen defined business as those efforts undertaken for pecuniary gain, and he distinguished them from the activities of industry (which produced goods of social value). In his view, business leaders too often pursued profit over productive industrial activity, and as a consequence benefits to society from generational technical advancement were displaced by conflict and competition.[70]

Rather than referring to them as daring figures of enterprise, Veblen slighted those business and industry leaders with diminutives such as "Captains of Solvency" and "Lieutenants of Finance." He thought little of the millionaires of his day, believing that they essentially reduced all business activity to the monotonous increase of wealth. Veblen noted their "short-sightedness and lack of insight," and he found absolutely nothing recondite about their business methods. [71] Self-interest made thoughtful curiosity alien to businessmen, and their pecuniary mindset and mercantile orientation rendered commercial skepticism impossible—attitudes leading them to become "necessarily conservative." [72] Unlike precapitalist businessmen and business-women who engaged in handicraft or trade to make a living, barons of business made profits through systematic investment and sought to attain control over some sizable portion of the industrial system—and to keep it. [73] Under the regime of large-scale enterprise, which made relations between producers and consumers remote and impersonal, business management could proceed by calculating "profit and loss, untroubled by sentimental considerations of human kindness." [74] When a pecuniary orientation becomes a "habit of thought," it sanctifies ownership and minimizes traditional religious appeals to morality and human dignity. [75] Discontent arises when the narrow focus on profit causes a demand for the restraint of business—which is often manifested in socialism or even more dramatically in anarchism.

Despite Henry Ford's quasi-socialist rhetoric, his record of labor relations was sometimes worse than the robber barons who preceded him. Widely applauded for introducing the $5 Day, which traded higher pay for increased productivity, Ford became the object of derision for his resistance to labor unions later in his life, and for the dehumanizing labor practices associated with the unparalleled mechanization of his factories. Executives and bean counters at Ford Motor Company loved the economies of scale that the assembly line created, but Ford, a notorious efficiency monger, also reduced the "necessity of thought on the part of the worker," limited their movements, reduced lunch and bathroom breaks to a total of fifteen minutes per day, and forbade sitting, squatting, whistling, leaning on machines, and conversation on the factory floor. While company "spotters" patrolled factory floors for rule breakers, Ford's Socialization Department regulated the lives, and the morality, of employees and their families outside of work and made compliance a necessary qualification for the profit-sharing bonus. That institution, later renamed the Education Department, was disbanded in 1921. In its place rose the Ford Service Department, staffed "by thugs and labor-spies under the leadership of an ex-boxer named Harry Bennett, charged with keeping Ford an open shop." [76]

During the Great Depression, Ford's responses to attempts to unionize his factories grew violent. In March 1932, police in Dearborn, Michigan, fired on marching workers at point-blank range, killing three people (including a *New York Times* photographer) and wounding fifty more. [77] Strikes continued across the automotive industry in 1935 and 1936, but Chrysler, General Motors, and Ford Motor Company continued to oppose collective bargaining. Finding sit-down strikes and other methods of work stoppage effective, the United Automobile Workers (UAW) organized a massive sit-down strike at a General Motors factory in Flint—infuriating chairman Alfred P. Sloan. As the strikes spread to Ford, one prominent newspaper observed that Harry Bennett's "service department" was the largest private army in the world.[78] Instead of ceding to the inevitability of unionization following passage of the Wagner Act, which established the National Labor Relations Board (NLRB) to enforce employee rights, Ford supported Bennett's pledge to keep union men and their leaflets away from his River Rouge plant. On May 26, 1937, labor organizers and their supporters approached an overpass to the massive facility, and they were surrounded by thirty to forty men who beat them to a pulp. Newspaper photographers captured the bloody scene, and in light of the public's negative attitude toward big business and its leaders after 1929, Ford's tactics were nationally and internationally condemned. Ford Motor Company was found guilty of violating the National Labor Relations Act in Detroit in 1939, and two years later the NLRB investigated incidents of corporate "terrorism" at the River Rouge plant, including thirty reported beatings of union sympathizers and a near fatal attack on a United Automobile Workers lawyer.[79]

In the early spring of 1941, the union called for a strike at the River Rouge plant, and it continued into May. Rather than relent, Henry Ford seemed willing to close the factory down and let Bennett fight it out to the end. However, when his wife, Clara, threatened to divorce him if he did not settle with the unions, he immediately capitulated.[80] Like many business capitalists of the late nineteenth and early twentieth centuries, Ford was a "complex, wayward, mercurial" man with "a streak of meanness engendered by his hard early life, and prejudices that arose from ignorance." One associate of forty years called Henry Ford "petty, ignorant, jealous, desirous of running a one-man show, devious, insincere, inconsistent, malicious, and friendless."[81] Perhaps such accusations have some basis in fact, for Ford penned noxious anti-Semitic tracts in the 1930s—and Adolf Hitler praised the American automaker in *Mein Kampf* and awarded him the Third Reich's Grand Cross of the Supreme Order of the German Eagle in 1938.[82] Ford was not nearly so generous as Rockefeller and Carnegie in later life, either. In fact, he gave little to charity, though that shortcoming was rectified eleven years before his death when his son, Edsel, established the Ford Foundation.

As a result of New Deal reforms, unionization, a pervasive spirit of egalitarianism, and a call for shared economic prosperity, the period between 1937 and 1975 stands out in American history as an unprecedented era of *declining inequality* in the United States. In contrast to our own time, when income inequality threatens to plunge the nation into the seas of social unrest, this thirty-eight-year era of tax reforms, of changes in regulation for the financial sector, of labor reforms that privileged unions, of civil rights breakthroughs, and of the modernization of the South—these remarkable advances decreased inequality.[83] Maximum tax rates reached 90 percent during World War II (and remained above 70 percent until 1981), union density reached 35 percent in 1950, higher education expanded rapidly from the 1950s to the 1970s, and American economic dominance in global markets generated high profits. A series of Great Society programs during the early 1970s were their capstone.[84] In place of tycoons, who single-handedly managed big companies such as Standard Oil or Ford Motor Company, the size of corporate management grew swiftly during the twentieth century. The ratio of administrators to production workers increased threefold from the beginning of the century to 1950.[85] Even so, from the mid-1940s to mid-1970s, the prevailing business ethos encouraged business leaders to find competitive advantage in caring for the health of its workforce, maintaining full employment during recessions, and protecting job security. Earl Willis at General Electric made maximizing employment security "a prime company goal," and the chairman of Standard Oil of New Jersey, Frank Abrams, advocated for "stakeholder capitalism" whereby corporations maintained an equitable and working balance among the competing interests of stockholders, employees, customers, and the public at large.[86]

Some trace the abandonment of that ethos of corporate social responsibility to Lewis Powell, who in 1971 warned (in a confidential memorandum to the chairman of the U.S. Chamber of Commerce) that anti-corporate sentiment had reached new heights in the United States, and he believed it was high time that corporations leverage the enormous advantages of their collective wealth and make long-term plans to effect better political outcomes for themselves through united action and national organization.[87] The *Powell Memorandum* galvanized American business leaders by convincing them that the American economic system was under broad attack. Capital quickly became hostile toward government regulation and intervention in the economy, and during the Reagan presidency, socially conservative voices found new ways to evangelize (via think-tanks, talk radio, television news channels, and magazines). According to Powell, a future Supreme Court justice, there should be "no hesitation to attack the [Ralph] Naders, the [Herbert] Marcuses and others who openly seek destruction of the system. There should not be the slightest hesitation to press vigorously in all political arenas for support of the enterprise system. Nor should there be reluctance to penalize politically those who oppose it."[88]

Powell maintained that government regulation "seriously impaired the freedom of both business and labor, and indeed of the public generally. But most of the essential freedoms remain: private ownership, private profit, labor unions, collective bargaining, consumer choice, and a market economy in which competition largely determines price, quality and variety of the goods and services provided the consumer."[89] In reality, Americans needed few additional motivations to consume, since an extended period of stagnant wages was well under way as big business sprang to life politically. Corporate think-tanks (such as the Heritage Foundation and the Cato Institute) generated favorable social and political analyses, and their political action committees (PACs) pooled campaign contributions dedicated to advancing a business perspective.[90] The economic theories of Milton Friedman accelerated the move away from corporate social responsibility and toward the political activism outlined in the *Powell Memorandum*. A prophet of self-interest, Friedman helped to make the dismantling of the social welfare state a political imperative. He desired to unwind New Deal regulations and to transform the marketplace into a matrix for fostering individualism over the common good. His dark capitalist vision untethered people from "ties of kin, home, locale, race, ethnicity, church, craft, and fixed moral order," and everything became a commodity to be bought and sold in an unforgiving marketplace.[91]

"Neutron Jack" Welch remained "the gold standard against which all other CEOs were measured" during the 1980s and 1990s. His stridently profit-orientated leadership of General Electric made him a darling of the business elite, but to many of those who worked under him, he was a scoundrel par excellence. In his first two years at the helm of General Electric, Welch laid off 70,000 people, and three years later, he let another 60,000 go. As a result, entire cities like Schenectady in New York and Erie in Pennsylvania suffered the "inexorable economic mechanics of deindustrialization" as local bars closed, trucking companies went bust, cars were repossessed, homes were foreclosed, and local and state governments reeled under shrunken tax revenues.[92] In spite of its negative social impact, Welch argued that downsizing, his trademark, saved General Electric $6.5 billion, and perhaps not surprisingly his abrasive management style included "criticizing, demeaning, ridiculing, and humiliating" his executives, rejecting the employee-friendly policies of previous company leaders, and eschewing the value of company loyalty.[93]

Al Dunlap, corporate executive and best-selling author of *Mean Business,* became a cult figure in the 1990s for practicing a form of predatory capitalism that found favor on Wall Street with big investors. Dunlap earned the unflattering moniker "Chainsaw Al" by amputating entire corporate divisions. In the competitive and imitative world of business, his merciless actions initiated a style of slash-and-burn management that was mimicked at IBM, General Motors, and AT&T.[94] Dunlap laid off 11,000 blue-collar workers, and he cut the white-collar ranks from 1,600 to just 300 people.[95] By combining those cuts with the elimination of charitable giving and a sustained focus on short-term profits, he doubled Scott Paper Company's stock price in a single year. Dunlap boasted that he created sixty-two millionaires at Scott in just eighteen months through grants of company stock. During the same period, he made a cool $166,000 per day.[96] His luck ran out at Sunbeam when his extreme cost-cutting measures crippled the company. Big write-offs during his first year made the company look more profitable than it really was, as did exaggerations of sales and income, but when that ruse became apparent Dunlap was sacked, and Sunbeam declared bankruptcy. The Securities and Exchange Commission barred "Chainsaw Al" from ever serving again as a corporate officer following allegations of his inflation of the company's stock price through fraudulent accounting.[97] Still, Dunlap walked away rich for his emphasis on the bottom line—whatever the cost.

CEO pay soared during the 1980s as corporate leaders were lionized for their renewed emphasis on shareholder interests, which legitimized the unraveling of the American Dream for millions of ordinary folk. The upper decile's share of national income increased from 30 to 35 percent in the 1970s to a whopping 45 to 50 percent in the 2000s—and if that trend continues, by 2030 "the upper decile will rake in 60 percent of national income."[98] Thomas Piketty, an eminent French economist who devoted fifteen years to understanding the historical dynamics of wealth and income in a global context, reserves "absolutely no doubt" that increasing inequality in the United States contributed to the nation's financial instability during the Great Recession of 2008, because stagnant purchasing power among the lower and middle classes made them take on more debt, and "unscrupulous banks and financial intermediaries, freed from regulation and eager to earn good yields on the enormous savings injected into the system by the well-to-do, offered credit on increasingly generous terms."[99] Wages for the bottom 90 percent in the United States rose only 0.5 percent per year from 1977 to 2007, making it "hard to imagine an economy and society that can function indefinitely with such extreme divergence between social groups."[100] Very high income earners are now about twice as common in the financial professions (i.e., among managers of banks and other financial institutions and traders operating on the financial markets) as in the economy overall, but 80 percent of top income earners are not in finance—meaning that "the skyrocketing pay packages of top managers of large firms in both the financial and nonfinancial sectors" squarely accounts for the increasing proportion of high-earning Americans.[101]

Take, for example, corporate raider Michael Milken who helped to jump-start rising social inequality in the United States by upsetting previous standards for executive compensation and changing the face of finance using the leveraged buyout. Only five years after completing an MBA program at the Wharton School of Business, "Milken had become a superstar."[102] He opened a trading desk in low-grade bonds at a Philadelphia investment bank and was soon turning a 100 percent profit by positioning himself as a middleman and capturing the difference between the price buyers were willing to pay and that sellers were willing to accept. Milken saw that enormous returns were possible by taking over corporations and paying their stockholders with capital from the sale proceeds of high yield "junk" bonds.[103] One could do even better by taking over a firm where the cost of labor could be cut significantly by eliminating workers, reducing wages, or delving into over-capitalized pension funds. In one 1985 scheme, Milken raised $1.5 billion in forty-eight hours to raid corporations, and the following year he gave himself a $550 million bonus—a sum never before paid to an American executive in a single year.[104] An impresario of the high-yield bond market, Milken inno-vated a notoriously aggressive style of entrepreneurism and raised the stan-dard for executive compensation.

As a result of guerrilla tactics deployed by Milken and his ilk, top execu-tives at large American corporations could no longer be confident in their ability to survive hostile takeovers. Described as "heroic" by some for engi-neering purchases that would "oust entrenched incompetent management and thereby raise prosperity for all," their hostile takeovers actually displaced competent managers and breached the trust of employees in regard to their "pay, benefits, work conditions, and pensions."[105] Because he transgressed the law in search of massive returns, Milken pled guilty to securities and tax violations, served time in prison, and suffered the bankruptcy of his trading operation and its parent company. He settled a civil case, in which he was accused of collusive use of other people's money, out of court for $500,000.[106] Milken turned his attentions to philanthropy after his release by helping to establish the Milken Family Foundation dedicated to education, medical research, and public health.

Another celebrated player in the era of "irrational exuberance," Jordan Belfort, also served time for fraud; gluttony became glamorous and money a new idol as the Reagan era came to a close. Belfort's eponymous memoir, *Wolf of Wall Street*, opens in 1987 just as that New York financial center "was in the midst of a raging bull market, and freshly minted millionaires were being spit out a dime a dozen. Money was cheap, and a guy named Michael Milken had invented something called 'junk bonds,' which had changed the way corporate America went about its business. It was a time of unbridled greed, a time of wanton excess."[107] Belfort learned the hard way that happiness cannot be found in material luxuries, in sensual pleasures, or at the bottom of a Quaalude bottle. He narrates his memoir, a "reconstruc-tion" of "one of the wildest rides in Wall Street history," in the "voice that was playing in my head at that very time. It's an ironic voice, a glib voice, a self-serving voice, and, at many times, a despicable voice. It's a voice that allowed me to rationalize anything that stood in my way of living a life of unbridled hedonism. It's a voice that helped me to corrupt other people—and manipulate them—and bring chaos and insanity to an entire generation of young Americans."[108] Belfort's journey into the heart of darkness, romanti-cized in the film by Martin Scorsese, began innocently enough at the investment banking firm LF Rothchild, where he started as a sober and serious phone operator for stockbrokers.

That corporate environment proved so corrupting that six years later, Belfort established his own brokerage house that acted as a boiler room selling penny stocks in small companies, and it defrauded investors by hyping those penny stocks before dumping them at inflated prices using deceptive high-pressure sales tactics. Belfort also utilized a "rathole" technique that permitted a partner to hold stock with a prearranged buyback at a profitable time. On one such deal, he writes, "I had locked in $12.5 million—12.5 million! In three minutes! I'd made another million or so in investment-banking fees and stood to make another three or four million a few days from now—when I bought back the bridge-loan units, which were also in the hands of my ratholes."[109] Through such dubious maneuvers, Belfort became incredibly rich, but his increasingly profligate lifestyle led to drug addiction. By 1997, he slept just three hours a week and started every day with four Quaaludes, a gram of cocaine, three milligrams of Xanax, and forty-five milligrams of morphine. The combination of these and other drugs ingested over the course of a day once caused such paranoia that he "took a few potshots at the milkman with a twelve-gauge shotgun."[110] When Belfort sobered up, he cooperated with law enforcement (betraying many business partners and executive employees in the process) and served nearly two years in prison for securities fraud. Today, he sells "Straight Line Persuasion" techniques to "ethically persuade anyone to take any action" (as if *any* action can be ethical).[111] As the old maxim has it, "Once a huckster, always a huckster."

An appeal to corrupt instincts combined with a cultural shift away from corporate social responsibility and resulted in a debauch remarkable even in the history of a business nation such as the United States. The exploits of other late twentieth-century American businesspersons include Bernie Madoff, who perpetrated the longest-running Ponzi scheme in history; the misappropriation of corporate funds at Tyco by Dennis Kozlowski; the deception of Bernard Ebbers at WorldCom; and the shocking securities and wire fraud committed at Enron by Kenneth Lay and Jeffrey Skilling. The neoliberal agendas of Margaret Thatcher and Ronald Reagan laid the groundwork for a dramatic rise in income inequality in later decades, in part by foisting a logic of competition on the public known as neoliberalism that rationalizes the transformation of institutions established for the common good into business enterprises. Neoliberal policies reduced state intervention in the economy, shrunk social protections, cut government tax revenues, facilitated privatization, battered labor unions, and significantly raised the federal deficit.[112] Federal spending remained high during the George H. W. Bush presidency, and Bill Clinton continued to stress spending for defense and the establishment of "strategic trade policies" (such as NAFTA), although deficits were reduced through growth under his administration.[113]

In the preceding chapters, we followed the transformation of medieval markets into national and international venues for commercial exchange; highlighted the European pillage of natural and human resources; noted the creation of joint-stock ventures to raise capital for risky voyages to the New World; and pondered the violent enslavement of Native Americans and African peoples for the sake of profit. The portraits of late nineteenth-century robber barons that followed illustrated how ruthless competitive tactics and exploitative labor practices magnified inequality during the Gilded Age. Although business and government worked together to create a society that shrunk inequality in the decades after World War II, by the 1980s an avaricious new breed of business leader sanctified greed under the rhetorical guise of individual freedom and laissez-faire economics—and they became celebrities in an age of conspicuous consumption and "affluenza." Our aim has been to underscore the yawning perils of wealth and income inequality in our own time. Before addressing those social ills in chapter 4, let us examine the nature of ambition—let us call it greed, which has generated such deep social, political, and economic divisions in contemporary American society. We may also call it the "mercantile mind."

NOTES

1. James Davis, *Medieval Market Morality: Life, Law and Ethics in the English Marketplace 1200–1500* (Cambridge: Cambridge University Press, 2012), 2.

2. Davis, *Medieval Market Morality*, 7–8.

3. Davis, *Medieval Market Morality*, 20.

4. Davis, *Medieval Market Morality*, 28–29.

5. Davis, *Medieval Market Morality*, 421.

6. Christopher Columbus, *The Diario of Christopher Columbus's First Voyage to America, 1492–1493* (Norman: University of Oklahoma Press, 1991), 65.

7. Columbus, *The Diario*, 65–67.

8. Columbus, *The Diario*, 67–69.

9. Julius E. Olson, *The Northmen, Columbus, and Cabot* (New York: Charles Scribner's Sons, 1906), 79.

10. Alex Alvarez, *Native America and the Question of Genocide* (Lanham, MD: Rowman & Littlefield, 2016), 47.

11. D. A. Brading, *Miners and Merchants in Bourbon Mexico 1763–1810* (Cambridge: Cambridge University Press, 1971), 1.

12. Grizzard and Smith, *Jamestown Colony*, xxii.

13. John Steele Gordon, *The Business of America* (New York: Walker & Co, 2001), 3–4.

14. Gordon, *The Business of America*, 5–6.

15. Gordon, *The Business of America*, 6.

16. Gordon, *The Business of America*, 6.

17. Gordon, *The Business of America*, 7.

18. Wiesner-Hanks, *Early Modern Europe*, 237.

19. Wiesner-Hanks, *Early Modern Europe*, 240.

20. Wiesner-Hanks, *Early Modern Europe*, 236.

21. Wiesner-Hanks, *Early Modern Europe*, 236–37.

22. Wiesner-Hanks, *Early Modern Europe*, 238.

23. Wiesner-Hanks, *Early Modern Europe*, 238.

24. Karen Ordahl Kupperman, *Providence Island, 1630–1641: The Other Puritan Colony* (Cambridge: Cambridge University Press, 1993), 172.

25. Kupperman, *Providence Island, 1630–1641*, x.

26. Kent G. Lightfoot, *Indians, Missionaries, and Merchants: The Legacy of Colonial Encounters on the California Frontiers* (Berkeley: University of California Press, 2005), 7.

27. Cochran, *Business in American Life*, 17.

28. Cochran, *Business in American Life*, 70.

29. Williams, *Capitalism and Slavery*, 110.

30. Mark S. Ferrara, *Barack Obama and the Rhetoric of Hope* (Jefferson, NC: McFarland, 2013), 46.

31. Cochran, *Business in American Life*, 71.

32. Cochran, *Business in American Life*, 70–71.

33. Ferrara, *Barack Obama and the Rhetoric of Hope*, 48.

34. Piketty, *Capital in the Twenty-First Century*, 159.

35. Piketty, *Capital in the Twenty-First Century*, 159.

36. Piketty, *Capital in the Twenty-First Century*, 160.

37. Piketty, *Capital in the Twenty-First Century*, 160–61.

38. Piketty, *Capital in the Twenty-First Century*, 161.

39. Michel Villette and Catherine Vuillermot, *From Predators to Icons: Exposing the Myth of the Business Hero* (Ithaca, NY: ILR Press, 2009), 18.

40. Villette and Vuillermot, *From Predators to Icons*, 18.

41. Villette and Vuillermot, *From Predators to Icons*, 21–28.

42. Beaud, *A History of Capitalism*, 129–30.

43. Villette and Vuillermot, *From Predators to Icons*, 10–11.

44. Beaud, *A History of Capitalism*, 127.

45. Beaud, *A History of Capitalism*, 61.

46. Beaud, *A History of Capitalism*, 99–100.

47. William Blake, "Milton: A Poem," in *The Complete Poetry and Prose of William Blake*, ed. David Erdman (Princeton: Princeton UP, 1991), 95.

48. Ron Chernow, *Titan: The Life of John D. Rockefeller, Sr.* (New York: Random House, 1998), 3.

49. Chernow, *Titan*, 4.

50. Chernow, *Titan*, 5–6.

51. Chernow, *Titan*, 6.

52. Chernow, *Titan*, 6–7.

53. Chernow, *Titan*, 8–9.

54. Chernow, *Titan*, 15.

55. Chernow, *Titan*, 19.

56. Chernow, *Titan*, 46–47.

57. Chernow, *Titan*, 54–55.

58. Chernow, *Titan*, 97.

59. Chernow, *Titan*, 97.

60. Chernow, *Titan*, 144.

61. Chernow, *Titan*, 136.

62. Means, *Money and Power*, 158.

63. Chernow, *Titan*, 575–79.

64. Means, *Money and Power*, 163.

65. Nasaw, *Andrew Carnegie* (New York: Penguin, 2006), 361.

66. Nasaw, *Andrew Carnegie*, 415.

67. Nasaw, *Andrew Carnegie*, 421–22.

68. Nasaw, *Andrew Carnegie*, 423.

69. Thorstein Veblen, *The Higher Learning in America: A Memorandum on the Conduct of Universities by Business Men* (Baltimore: Johns Hopkins University Press, 2015), 192.

70. Clare Virginia Eby, *Dreiser and Veblen: Saboteurs of the Status Quo* (Columbia MO: University of Missouri Press, 1998), 66–71.

71. Eby, *Dreiser and Veblen*, 85–86.

72. Eby, *Dreiser and Veblen*, 80.

73. Thorstein Veblen, *The Theory of Business Enterprise* (New York: Augustus M. Kelley, 1965), 30.

74. Veblen, *The Theory of Business Enterprise*, 53.

75. Veblen, *The Theory of Business Enterprise*, 358–59.

76. Means, *Money and Power*, 177.

77. Means, *Money and Power*, 181.

78. Brinkley, *Wheels for the World*, 425–27.

79. Brinkley, *Wheels for the World*, 430.

80. Brinkley, *Wheels for the World*, 432.

81. Krooss and Gilbert, *American Business History*, 301.

82. Means, *Money and Power*, 182–83.

83. Jeff Manza, "Unequal Democracy in America," in *The New Gilded Age: The Critical Inequality Debates of Our Time*, ed. David Grusky and Tamar Kricheli-Katz (Stanford: Stanford University Press, 2012), 145.

84. Manza, "Unequal Democracy in America," 146–47.

85. Cochran, *Business in American Life*, 245.

86. Hedrick Smith, *Who Stole the American Dream?* (New York: Random House, 2013), 36–37.

87. Smith, *Who Stole the American Dream?*, 6–7.

88. Smith, *Who Stole the American Dream?*, 464.

89. Smith, *Who Stole the American Dream?*, 466.

90. Smith, *Who Stole the American Dream?*, 11.

91. Fraser, *The Age of Acquiescence*, 217.

92. Fraser, *The Age of Acquiescence*, 227.

93. Smith, *Who Stole the American Dream?*, 58–59.

94. Smith, *Who Stole the American Dream?*, 50.

95. Fraser, *The Age of Acquiescence*, 244.

96. Smith, *Who Stole the American Dream?*, 51.

97. Smith, *Who Stole the American Dream?*, 56.

98. Piketty, *Capital in the Twenty-First Century*, 294.

99. Piketty, *Capital in the Twenty-First Century*, 297.

100. Piketty, *Capital in the Twenty-First Century*, 297.

101. Piketty, *Capital in the Twenty-First Century*, 302–3.

102. George A. Akerlof and Robert J. Shiller, *Phishing for Phools: The Economics of Manipulation and Deception* (Princeton, NJ: Princeton University Press, 2015), 124.

103. Akerlof and Shiller, *Phishing for Phools*, 125–26.

104. Akerlof and Shiller, *Phishing for Phools*, 128 & 131.

105. Akerlof and Shiller, *Phishing for Phools*, 131.

106. Akerlof and Shiller, *Phishing for Phools*, 132.

107. Jordan Belfort, *Wolf of Wall Street* (New York: Bantam, 2007), 3.

108. Belfort, *Wolf of Wall Street*, 10–11.

109. Belfort, *Wolf of Wall Street*, 99–100.

110. Belfort, *Wolf of Wall Street*, 414–15.

111. http://jordanbelfort.com/

112. Beaud, *A History of Capitalism*, 272.

113. Beaud, *A History of Capitalism*, 173.

Chapter Three

Madness and the Mercantile Mind

In *The Power of Now* (1997), writer Eckhart Tolle describes an early encounter between Native Americans and white Europeans, one that highlights the perplexity of indigenous peoples at the destructive avarice latent in the minds of many colonists. Because they did not subscribe to European notions of capital and private property, or value what we call "precious metals" to the same extent, Native Americans were unprepared for the barbarous methods that colonists deployed to realize a profit from their commercial endeavors. The following passage from Tolle's best-selling book is superbly illustrative of the "mercantile mind" to which this chapter is dedicated:

> Carl Jung tells in one of his books of a conversation he had with a Native American chief who pointed out to him that in his perception most white people have tense faces, staring eyes, and a cruel demeanor. He said: "They are always seeking something. What are they seeking? The whites always want something. They are always uneasy and restless. We don't know what they want. We think they are mad."

The undercurrent of constant unease started long before the rise of Western industrial civilization, of course, but in Western civilization, which now covers almost the entire globe, including most of the East, it manifests in an unprecedentedly acute form. It was already there at the time of Jesus, and it was there 600 years before that at the time of Buddha, and long before that. Why are you always anxious? Jesus asked his disciples. "Can anxious thought add a single day to your life?" And the Buddha taught that the root of suffering is to be found in our constant wanting and craving. [1]

Tolle draws attention to the "collective dysfunction" and "loss of awareness of Being" that constitute the basis of our "very unhappy and extraordinarily violent civilization that has become a threat not only to itself but also to all life on the planet."[2] He points out that the hatred, violence, and oppression that we countenance every day are a reflection of our minds, which the Native American chief in Tolle's story observed are suffused with desire, competition, self-interest, intolerance, acquisitiveness, and cruelty. Tolle's observation has important ramifications since it ties social amelioration to psychological evolution beyond the dictates of the ego, a truism that many of the world's religious traditions understood centuries ago: "As within, so without."[3]

In order to foreground the specific and troubling nature of the mercantile mind, let us take an overview of the field of global cultures to examine the spiritual traditions that have shaped the world's great civilizations, for their admonitions and ethical prescriptions provide the standards against which our present economic practices may be considered. The Book of Genesis artfully illuminates the perils of afflictive desire and the effects of egoic consciousness in the world. In this primal myth, the Lord God "formed man of the dust of the ground, and breathed into his nostrils the breath of life," and God placed him in a garden paradise where "every tree that is pleasant to the sight, and good for food" provisioned him amply; he needed only "to dress it and to keep it."[4] From any of the trees in the garden Adam could eat freely, except "of the tree of the knowledge of good and evil," since God forewarned him, "In the day that thou eatest thereof thou shalt surely die."[5] Eve transgressed that injunction when the serpent duped her into believing that "the tree was good for food, and that it was pleasant to the eyes, and a tree to be desired to make one wise."[6] Contrary to the serpent's claims, her mind—along with Adam's, who also ate of the fruit—suffered diminution, loss. There are many interpretations of this rich story, but here is the one, for our purposes, which I find illuminating.

That "Fall" indicates the loss of unitive perception indicative of innocence after eating from the tree of the knowledge of good and evil. Adam and Eve's consciousness became divided, and they perceived the world in terms of dualities (male and female, self and other, right and wrong, innocence and experience). The "eyes of them both were opened, and they knew that they were naked"; they covered themselves and hid from "the presence of the LORD God amongst the trees of the garden."[7] Their desire to eat the fruit, and the thirst for a new mode of discerning, turn a life of ease in the Garden of Eden into one of toil and pain since it estranges the first couple from the divine, along with the generations that follow. The male took precedence over the female, human lives grew shorter, and people toiled to survive until they returned "unto the ground."[8] Cain's killing of his brother Abel exemplifies the enmity that fallen consciousness instills. Mercifully, at the east of the garden of Eden the Lord places "Cherubims, and a flaming sword which turned every way, to keep the way of the tree of life." But, if man "put forth his hand, [to] take also of the tree of life, and eat," he might "live for ever."[9]

Read as a map of human consciousness, the text encodes the possibility of a return to prelapsarian consciousness and an escape from estrangement and suffering. Given this opportunity for the recovery of unified perception, it behooves us to inquire how afflictive desire, which in Genesis begets transgression, might be rooted out of our minds.

Consider the application of this archetypal story to the mercantile mind, the tendency to weigh the world solely in terms of profit and loss, to seek personal advantage, and to transgress social norms of fairness in pursuit of private gain. During the Middle Ages in Europe, the concept of a just price for a commodity or service meant that guild members who sold products for more or less than their "natural price" (i.e., the cost of that commodity plus a fair profit for the maker), put the welfare and reputation of everyone belonging to that guild in jeopardy.[10] As a moral and economic formulation, the concept of just price has a foundation in the Golden Rule: "All things whatsoever ye would that men should do to you, do ye even so to them."[11] The great theologian Thomas Aquinas later affirmed that commandment, arguing: "It is wholly sinful to practice fraud for the express purpose of selling a thing for more than its just price, inasmuch as a man deceives his neighbor to his loss."[12] In the agrarian and small-town cultures of Western Europe, where life was envisioned as a zero-sum game and individual profit inevitably came at the expense of others, this guiding altruistic principle was especially germane to social well-being.[13] By controlling prices, guilds ensured the recovery of production costs plus a reasonable reward for labor, and that permitted little room for price gouging—particularly in respect to the foodstuffs on which the lives of community members depended.

Merchants and guildsmen who conducted their affairs with honesty and integrity, and observed the dictates of the Golden Rule, benefited themselves along with society. The challenge for those working in enterprise was not allowing avarice to make them cunning and calculating, exploitative of labor, and overly desirous of material gain, because these personality traits led to deceptive practices that turned human relationships into transactional ones. The Church regarded business as morally suspect, since it could lead to mortal sin. Disdain for the mercantile arts persisted for many centuries, even after aristocrats effectively engaged in commerce.[14] According to the medieval conception of the social body, envisioned as an interdependent hierarchy, the "ruler was always the head, but the eyes and ears were the king's advisors or the clergy, the hands knights, the thighs merchants, the feet peasants, the toes servants, and so on."[15] Like the physical body, the social body could become ill when one or more of its component parts failed to function properly (resulting in social conflict). Given the interdependence of members of society, when the Golden Rule was honored throughout the manufacture, marketing, and distribution of wares, business activity became advantageous to merchant purses and to society writ large, whereas unchecked greed led to ethical lapses with deleterious effects on self and other.

Concerned about the social consequences of cupidity, Jews and Christians regarded avidity a form of idolatry (in Job, Matthew, and Luke, as well as the apocryphal Philo), since it implied the worship of worldly wealth instead of the Lord.[16] In the Book of Jeremiah, the pursuit of economic gain, and the greed that underpins it, come under scrutiny. Since "every one from the least even unto the greatest is given to covetousness, from the prophet even unto the priest every one dealeth falsely," the Lord sends Jeremiah into the streets of Jerusalem to preach.[17] Appointed to announce the approaching calamities of Jerusalem and Judea, Jeremiah condemns the wickedness of the Israelites who hold fast to deceit, rather than repenting and building a nation of peace and shared prosperity. The Lord rues that among his people "are found wicked men" who "lay wait," "setteth snares," and "set a trap" to "catch men. As a cage is full of birds, so are their houses full of deceit: therefore they are become great, and waxen rich."[18] By acquiring wealth through duplicity, those engaged in commerce and trade "overpass the deeds of the wicked" for failing to consider "the cause of the fatherless" or "the right of the needy." Sick at heart about those who dismiss virtue and transgress his commandments, who revel in their own works forgetting who formed their bodies from the earth, God asks, "Shall not my soul be avenged on such a nation as this?"[19]

To bring his errant flock back into the fold, God sets Jeremiah "over the nations and over the kingdoms, to root out, and to pull down, and to destroy, and to throw down, to build, and to plant."[20] Using the prophet Jeremiah as a spokesperson, God admonishes the people of Israel for their "perpetual back-sliding" and failure to succor the indigent, ill, scorned, and orphaned in their midst. He commands Jeremiah to stand in the gate of the temple, and to petition those who enter to worship to amend their "ways and doings":

> Will ye steal, murder, and commit adultery, and swear falsely, and burn incense unto Baal, and walk after other gods whom ye know not; And come and stand before me in this house, which is called by my name, and say, We are delivered to do all these abominations? Is this house, which is called by my name, become a den of robbers in your eyes?[21]

Indicted for acting selfishly, and without sympathy for the most vulnerable members of society, priests, judges, and business leaders are advised to change their ways or be cast out for breaking their covenant with the Lord and violating the principles upon which inner divinity and social amelioration depend. Profane desire, the text makes explicit, leads to estrangement from God and therefore should be expunged from consciousness.

Exhortations against the negative repercussions of desire, particularly in the mercantile mind, recur in biblical wisdom literatures, too. The Book of Proverbs (an anthology of aphorisms attributed to Solomon, son of King David) addresses subjects such as moral propriety and the meaning of human life with the purpose of teaching the wisdom that, when practiced by social leaders, transmutes nations into realms of peace and prosperity. As Solomon discourses on trade and commerce, he emphasizes honesty and integrity in all transactions and the ephemeral nature of worldly riches. He asserts that a "false balance is abomination to the Lord" because it violates the Golden Rule, whereas "a just weight is his delight." Moreover, since they are transitory, great riches will "profit not in the day of wrath" (Last Judgement), for only righteousness "delivereth from death." [22] Hence, Solomon argues: "Better is the poor that walketh in his uprightness, than he that is perverse in his ways, though he be rich." Like the false balance in the marketplace used to swindle, the person who "by usury and unjust gain increaseth his substance" gathers a fortune only to surrender it "to him that will pity the poor." [23] So that the need for moral integrity in the marketplace be apprehended, and the dangers of pursuing wealth not go unheeded, the poet-king explains that the person who "tilleth his land shall have plenty of bread" for his contentment in honest work, while the person who hastens to become rich "hath an evil eye, and considereth not that poverty shall come upon him" due to his avarice. [24] Wisdom and righteousness are more valuable than gold, for with them, one "shall stand before kings," rather than before "mean men." [25]

In Ecclesiastes, an anonymous biblical work of fictional biography, a wise aged speaker offers a view of life that abjures endless striving for gain in an impermanent world. As "king over Israel," the narrator of Ecclesiastes experienced all forms of pleasure, acquired great wealth, pursued knowledge, and strove to bring to fruition great building projects (orchards, gardens, vineyards, and houses). Being wise, he perceived that those works, together with his treasure, would pass to a successor when he died—and who knows "whether he shall be a wise man or a fool? Yet shall he have rule over all my labour wherein I have laboured, and wherein I have shewed myself wise under the sun." [26] Human lives are short and material things temporary, so why should consciousness be so full of craving for worldly gain that "the eye is not satisfied with seeing, nor the ear filled with hearing"? [27] His awakening to transitoriness prompts the reader to internalize the folly of accumulating treasure, of seeking fame, or of striving to build works doomed, along with everything in the material world, to disintegration. The following verses highlight the pestiferous nature of desire and the futility of organizing one's life around acquisition:

He that loveth silver shall not be satisfied with silver; nor he that loveth abundance with increase: this is also vanity.
When goods increase, they are increased that eat them: and what good is there to the owners thereof, saving the beholding of them with their eyes?
The sleep of a labouring man is sweet, whether he eat little or much: but the abundance of the rich will not suffer him to sleep.
There is a sore evil which I have seen under the sun, namely, riches kept for the owners thereof to their hurt.
But those riches perish by evil travail: and he begetteth a son, and there is nothing in his hand.
As he came forth of his mother's womb, naked shall he return to go as he came, and shall take nothing of his labour, which he may carry away in his hand.
And this also is a sore evil, that in all points as he came, so shall he go: and what profit hath he that hath laboured for the wind?[28]

A mind full of craving never finds gratification in the physical world. At best, Ecclesiastes suggests, acquisition offers brief moments of pleasure so ephemeral that lusting after wealth and pleasure constitutes a form of madness. Most of us will recognize in ourselves a mental susceptibility to privileging the transitory over the eternal, and to fulfilling desires rather than leading meaningful lives.

In a like manner, Christian scriptures exhort readers to avoid the perils of greed and acquisition since they distort perception and obscure the Kingdom of God, which is "spread out upon the earth, and men do not see it."[29] The Synoptic Gospels (Matthew, Mark, and Luke) single out the well-to-do and those engaged in mercantile activities and utilize fable and allegory to reconnoitre a psychology of greed. In the Gospel of Luke, someone asks Jesus to "speak to my brother, that he divide the inheritance with me." Immediately intuiting the craving mind of the questioner, Jesus warns him to "beware of covetousness: for a man's life consisteth not in the abundance of the things which he possesseth," but in realizing the Kingdom of God.[30] The parable of the rich fool blinded by his own wealth follows that stinging retort. In it, Jesus tells of a wealthy man whose fields brought forth such abundance that he had nowhere to store that largesse. "I will pull down my barns, and build greater," decides this fellow, "and there will I bestow all my fruits and my goods."[31] Imagining that he would enjoy those goods for years, and that his prosperity would always increase, he stored them away rather than sharing them with the poor. "Thou fool," God says to the rich man, "this night thy soul shall be required of thee: then whose shall those things be, which thou hast provided?" Truly, he "layeth up treasure for himself, and is not rich toward God."[32]

Through this parable, Jesus encourages his listeners to relinquish the egoic grasping that constitutes so much of ordinary consciousness, and he points to a new way of being in the world—one more conducive to finding contentment in the here-now. Instead of mimicking the rich fool, who stows treasure that he will not live to enjoy, Jesus tells his disciples to take "no thought for your life, what ye shall eat; neither for the body, what ye shall put on."[33] The prophet points to the ravens that "neither sow nor reap; which neither have storehouse nor barn; and God feedeth them."[34] Likewise, the lilies of the field grow into beautiful flowers without the toil that characterizes human lives dedicated to mammon. To achieve the state of natural equipoise represented by the crows and field lilies, Jesus suggests amassing heavenly provisions by selling material surpluses and giving alms, for heavenly treasure cannot be stolen by thieves or corrupted by moths. If one seeks the Kingdom of God instead of the treasure that all the "nations of the world seek after," Jesus shrewdly observes: "All of these things shall be added unto you."[35] Selfishness brings loss, whereas altruism insures plenty—a radical teaching that challenges traditional notions of acquisition and rebukes the impulse toward "security" in a world where life is so provisional.

When Jesus is teaching on the coast of Judea in the Gospel of Mark, a man runs up to the rabbi, kneels down, and asks: "What shall I do that I may inherit eternal life?" Jesus asks the man if he keeps the Lord's commandments (meaning not committing adultery; defrauding anyone; and killing, stealing, or bearing false witness). When the man affirms that he has observed the precepts from his youth, Jesus encourages the seeker to "go thy way, sell whatsoever thou hast, and give to the poor" (so that he might earn "treasure in heaven") and then to "come, take up the cross, and follow me."[36] Vexed by that advice, the man departed. Already rich, he proved unwilling to part with hard-won capital for the sake of salvation, let alone for the welfare of others in the community. Amused at his reaction, Jesus exclaims, "How hardly shall they that have riches enter into the kingdom of God!" Truly, it is "easier for a camel to go through the eye of a needle, than for a rich man to enter into the kingdom."[37] When Jesus in Mark overthrows the tables of exchange belonging to the merchants, because they bought and sold on the temple grounds, it was no mere symbolic act. It disrupted mercantile activity in the city, but Jesus was outraged that these dealers had made the house of the Lord into a den of thieves.[38] In John, the incident is told in greater detail. On the eve of Passover, Jesus enters the temple and notices those who "sold oxen and sheep and doves, and the changers of money" sitting down. With a "scourge of small cords," he drives them away, and then he "poured out the changers' money, and overthrew the tables" shouting: "Make not my Father's house a house of merchandise."[39]

We may marvel at the vehemence with which Jesus rebuked the merchants, but the expanded perception that marks entry into the Kingdom of God is not available to acquisitive minds heedless of the sorrow that their greed generates. No wonder, when the great city of commerce and vice, Babylon, comes crashing down at the end of time in the Book of Revelation, "the merchants of the earth shall weep and mourn," for those who once grew rich shall endure "torment, weeping and wailing" instead, and in just one hour, they will see their great riches "come to nought."[40] The epistles of Paul contain similar cautions against the corrosive effects of material acquisition on the individual and on society. In Colossians, Paul writes to the congregation at Colossae in Anatolia with the intention of persuading them to eliminate "fornication, uncleanness, inordinate affection, evil concupiscence, and covetousness, which is idolatry" among congregation members.[41] Covetousness and concupiscence are idolatry because they estrange the mind from God and turn it toward material possessions and sensual pleasures. In Ephesians, the apostle identifies the mind as the seat of separation (allegorized in the story of the Fall in Genesis) when he asserts that no "covetous man, who is an idolater, hath any inheritance in the Kingdom of Christ and of God." Paul implores members of the church at Ephesus to be "renewed in the spirit of your mind," and to "put on the new man, which after God is created in righteousness and true holiness," by speaking truth with neighbors, letting go of wrath, and banishing malice.[42] In these epistles, Paul shows how the rooting out of wrath, greed, and malice from our minds can constructively transfigure human relationships and bring beneficial social change.

To further explore the effects of desire, the mercantile mind, and profit-oriented enterprise on society, we leave these religious exhortations against greed to analyze unflinching depictions of merchants, entrepreneurs, capitalists, and tycoons in key works of literature. Literary fiction, particularly in the realistic mode, permits scholars and laypersons to probe the unspoken assumptions of a society in ways that other avenues of inquiry cannot—in allowing historians, for example, a window into past (and present) problems besetting a civilization, as well as illustrating how contemporaries viewed those tribulations. The study of literature assists scholars in different disciplines in understanding the process of social development by showing them the peculiar state of consciousness that emerges when a society has outgrown an old ideology, but has not yet formulated a new one.[43] By "thus investigating *how* (as opposed to *what*) people thought about religious, social, psychological, and moral issues, the historian develops an understanding of the mentality of his subjects" through literature.[44] The creative writer who reflects upon the imaginary actions of imaginary characters can isolate various social or psychological issues (love, hate, ambition, social rivalry) from their everyday contexts and consider them without having to deal with their practical consequences.[45]

Geoffrey Chaucer's "Pardoner's Tale," for instance, satirizes the vices of the medieval marketplace, lambasting the corrupting influence of greed in an ecclesiastical figure who employs deception to sell false relics and heavenly pardons to gullible churchgoing folk. His fraudulent sales techniques and counterfeit wares (condemned in many contemporary treatises and sermons) bear witness to the outrageous ends of such con men.[46] He also provides a vehicle for critiquing the dubious theory behind indulgences: that Christ and the saints laid up an infinite treasury of merit, under the guardianship of the pope, upon which Christians could draw checks in return for a cash payment—a payment that supposedly demonstrated the penitence required as reparation for sin. Although indulgences did not normally absolve guilt (which required confession and contrition), the system was rife with abuse, as the Pardoner's claim to the power of absolution demonstrates.[47] In pursuing material gain rather than laying up treasure in heaven, the Pardoner gives expression to the most common desire among the Canterbury-bound pilgrims.

The frame story of a pilgrimage permits the inclusion of voices from a professional and moral cross section of medieval English society, from members of the gentry to peasants, and the storytelling that they engage in as a pastime is set up as a competition—a game that gives the medley of pilgrims a common interest and purpose.[48] Taken together, their stories raise questions about fortune and providence, the suffering of the innocent, the nature of desire, perfidy in the marketplace, and false trading practices, as well as the choices people make and the intentions behind them.[49] When host Harry Bailly requests a merry story (after the macabre one told by the Physician), the Pardoner obliges with a sermon in the vernacular mode that features a biblical text, indicts sin, offers a main story as an illustrative exemplum, applies that tale to the congregation, and closes with a concluding prayer.[50]

The alcohol-fueled confession that forms his prologue makes clear that the Pardoner practices the very vices against which he preaches. He brags of his strong clear voice that inspires confidence in his audience and how he takes *radix malorum est cupiditas* (greed is the root of evil) as the perennial theme of his sermons.[51] The Pardoner begins sermonizing by flashing his papal bulls of indulgence sealed by the bishop before credulous parishioners, and by advertising the patent authorizing his sale of pardons. Next, he stirs their religious devotion with stories of patriarchs and cardinals, and he trots out glass cases stuffed with false relics made from rags and bones. He offers up potions that multiply livestock and cure jealousy, and he assures them of the virtues of a mitten that when worn bolsters grain harvests. By preaching such poisonous "venym" under the pretense of holiness, and repeating those falsehoods year after year, the Pardoner admits to becoming quite wealthy.[52] His blatant hypocrisy is matched only by the utter contempt that he reserves for the uneducated who fall for his rhetoric of deceit.

The Pardoner's skill as a preacher derives in part from embellishing his sermons with stories (fictions) and a smattering of Latin phrases. While his homilies might, as an unintended side effect, bring people to repentance, his main concern is with lining his own pockets.[53] He preaches against the vice of avarice ("though myself be gilty in that synne"), he begs and lectures in sundry lands to avoid laboring with his hands, and he eschews the examples of the apostles of Jesus by coveting money, wool, cheese, wheat—and keeping a "joly wenche" in every town.[54] To demonstrate the art of his duplicity, the Pardoner tells a morality tale set in the commercial center of Flanders that condemns the vices of gluttony, drunkenness, gambling, and blasphemy (the so-called "tavern sins").[55] It starts with three intoxicated youths in a pub who hear a death knell well before 6 a.m. (the first hour of the day) and watch the corpse carried to the grave. After asking the unfortunate fellow's name, they discover that Death found their drinking buddy sitting bolt upright on his bench. Appalled at Death's cheekiness, the three rioters swear an oath to kill Death for taking men and women of their village (including children, farmworkers, and serving boys) during the past year.

Before the three rioters travel a half mile, they encounter an old man who greets them with the ominous salutation: "God yow see" ("May God look after you").[56] When the proudest of the rioters asks him how he became so withered, the mysterious elder replies that he has yet to meet a man who would exchange his youth for age, and so he lives on despite knocking at Death's door. Amazed to hear him speak of the traitor, they ask the old man where to find Death. He directs them up a crooked path to a wooden grove where under an oak tree the Grim Reaper was last spied. Arriving there posthaste, the rioters discover eight bushels of fine gold coins, so shiny and alluring that they soon forget the purpose of their quest. The worst among these three rascals cunningly observes that their newfound treasure must be carried away under the cover of night to escape suspicion of thievery, and he proposes that they draw straws to determine who should go stealthily to town for provisions of bread and wine.[57] The youngest of them draws a short stick, and as soon as he departs, his two comrades plot to murder him and split his share.

Meanwhile, the young man who walks to town becomes enraptured with the gold coins in his possession, and he contrives to kill his two drinking companions and keep the cache of coinage for himself. To that end, he visits an apothecary shop and purchases a "strong and violent" rat poison, finds three empty bottles elsewhere, and pours poison into two of them (keeping the third clean for himself as a drinking vessel).[58] With all three bottles filled with wine, the young man returns to his mates, who promptly slay him. Before burying his body, they decide to drink and make merry for a bit. By chance, they select a poisoned bottle to slake their thirst, and soon all three who set out to kill Death succumb to the greed that destroys them. At this point, the wily Pardoner thoroughly condemns the lechery, gluttony, drunkenness, and villainy that led to the murders, and he convincingly bemoans the degenerate condition of humankind more generally.

Ever the grifter, the Pardoner closes by offering members of his pilgrim audience, who might be suffering under the weight of similar sins, to purchase one of his holy bulls with coins large or small, silver broaches, spoons, rings, and wool. Once the Pardoner enters their names into his roll, he contends, they shall enter the bliss of heaven.[59] After repeated assurances of his honesty and integrity, the crooked ecclesiastic offers pardons for events yet to happen and security for souls taken unexpectedly. With all the slickness of the quick-change artist, the Pardoner artfully employs multiple rhetorical figures to persuade, but these flourishes only serve to underscore his lack of genuine spirituality.[60] By his own account, the Pardoner makes a rich living from corrupt preaching, and he values material gain over heavenly manna.

Although writers in Europe initially chose to depict moneymaking activities in the worst possible light, with the economic realities that accompanied a growing middle class, individuals engaged in mercantile activities were regarded less negatively.[61] That move away from portraying moneymaking activities as morally condemnable started in the Renaissance as Europeans adjusted to expanding roles for business, international trade, and capital in society. Portrayals of street peddlers, hucksters, and local shopkeepers continued to differ a good deal during the Enlightenment, but the clear trend was to depict merchants as figures who could act as heroic guides in an economic crisis and who were well positioned to change society for the better.[62] This change in the characterization of merchants reflected shifting European attitudes toward business accompanying the rise of the bourgeois entrepreneur. During the English Renaissance, however, lingering suspicions about business and finance persisted among certain writers and their audiences (for example *The Jew of Malta* by Christopher Marlowe), and no play of the period better reflects the increasing importance of capital, credit, and finance than William Shakespeare's *Merchant of Venice*.

Shakespeare makes the mercantile mind a main theme of the play, and he explores it through the characterizations of Antonio and Shylock, sixteenth-century businessmen occupied in commerce and finance in bustling Venice. Rather than the two-dimensional caricatures they might have been during the Middle Ages (in sermons condemning avarice, in satires exposing greed and dishonesty, and in chronicles lamenting the fickleness of the commonality), new representations replaced stock figures of the usurer in popular fiction during the Renaissance.[63] The play nevertheless retains some of the features of the morality plays that preceded it, but it sufficiently complicated the stock formula of charity and greed that the playwright inherited. The *Merchant of Venice* (1600) articulates ambivalent social attitudes concerning new roles for business, and it confronts the controversial practice of usury (discussed earlier in regard to Christian prohibitions against lending money at interest and the resourceful ways of skirting that prohibition).

The action commences with Antonio, who initially appears quite the charitable gentleman for lending money gratis to fellow Christians. Such acts of generosity, however, lower the rates that Jewish moneylenders depend upon to offset the risk of default associated with their loans. More likely a deliberate slight of moneylenders and their usury, Antonio's benevolence does not extend to Shylock, whom he spat upon in public and called a "misbeliever, cut-throat dog."[64] When forced to petition Shylock for a loan on behalf of his Christian friend Bassanio, Antonio offers to pay interest. Shylock agrees on the condition that if the bond is forfeit, any penalty due would not be payable in currency, but rather as a pound of Antonio's flesh. When his mercantile vessels fail to return to port as Antonio anticipated, Shylock insists on the grisly payment stipulated by the contract—even in the face of offers by Antonio's friends to settle for three times the original sum. Shylock's stubborn insistence on justice in a Venetian court of law, where he believes that his bond will be honored, sets the stage for a miscarriage of justice when Bassanio's wife, Portia, disguises herself as a doctor of law and thwarts Shylock's attempts at a fair hearing. His refusal to accept any terms other than those agreed upon, which would cause Antonio's death from blood loss, makes Shylock the villain, but the reader cannot help but feel compassion for this man, who by the final act has lost his daughter, Jessica, his ducats, and his religion (when he is forced to convert to Christianity).

The play also highlights the increasingly important role of credit in Renaissance commerce and exposes the hypocrisies of those professing to hold higher ethical codes than non-Christians. After all, is it "right to steal treasure from Shylock's house along with his eloped daughter?" Does Shylock's "insistence on law justify the quibbling countermeasures devised by Portia," as she rattles on about Christian "mercy?"[65] Shakespeare put commerce and merchants at the heart of the play, and the figures of the Christian businessman Antonio, Jewish moneylender Shylock, and financial opportunist Bassanio elucidate the individual and social costs of greed. That moral lesson is troped in the riddle of the three caskets that Portia's father devises to prevent his daughter from becoming the object of suitors who thirst after her wealth and beauty. In these ways, Shakespeare probes the mercantile mind using characters who, despite their actions, repeatedly profess adherence to moral codes of conduct informed by religion. In fact, "the moneylenders of England were Christians, and few Jews were found in any professions,"[66] a point that brings us back to the author. Shakespeare was a shareholder in the Lord Chamberlain's Men, "the most successful theatrical organization in England," and his subsequent prosperity appears in the first record of his residence and other properties acquired in Stratford and London.[67] Shakespeare purchased land in Shottery and appeared listed as a chief holder of corn and malt in Stratford in 1598, and he "sold a load of stone to the Stratford corporation" the following year.[68] Little surprise that the Bard so knowledgeably depicted the mercantile mind from multiple points of view given his own personal commercial activities at a time when modern consumer culture was in its infancy.

Halfway around the world, the seventeenth-century writer Ihara Saikaku bore witness to busy mercantile markets of the Tokugawa Shogunate, a stable and peaceful time in Japan resulting from the ousting of ambitious traders and Christian missions from the country and the adoption of an isolationist and exclusionist policy that kept Japanese people inside the country, prohibited the construction of seagoing vessels, and banned foreign trade (save for exchange carried out by a handful of Chinese and Dutch traders who lived under strict control on an island off the coast of Nagasaki).[69] Supported by Confucian principles from China (reinterpreted according to the needs of a feudal society containing a strict hierarchy of samurai warriors, peasants, artisans, and merchants), the status quo put nonproductive warriors, who made up eight percent of the population, at the top of the social hierarchy. At the bottom, the "despised bourgeois money-makers, who were theoretically devoid of both power and rights," were known as *chōnin*.[70] After the introduction of gold and silver currency, commercial capitalism inside Japan developed rapidly, as land reclamation bolstered agricultural production and improved communications led to an expansion of domestic markets and gave rise to the formation of great urban centers like Edo (Tokyo). As increasingly prosperous merchants broke free from their provincial lords and relocated to the cities, they established production and the free exchange of commodities.[71] By the end of the seventeenth century, merchant-townsmen (*chōnin*) accumulated fortunes that exceeded those found in most feudal societies, a development that helped to blur class boundaries in Japan.

However, the immense wealth accrued by prosperous merchants during the Tokugawa period failed to result in the formation of a middle class resembling the one emerging contemporaneously in the West, for a rigid and hierarchical guild structure in Japan prevented an individualist spirit of free enterprise and open competition from flowering. Because Tokugawa merchants lived in a closed economy, they remained "unable or unwilling to provide the initiative for converting the mercantile economy into industrial capitalism," and as a consequence economic stagnation followed in the eighteenth century.[72] Saikaku chronicled the business activities of the *chōnin* and recorded their hedonistic exploits in the "floating world" of pleasure and fashion known as the "gay quarters," which offered a "ribald escape from the gloom of [Japanese] Buddhism, the rigid codes of Confucianism and the draconian laws that governed sexual morality."[73] In a collection of thirty stories entitled *The Eternal Storehouse of Japan* (1688), Saikaku inventoried the varied means by which ingenious men accumulated money—and the countless ways that feckless ones squandered it.[74] With realistic precision, Saikaku illustrated the deleterious impact that money could exert on people, and many of the stories in his collection took on moral issues and adopted didactic stances.

For instance, in "Ten Virtues of Tea That Disappeared at Once," a man of ready wit, Risuké of Kobashi, invested in a handsome portable tea stall, and he set out every morning with it calling: "Ebisu morning tea for sale!" [75] Fortune shined on him, and soon he accumulated enough capital to employ his own clerks and become a wholesaler in town. Sadly, he became an incredibly avaricious person, and as lonely years passed, the continual accrual of wealth became his sole pleasure. As his avarice grew, he eventually stooped to "some base trickery" in buying discarded tea leaves, cutting the fresh tea leaves in his shop with their grounds, and selling them to unsuspecting customers. To his amazement, his business flourished despite that duplicity, until heaven "wished to rebuke him" for his immoral business practices, and "Risuké suddenly went mad and himself began to spread abroad an account of his own misdeeds." [76] When people learned of the knavish means by which he increased his fortune, they would no longer do business with him. Risuké's health rapidly declined, and as his final breath approached, he told attendants to fetch his life savings from a nearby indoor storehouse. At death's door, Risuké spread that stash out around his pillow and in agony bemoaned the fact that others would get all his money. "Alas, alas, how grievous it all is!" he exclaimed:

> With these words he clung to his money and gnashed his teeth. The tears gushed from his eyes like scarlet streaks of blood and his expression was that of a hornless blue devil. Next he began to run round the room like some sort of phantom. When he collapsed, his attendants held him. Again and again he revived, and each time he insisted on examining his money to make sure that it was all there. [77]

Risuké died with his eyes wide open—and his money clasped firmly to his breast. When people heard about his demonic obsession with wealth, and the signs of karmic retribution in his demise, even distant relatives who arrived for the distribution of his property would have nothing to do with his money. With little recourse, the proceeds of Risuké's estate were donated to a local parish, where they funded an extravagant debauch for priests in Kyoto! So wicked was his avarice, Risuké's ghost haunted the shops of wholesalers demanding debts from years past. In the story of this tea merchant, the narrator explains:

> We see certain practices must be eschewed, however profitable they may be. To pawn worthless objects with no intention of redeeming them, to deal in various forms of counterfeit, to trick a girl into marriage in order to lay hands on her dowry, to borrow Mass money from temples and to avoid repayment by going into bankruptcy, to join a gang of gamblers, to sell worthless mines by means of trickery, to force people into buying ginseng against their will, to arrange for a man to commit fornication with a married woman and then to blackmail him with the threat of exposure, to sell stolen dogs, to receive

money for looking after babies and then to let them starve to death, to pluck the hair from the heads of drowned people and sell it—all these may be a way of making a living; but for him who indulges in such brutish ways, it were better that he had never enjoyed the small chance of having been born into this world in human form.[78]

This comprehensive accounting speaks to the forms of greed and deception looming in hustling Tokugawa marketplaces, as much as it does to Buddhist notions of karma and reincarnation.

The equation of money with madness is an old trope in Chinese literature used to illustrate the effects of an obsession with profit and wealth on the thoughts and behaviors of people. Variously interpreted as a roman à clef, a work of pornography (still banned in mainland China), and a Buddhist morality tale, the Ming dynasty novel *Golden Lotus* (*Jin Ping Mei*, 1618) describes the decadent exploits of the wealthy merchant Ximen Qing and his six wives. These characters exemplify the extravagance, corruption, and ineptitude that led to the fall of the (Han Chinese) Ming dynasty and the establishment of the foreign (Manchu) Qing dynasty. The six traitor ministers traditionally blamed for the fall of the Northern Sung dynasty, for example, have counterparts in Ximen Qing's six wives, and by setting this realistic novel in the twelfth century rather than the fourteenth, the anonymous author suggested stereotypical traits of incompetent rulers and prosperous merchants, while implicitly taking aim at the Jiajing or Wanli emperors and the unethical mercantile practices of the Ming dynasty.[79]

Ximen Qing's status, wealth, corruptibility in a city suggestive of Peking, the Ming capital, makes for a caustic appraisal of political and business leaders who fail to assume moral responsibility for their actions and therefore infect the social system from top to bottom. Ethical lapses are particularly regrettable among the wealthy, for through their waywardness these prominent citizens "encourage the lower orders of society to follow suit."[80] Ximen Qing's servants, for instance, pander to his decadent tastes, take no responsibilities for their actions, and "sedulously imitate the examples of immorality set for them by their master and his wives"; in this respect, they also "function as surrogates for the eunuchs and lesser officials in the imperial administration."[81] As the narrative progresses, Ximen Qing's shady business dealings provision him with income enough to gratify his every sexual, economical, and political aspiration. Through lavish gift giving, he obtains a high-ranking official post, sires a son by way of an incestuous relationship, and brings that paramour into his home against the protests of his legitimate wife. In this manner, he alienates many members of the household.[82]

A strong correlation between economic and political power and sexual prolificacy persists throughout the novel. The following epigraph from chap-

ter 27 for instance, an indictment of Ximen Qing's immoral behaviors, links
states of consciousness with the outer world:

> The Azure Heaven over our head he would wantonly defy;
> Taking people's lives to gain possession of their wives.
> You must know that his thousands of crafty and evil schemes;
> Will only result in putting his own household in jeopardy.
> Excess and debauchery have always arisen from ill-gotten wealth. [83]

Ximen's depravity is put on display when he participates in an orgy in his
garden, during which he ties the naked Pan Jinlian to the crossbeams of a
grape arbor with her legs apart and performs the "Old Monk Rings the
Dinner Bell" maneuver, by thrusting himself inside her until the tip of his
organ penetrated all the way to her cervix," where it broke the "sulfur-
imbued ring" inserted in her vagina before intercourse. Almost immediately
after that rupture, Jinlian's eyes dimmed, her respiration slowed, and her
tongue became ice cold. Only after Ximen retrieves the ring does she begin
to revive—after about half a day. [84]

True to the epigraph above, Ximen Qing's dissoluteness sets in motion
his own demise, as well as that of everyone and everything around him. He
suffers a gruesome death after an insatiable lover gives him an overdose of a
powerful aphrodisiac given to the debauched merchant by a mysterious In-
dian monk. When she discovers blood in his semen, Ximen Qing collapses,
at which point the narrator intrudes to warn the reader: "There is a limit to
our energy, but none to our desires. A man who sets no bounds to his passion
cannot live more than a short time." Ximen "had given himself to the enjoyment of women and did not realize that he was like a lantern whose oil is
exhausted and whose light is failing. Now his seed was used up, there was
nothing in store for him but death." [85] Five days later, his testicles swelled
and burst open, soaking the bedsheets. As death neared, Ximen summoned
his son and went over his financial holdings and business dealings with the
young man. His silk shop was worth 50,000 taels, the thread shop 6,500 taels,
the pawn shop 25,000 taels, and the medicine shop another 5,000 taels.
Ximen recorded his debtors well, including Li and Huang who still owed him
150 taels (with interest doubling that sum), and then he died a sordid man at
just thirty-three years of age. [86] In the final twenty of one hundred chapters,
Ximen's household is scattered to the winds, and the remaining characters
meet fates corresponding to their thoughts and actions in the red-dust human
world.

Joseph Conrad's novel *Heart of Darkness* (1899) uncovers the violent
excesses of imperial capitalism during the European colonial period, and it
provides a gruesome accounting of the destructive nature of the mercantile
mind. When Conrad visited the colonial territory later known as the Belgian
Congo in the late nineteenth century, he observed one of the most brutal

exploitations of land, animal, and human resources the world has ever known. The title phrase "heart of darkness" refers not simply to unexplored, and therefore unknown or "dark," reaches of the African continent, or to the skin color of its native peoples, but to a state of mind so bereft of light that it creates a living hell, its own true reflection, in the physical world. In the novel, which confirms a profit pathology recognizable in the twenty-first century, a company agent named Kurtz turns a tidy profit for himself and his employer in the African ivory and rubber trade, but he slips into madness when he tries to justify the violence required to realize lucrative returns with his own humanity. Once a painter, man of letters, and lover of poetry, his mental devolution from aesthete to money-driven monster to megalomaniac is a study in horror (famously his last words).

Sitting cross-legged, in a meditative posture, aboard a cruising yawl slowly making its way up the Thames, Charlie Marlow, the skipper of a Congo river steamboat sent to retrieve the remains of Kurtz, narrates that man's tragic descent into madness. As darkness placidly descends upon the river, Marlow's sunken cheeks and yellowed complexion match the setting sun. Addressing a group of fellow wayfarers, Marlow explains how Kurtz operated profitably deep in the hinterlands beyond company control in "one of the dark places on earth." The company men drawn to despoil the Congo "were no colonists," he affirms—their administration was "a squeeze, and nothing more."[87] They savaged that unexplored land for their companies with a zeal reflective of the maniacal cult of efficiency to which they subscribed, but it was so inhumane that it forever darkened the minds of those who ventured there in the quest for money. These were men of business, but "they were conquerors" too, Marlow notes, "and for that you want only brute force— nothing to boast of, when you have it, since your strength is just an accident arising from the weakness of others. They grabbed what they could get for the sake of what was to be got. It was just robbery with violence, aggravated murder on a great scale, and men going at it blind—as is very proper for those who tackle a darkness. The conquest of the earth, which mostly means the taking it away from those who have a different complexion or slightly flatter noses than ourselves, is not a pretty thing when you look into it too much."[88]

Marlow's "sad pilgrimage" into the heart of darkness began with a required mental and physical health examination. The old doctor who performed that task saw many people become deranged "out there," and he believed it would be quite interesting "for science to watch the mental changes of individuals, on the spot" in the Congo.[89] It was a prescient assertion, for after a prolonged journey to the Inner Station to retrieve Kurtz, Marlow found the man at the point of death. Kurtz entered the dark continent a genius but left it as a madman. "I had immense plans," Kurtz muttered dementedly. "I was on the threshold of great things." Marlow tells us that his "intelligence was perfectly clear—concentrated," but it was focused "upon himself with horrible intensity."[90] As he lay dying, "images of wealth and fame" filled Kurtz's head: "My intended, my station, my career, my ideas." On his ivory face, Marlow spied an "expression of somber pride, of ruthless power, of craven terror—of an intense and hopeless despair," and he wondered: "Did he live his life again in every detail of desire, temptation, and surrender during that supreme moment of complete knowledge? He cried in a whisper at some image, at some vision—he cried out twice, a cry that was no more than a breath: 'The horror! The horror!'"[91] Kurtz's agonizing death suits a man who made himself into a white idol and terrorized indigenous inhabitants into submission. In those demonic acts, he represented the crimes of European colonial states in Africa and around the world. "All of Europe," Marlow affirms, "contributed to the making of Kurtz."[92]

Like the *Merchant of Venice, Eternal Storehouse of Japan, Golden Lotus,* and *Heart of Darkness,* the late twentieth-century novel *American Psycho* (1991) probes the excesses of greed, and it highlights a propensity for avarice in business to fall into psychopathy. At first glance, Patrick Bateman seems a prototypical young Wall Street investment banker whose lifestyle is enviable, but he lives in a shallow world of materialism where conspicuous consumption defines identity. Able to afford almost anything he desires, Bateman partakes of gourmet meals at restaurants where reservations are nearly impossible, and he is meticulous in appearance and proud of his upscale Manhattan address. Bateman and his yuppie colleagues snort cocaine, visit nightclubs, and generally endure hollow self-indulgent existences and compete amongst themselves for luxury items that buoy their status with the in-group. Obsessed with his hero Donald Trump and first wife, Ivana, *Art of the Deal* is one of Bateman's favorite books.[93] Emblematic of the spiritual vacuity of the lifestyles that Bateman and his colleagues admire, everything around them, even other people's bodies, was a commodity to be bought and sold. Such an erroneous supposition, the title *American Psycho* indicates, leads to a form of madness discernable in Bateman's obsessive compulsive behavior, lack of moral values, morose runaway imagination, social alienation, and multiple addictions. For this reason, the graffiti on the side of Chemical Bank at the opening of the novel alludes to the inscription over the gates of hell in Dante's *Inferno*: "Abandon All Hope Ye Who Enter Here."[94]

When Bateman phones his lawyer, Harold Carnes, to make a full confession of his (imagined) crimes on that man's answering machine, the full extent of his derangement—and the unreliability of his narrative—becomes clear to readers. Bateman explains dementedly: "I leave a message, admitting everything, leaving nothing out, thirty, forty, a hundred murders, and while I'm on the phone with Harold's machine a helicopter with searchlight appears, flying low over the river, lightning cracks in the sky open in jagged blots behind it, heading toward the building I was last at." After ten minutes of rambling, he concludes, "I'm a pretty sick guy."[95] In drawing our attention to his unreliability, the author implies that the brutal violence that Bateman relates (often against women and involving masochistic sex)—and the subject of great controversy at the time of the novel's publication—puts his psychopathy beyond question, and Bateman's confession demonstrates a lack of empathy associated with narcissistic and Machiavellian personality disorders: "It did not occur to me, *ever*," he declares, "that people were good or that a man was capable of change or that the world could be a better place through one's taking pleasure in a feeling or a look or a gesture, of receiving another person's love or kindness."

In Bateman's yuppie worldview, simple generosity of spirit "applied to nothing, was a cliché, was some kind of bad joke."[96] In spite of his upscale purchases and lavish lifestyle, Bateman no longer finds anything worth looking forward to—his repeated attempts at satiating every physical and material desire notwithstanding. Amazingly, that metaphysical angst leads him to a new understanding, which falls just short of religious epiphany:

> There is an idea of a Patrick Bateman, some kind of abstraction, but there is no real me, only an entity, something illusory, and though I can hide my cold gaze and you can shake my hand and feel flesh gripping yours and maybe you can even sense our lifestyles are probably comparable: I *simply am not there*. It is hard for me to make sense on any given level. Myself is fabricated, an aberration. I am a noncontingent human being. My personality is sketchy and unformed, my heartlessness goes deep and is persistent. My conscience, my pity, my hopes disappeared a long time ago (probably at Harvard) if they ever did exist. All that I have in common with the uncontrollable and the insane, the vicious and the evil, all the mayhem I have caused and my utter indifference towards it, I have now surpassed. I still, though, hold on to one single bleak truth: no one is safe, nothing is redeemed.[97]

In this passage, Bateman voices an existential anguish born of material craving, a desire for business success, and a passion for fleeting pleasures. The dark vacuity that Kurtz witnessed in the trafficking of ivory and denigration of human beings drives him mad, but for Bateman it is the superficiality of corporate culture, the excesses of overconsumption, and the numbness to exploitation. The remainder of this chapter analyzes competition and greed from the perspective of modern psychology, and it asks at what point individuals motivated by them fall into psychopathy.

As earlier chapters show, competition is venerated as an engine of innovation in American culture, and it motivates individual and institutional behaviors that have social repercussions. Most people exhibit some competitive inclination—and no book, sermon, movement, or political party will change the human compulsion for status and distinction.[98] However, most of us are not only competitive but also collaborative beings cognizant of group needs and dynamics. Competition may be innate or learned, but healthy competition leads to positive achievements and outcomes, while sociopathic forms bring social disorder. One might say that societies become sociopathic when destructive institutional and individual behaviors become accepted as "the outcome of dominant social values and power arrangements."[99] A sociopathic society creates dominant social norms that are paradoxically antisocial, meaning that they *"assault the well-being and survival of much of the population and undermine the social bonds and sustainable environmental conditions essential to any form of social order."*[100]

The myth of the American Dream (which celebrates competitive entrepreneurialism, individualism, and material acquisition) may ironically be a "master sociopathic script corrupting everyday life and social interaction," argues sociologist and writer Charles Derber, because of the way that it normalizes profit maximizing and permits the self-destructive and socially damaging consequences of adopting a profit-driven orientation. For Derber, the sociopathic society is structural and "rooted in the political and economic system rather than in psychiatry."[101] For this reason, sociopathic people in the United States are frequently "successful and well-adjusted, most of them sane and socially integrated," and they are more likely to conform to the values and rules of conduct of society than to violate them.[102] As a result, we might think of some American values, which enable and sometimes acclaim socially destructive forms of competition, as at least metaphorically "sick."

Robert Hare's Psychopathy Checklist—the revised (PCL-R)—remains the most frequently used and validated measure of persistent antisocial behavior, and it is grounded in a clinical tradition that long described psychopathy in terms of a constellation of affective, interpersonal, and behavioral characteristics. Each item on the PCL-R, a twenty-item clinical construct rating scale completed in a semi-structured interview or file, is scored on a three-point scale according to specific criteria. Total scoring, ranging from 0 to 40, provides an estimate of the extent to which individuals match the prototypical psychopath (with 25 to 30 being indicative of psychopathy).[103] Its psychometric properties are well established with male offenders and psychiatric patients, and there exists increasing evidence of its reliability and validity with female offenders and patients, as well. The PCL-R measures affective and interpersonal features such as egocentricity and callousness, which correlate positively with narcissism and Machiavellianism. Factors of social deviance such as impulsiveness, unstable lifestyles, and risks for violence are strongly correlated with antisocial personality disorder, criminal and antisocial behaviors, and substance abuse.[104]

In his pioneering research, Hare found that "conceptualizing psychopaths as remorseless predators" helped him "to make sense of what often appeared to be senseless behavior. These are individuals who, lacking in conscience and feelings for others, find it easy to use charm, manipulation, intimidation, and violence to control others and satisfy their own selfish needs."[105] They violate social norms and expectations without remorse, guilt, or regret, and therefore they "form a significant proportion of persistent criminals, drug dealers, spouse and child abusers, swindlers and conmen, mercenaries, corrupt politicians, unethical lawyers, terrorists, cult leaders, black marketeers, and radical political activists. They are well represented in the business and corporate world, particularly during chaotic restructuring, where the rules and their enforcement are lax and accountability is difficult to determine."[106] Many psychopaths even emerge as heroes during periods of social, economic, and political upheaval, and they "wrap themselves up in the flag, enrich themselves by callously exploiting ethnic, cultural, or racial tensions, and grievances."[107] Anyone following American politics during the 2016 presidential election cycle saw these characteristics on bold display.

The PCL-R also evaluates individuals for traits such as responsibility, remorse, pathological lying, manipulativeness, cunning, promiscuity, general impulsiveness, superficial charm, and grandiosity. Individuals who score high enough to be deemed psychopathic fail to process emotion as other people do—and according to one estimate, they make up about 1 percent of the male population—or approximately one out of every hundred men that you meet.[108] As much as another 10 percent or so fall into a gray zone and exhibit sufficient psychopathic features to be of concern to others.[109] Few women score in the psychopathic range on the PCL-R (which may explain their relative absence from our survey of business villains in chapter 2). As a biological predisposition leading to many of the behaviors associated with the confidence artist, the grifter, and the con man, psychopathology is usually triggered by society or the environment.[110]

Narcissism (entitlement, self-enhancement, intolerance for being viewed as inferior) and Machiavellianism (ruthlessness, practiced duplicity, aggressive deviousness to achieve personal and corporate goals, and the manipulation of others for the same objectives) are two personality traits associated with deception and deceptive business practices.[111] In one extensive study of academic faculty, students, parents, athletes, mental hospital staff, and business employees, the Machiavellians among them were more likely to attempt to bluff, cheat, and ingratiate themselves with others—and they were actually more successful in these disingenuous and obsequious endeavors than their peers.[112] Another study found that Machiavellian students were more likely to specialize in business and law; however, such decisions alone do not compel people to exercise manipulative behavior to the extent that it becomes socially transgressive. In other words, politicians, lawyers, businessmen, advertising executives, and marketers are not simply born "grifters," but rather the environment provides triggers for psychopathology.[113]

Paul Babiak and Robert Hare regard psychopathy as a personality disorder (not a mental illness) whereby a limited range of stereotyped "solutions" are applied to most problems encountered in life.[114] Among ten personality disorders recognized by psychologists, narcissistic personality and histrionic personality correspond most closely to psychopathy. Many psychopaths operate within the parameters of the law, and some professions, including business, even reward psychopathic behavior. In 2009, *Forbes*, a biweekly American business magazine, observed that "the incidence of psychopathy among CEOs is about 4 percent, four times what it is in the population at large," and they wondered why some psychopaths make great CEOs.[115] Journalist Jon Ronson cites "Chainsaw" Al Dunlap as a highly successful business executive who might suffer from psychopathy, since he seemed to enjoy firing people, failed to attend his parents' funerals, and told his first wife about his desire to taste human flesh.[116] In the sociopathic capitalistic society in which we live, however, those psychopathic traits were highly regarded: the more ruthlessly Dunlap's administration behaved, the more his share price shot up.

Individuals with narcissistic personality disorders display, among other traits, an excessive need for admiration, pervasive patterns of grandiosity in fantasy or behavior, a sense of entitlement, and a lack of empathy. Narcissists may learn to moderate their behaviors, but when a sense of entitlement and a lack of empathy augment antisocial behaviors, the "pattern might be described as aggressive or malignant narcissism, which is difficult to distinguish from psychopathy."[117] In business, Babiak and Hare found that a small number of highly motivated individuals with psychopathic personalities could ably "enter an organization, evaluate strengths and weaknesses in its culture (processes, communication networks, corporate politics), use and abuse coworkers, 'deal with' opposition, and climb the corporate ladder."[118] They entered the corporation following a successful interview process, adapting to its culture, and manipulating coworkers and executives. Psychopaths built power bases inside the organization by convincing a large number of people that they were "best friends, trusted confidants, loyal coworkers, and all-around good people with whom to associate."[119]

In fact, psychopaths "do naturally what some politicians, salesmen, and promoters have to work hard to achieve: impress listeners with how they say something. In criminal cases, it is sometimes only after the authorities uncover some heinous crime or masterful deceit that a psychopath's charming mask of sincerity, integrity, and honesty is questioned. In less dramatic cases, it may take repeated exposure before the façade becomes transparent to a few studious observers, but this rarely happens with most people with whom they interact."[120] Many psychopaths demonstrate mastery at finding and exploiting the weaknesses and vulnerabilities of others, and they build careers that lead them to ever-higher positions in the organization. Their game plans involve "manipulating communication networks to enhance their own reputation, to disparage others, and to create conflicts and rivalries among organization members, thereby keeping them from sharing information that might uncover the deceit. They also spread disinformation in the interest of protecting their scam and furthering their own careers."[121] Such players take satisfaction in the "fast-paced manipulation of coworkers, executives, vendors, or customers," and for them winning almost always involves "financial and power rewards, such as a steady paycheck for work rarely completed, and promotions into increasing levels of authority," and it might include derailing the careers of coworkers up to and including their unjust termination.[122]

While some psychopaths use charm to deceive, abusive corporate bullies, not as sophisticated or as smooth as the manipulative type, rely on coercion, abuse, humiliation, harassment, aggression, and fear to get their way. They find reasons "to engage in conflict, to blame others for things that go wrong, to attack others unfairly (in private and in public) and tend to be generally antagonistic."[123] Should they not get what they want, psychopaths become vindictive, maintain a grudge for a considerable amount of time, and take every opportunity to seek revenge. They often select and attack targets who have the least power and are the most vulnerable. Yet Babiak and Hare note that some business organizations "actively seek out and recruit individuals with at least a moderate dose of psychopathic features," and some executives they interviewed argued that many of their psychopathic traits "seem to be valued" by their company.[124] Given access to unrestricted power and resources of startling proportions, combined with the erosion of ethical standards and a tendency for executives to allow the perks of power to override their moral sensibility, the recent rise in the number of reports of abuse in major corporations stands to reason. In the next chapter, we take a hard look at the social impact of psychopathic corporate leadership, and the privileging of profit over people, during the last fifty years.

NOTES

1. Eckhart Tolle, *The Power of Now* (Vancouver: Namaste, 2004), 76.
2. Tolle, *The Power of Now*, 63.
3. Tolle, *The Power of Now*, 65.
4. "Genesis," *The Bible: Authorized King James Version* (Oxford: Oxford University Press, 2008), 2.
5. "Genesis," 3.
6. "Genesis," 4.
7. "Genesis," 4.
8. "Genesis," 4.
9. "Genesis," 4.
10. John M. Riddle, *A History of the Middle Ages, 300–1500* (Lanham, MD: Rowman & Littlefield, 2016), 341.
11. "Gospel of Matthew," *The Bible: Authorized King James Version* (Oxford: Oxford University Press, 2008), 10.
12. Charles R. Geisst, *Beggar Thy Neighbor: A History of Usury and Debt* (Philadelphia: University of Pennsylvania Press, 2013), 67.

13. Hunt and Murray, *A History of Business in Medieval Europe*, 70.
14. Hunt and Murray, *A History of Business in Medieval Europe*, 53.
15. Wiesner-Hanks, *Early Modern Europe*, 254.
16. Brian S. Rosner, *Greed as Idolatry: The Origin and Meaning of a Pauline Metaphor* (Grand Rapids, MI: Eerdmans, 2007), 111.
17. "Book of Jeremiah," *The Bible: Authorized King James Version* (Oxford: Oxford University Press, 2008), 837.
18. "Book of Jeremiah," 833.
19. "Book of Jeremiah," 833.
20. "Book of Jeremiah," 827.
21. "Book of Jeremiah," 835.
22. "Proverbs," *The Bible: Authorized King James Version* (Oxford: Oxford University Press, 2008), 731.
23. "Proverbs," 747.
24. "Proverbs," 747.
25. "Proverbs," 743.
26. "Ecclesiastes," *The Bible: Authorized King James Version* (Oxford: Oxford University Press, 2008), 753.
27. "Ecclesiastes," 751.
28. "Ecclesiastes," 754–55.
29. James M. Robinson, ed., *Nag Hammadi Library in English* (Leiden: Brill, 1990), 138.
30. "Gospel of Luke," *The Bible: Authorized King James Version* (Oxford: Oxford University Press, 2008), 93.
31. "Gospel of Luke," 93.
32. "Gospel of Luke," 93.
33. "Gospel of Luke," 93.
34. "Gospel of Luke," 93.
35. "Gospel of Luke," 93.
36. "Gospel of Mark," *The Bible: Authorized King James Version* (Oxford: Oxford University Press, 2008), 59.
37. "Gospel of Mark," 59.
38. "Gospel of Mark," 61.
39. "Gospel of John," *The Bible: Authorized King James Version* (Oxford: Oxford University Press, 2008), 117.
40. "Revelation," *The Bible: Authorized King James Version* (Oxford: Oxford University Press, 2008), 314–15.
41. "Colossians," *The Bible: Authorized King James Version* (Oxford: Oxford University Press, 2008), 251.
42. "Ephesians," *The Bible: Authorized King James Version* (Oxford: Oxford University Press, 2008), 242.
43. Laura Caroline Stevenson, *Praise and Paradox: Merchants and Craftsmen in Elizabethan Popular Literature* (Cambridge: Cambridge University Press, 2002), 5.
44. Stevenson, *Praise and Paradox*, 3–4.
45. Stevenson, *Praise and Paradox*, 4.
46. Helen Cooper, *Oxford Guides to Chaucer: The Canterbury Tales* (Oxford: Oxford University Press, 1996), 260.
47. Cooper, *Oxford Guides to Chaucer*, 58.
48. Cooper, *Oxford Guides to Chaucer*, 19.
49. Cooper, *Oxford Guides to Chaucer*, 17–18.
50. Cooper, *Oxford Guides to Chaucer*, 263–64.
51. Geoffrey Chaucer, *The Canterbury Tales by Geoffrey Chaucer* (New York: Houghton Mifflin, 2000), 176.
52. Chaucer, *The Canterbury Tales*, 177.
53. Cooper, *Oxford Guides to Chaucer*, 262.
54. Chaucer, *The Canterbury Tales*, 177.
55. Cooper, *Oxford Guides to Chaucer*, 265.

56. Chaucer, *The Canterbury Tales*, 181.

57. Chaucer, *The Canterbury Tales*, 182.

58. Chaucer, *The Canterbury Tales*, 183.

59. Chaucer, *The Canterbury Tales*, 183.

60. Cooper, *Oxford Guides to Chaucer*, 273–74.

61. John Walter Van Cleve, *The Merchant in German Literature of the Enlightenment* (Chapel Hill: University of North Carolina Press, 1986), xiv.

62. Van Cleve, *The Merchant in German Literature of the Enlightenment*, xiv.

63. Stevenson, *Praise and Paradox*, 2.

64. Stevenson, *Praise and Paradox*, 101.

65. David Bevington, ed., *The Complete Works of Shakespeare* (New York: HarperCollins, 1992), 180–81.

66. Bevington, *The Complete Works of Shakespeare*, 180.

67. Bevington, *The Complete Works of Shakespeare*, lxiv.

68. Bevington, *The Complete Works of Shakespeare*, lxv.

69. Ivan Morris, ed., *The Life of an Amorous Woman and Other Writings*, by Ihara Saikaku (New York: New Directions, 1969), 3–4.

70. Morris, *The Life of an Amorous Woman*, 6.

71. Morris, *The Life of an Amorous Woman*, 6–7.

72. Morris, *The Life of an Amorous Woman*, 7–8.

73. Morris, *The Life of an Amorous Woman*, 10.

74. Morris, *The Life of an Amorous Woman*, 27.

75. Ihara Saikaku, *The Life of an Amorous Woman and Other Writings* (New York: New Directions, 1969), 226–27.

76. Saikaku, *The Life of an Amorous Woman*, 227.

77. Saikaku, *The Life of an Amorous Woman*, 228.

78. Saikaku, *The Life of an Amorous Woman*, 229–30.

79. David Tod Roy, ed., *The Plum in the Golden Vase or, Chin P'ing Mei: The Gathering* (Princeton: Princeton University Press, 1993), xxxi.

80. Roy, *The Plum in the Golden Vase or, Chin P'ing Mei: The Gathering*, xxxi.

81. Roy, *The Plum in the Golden Vase or, Chin P'ing Mei: The Gathering*, xxxi.

82. Roy, *The Plum in the Golden Vase or, Chin P'ing Mei: The Gathering*, xxxiii.

83. David Tod Roy, *The Plum in the Golden Vase or, Chin P'ing Mei: The Rivals* (Princeton: Princeton University Press, 1993), 127.

84. Roy, *The Plum in the Golden Vase or, Chin P'ing Mei: The Rivals*, 147–48.

85. Clement Egerton, ed., *The Golden Lotus: Volume Four* (New York: Routledge, 1959), 85–86.

86. Egerton, *The Golden Lotus: Volume Four*, 97–98.

87. Joseph Conrad, *Heart of Darkness* (New York: St. Martin's, 1989), 21.

88. Conrad, *Heart of Darkness*, 1989), 21.

89. Conrad, *Heart of Darkness*, 35.

90. Conrad, *Heart of Darkness*, 82.

91. Conrad, *Heart of Darkness*, 84–85.

92. Conrad, *Heart of Darkness*, 65.

93. Bret Easton Ellis, *American Psycho* (New York: Vintage, 2010), 121 & 276.

94. Michael P. Clark, "Violence, Ethics, and the Rhetoric of Decorum in *American Psycho*," in *Bret Easton Ellis: American Psycho, Glamorama, Lunar Park*, ed. Naomi Mandel (London: Continuum, 2011), 24.

95. Ellis, *American Psycho*, 352.

96. Ellis, *American Psycho*, 375.

97. Ellis, *American Psycho*, 377.

98. Margaret Heffernan, *A Bigger Prize: How We Can Do Better than the Competition* (Philadelphia: PublicAffairs, 2014), xiii–xiv.

99. Charles Derber, *Sociopathic Society: A People's Sociology of the United States* (New York: Routledge, 2013), 4.

100. Derber, *Sociopathic Society*, 4.

101. Derber, *Sociopathic Society*, xi.
102. Derber, *Sociopathic Society*, xi.
103. D. J. Cooke, Adelle E. Forth, and Robert D. Hare, *Psychopathy: Theory, Research and Implications for Society* (New York: Springer Science, 1997), 3–4.
104. Cooke, Forth, and Hare, *Psychopathy*, 4–5.
105. Cooke, Forth, and Hare, *Psychopathy*, 128.
106. Cooke, Forth, and Hare, *Psychopathy*, 129.
107. Cooke, Forth, and Hare, *Psychopathy*, 129.
108. Maria Konnikova, *The Confidence Game: Why We Fall for It . . . Every Time* (New York: Viking, 2016), 22.
109. Paul Babiak and Robert D. Hare, *Snakes in Suits: When Psychopaths Go to Work* (New York: HarperCollins, 2006), 177.
110. Konnikova, *The Confidence Game*, 22–23.
111. Konnikova, *The Confidence Game*, 24.
112. Konnikova, *The Confidence Game*, 25.
113. Konnikova, *The Confidence Game*, 26–27.
114. Babiak and Hare, *Snakes in Suits*, 40.
115. Jeff Bercovici, "Why (Some) Psychopaths Make Great CEOs," *Forbes*, June 14, 2011, http://www.forbes.com/sites/jeffbercovici/2011/06/14/why-some-psychopaths-make-great-ceos/#2f4b16994fac
116. Jeff Bercovici, "Why (Some) Psychopaths Make Great CEOs."
117. Babiak and Hare, *Snakes in Suits*, 41.
118. Babiak and Hare, *Snakes in Suits*, 103
119. Babiak and Hare, *Snakes in Suits*, 125.
120. Babiak and Hare, *Snakes in Suits*, 50.
121. Babiak and Hare, *Snakes in Suits*, 129.
122. Babiak and Hare, *Snakes in Suits*, 128.
123. Babiak and Hare, *Snakes in Suits*, 188.
124. Babiak and Hare, *Snakes in Suits*, 194.

Chapter Four

Corporation as Supervillain

To delineate the contours of the mercantile mind in the last chapter, we sketched cross-cultural warnings about the corruptive effects of afflictive desire, and pondered a modern corporate cultural landscape that rewards executives for decisions and actions that—outside of business at least—suggest psychopathy. Since the nation's founding, popular opinion in the United States has vacillated between depictions of merchants, tycoons, and executives as cultural heroes who embody an American Dream of success and material prosperity, and rascals whose blind pursuit of wealth and power leads to the exploitation of labor and natural resources and to the transgression of commonly held conceptions of fairness and equality. In this chapter, we scrutinize the implications of extolling business and commerce as engines of shared prosperity and enshrining that celebration in the nation's symbolic narratives—and we contemplate the real possibility that our business heroes may be killing us.

"If there is no religion then the culture dies, civilization goes to pieces," the philosopher Jiddu Krishnamurti asserts, and "considering what the world is like, with all its brutality, violence, wars, divisions, class hatreds and so on, which all indicate degeneration of the human mind, it behooves us to discover for ourselves what is religion," a foundational force for order in society and life.[1] Yet, rather than heeding these symptoms of mental deterioration, Americans continue to tacitly permit the perpetuation of what looks like sociopathy, a system resulting in economic inequality, profit maximization, and self-regarding greed that devastates lives and undermines democracy. Consider the attitudes that Americans hold concerning such evident narcissists as "O. J. Simpson, Donald Trump, Lance Armstrong, or Bernie Madoff," who can "appear entirely normal, since they are often pillars of the community and know how to succeed under existing rules of the game."[2]

When those rules endorse destructive institutional and employee behaviors, and become encoded as dominant social values, then they undermine the well-being of much of the population and cut asunder the social bonds and sustainable environmental conditions essential to social stability. Much like an autoimmune disease, antisocial attitudes weaken society—and in extreme cases, as Charles Derber observes, "kill the society itself."[3]

But social norms are not permanent, and evolving cultures may replace antisocial norms with ones that encourage health, sustainability, inclusion, and order. Regrettably, many Americans are grievously harmed by greedy cultural values—and that current levels of inequality are untenable makes the replacement of antisocial norms more imaginable. Signs of a shift away from sociopathy and toward health are already emerging, for we may cite the presidential candidacy of Bernie Sanders in 2016 and 2020 on a platform more socially progressive than many of his democratic contenders, possibly indicating a citizenry eager for a return to more equitably shared prosperity. Moreover, current pro-business values—largely constructed by elites—do not represent the ideals or interests of the general population. We define elites as the "1 percent." The United States instituted policies to reduce the influence of private capital after the Great Depression and took the progressive tax further than Europe in the effort to reduce inequality. We might recapture that democratic spirit, since the country "has become noticeably more inegalitarian than France (and Europe as a whole)" from the turn of the twentieth century to the present day—with inequality in 2010 as quantitatively extreme as in old Europe in the first decade of the twentieth century.[4] From that backward slide, it is clear that the neoliberal policies touted by the Reagan administration, and sustained by subsequent presidents, imperil the egalitarian promise enshrined in American founding documents (e.g., the Declaration of Independence).

The Reaganomics of the 1980s promoted neoliberal political and economic policies with the belief that "human well-being can best be advanced by liberating individual entrepreneurial freedoms and skills within an institutional framework characterized by strong private property rights, free markets, and free trade."[5] The state, in this view, existed to create and preserve an institutional framework supportive of those notions; otherwise it did well to get out of the way of entrepreneurial freedom, which in practice meant deregulation, privatization, and withdrawal of the state from many areas of social provision. Reagan and Thatcher preached the virtues of free trade, self-interest, and the power of the market to deliver justice and prosperity, as they disparaged social welfare programs as misguided. They promised jobs to those upgrading their skills in the knowledge economy, but pushed the cost of higher education onto students (who they claimed would be financially rewarded for taking on the necessary debt).[6] In reality, the retreat of state and federal funding for tertiary education from the Reagan era onward resulted in massive hikes in tuition and fees. College graduates have seen no substantial increase in income since the 1970s, and the average American undergraduate now leaves school with almost $40,000 in debt.[7] In addition, the demand for professional jobs that neoliberals guaranteed failed to materialize, and the global auction for cut-priced brainpower shattered the dream of working hard and earning a fair living wage in return.[8]

In dismantling the social safety net that characterized the mid-twentieth-century United States (and Europe), neoliberalism toppled the pillars of shared prosperity, security, and opportunity embedded in relationships among employers, unions, and the state. Neoliberal assertions regarding consumer freedom, free trade, and market individualism proved rhetorical devices designed to characterize government regulation of business as a relic of the past. During the Reagan era, dominant cultural values encouraged the pursuit of self-interest, and "greed was treated as a virtue in the vain hope that the hidden hand of the market would miraculously benefit all through the trickle down of resources from the winners to the losers."[9] Corporate CEOs emerged the clear victors on that unequal neoliberal playing field. Piketty estimates that the "vast majority" of the top *0.1 percent* in the income hierarchy between 2000 and 2010 consisted of supermanagers. By comparison, athletes, actors, and artists made up just 5 percent of this most elite group, which suggests that current levels of income inequality have more to do with "supermanagers" than "superstars."[10]

Between 1997 and 2007, the richest 1 percent of Americans appropriated three-quarters of growth, a jaw-dropping figure reflecting the emergence of top executives at large firms who obtained unprecedented compensation packages. Financial professionals (bank managers and traders in financial markets) are now "twice as common in the very high income groups as in the economy."[11] Still, since 80 percent of top income groups are not in finance, skyrocketing pay packages of top managers of large firms (in both the financial and nonfinancial sectors) best explain the recent increase in the proportion of high-earning Americans.[12] Public opinion supports high salaries for supermanagers, considering the size and complexity of large organizations, but Piketty argues that their salaries represent a form of "meritocratic extremism" through which American society designates certain individuals as "winners" deserving great riches.[13] In truth, data collected about publicly owned corporations demonstrate that firm performance is more the consequence of external variables (the overall state of the economy, raw material prices, exchange rates) than its leadership. That is to say, disproportionally high executive compensation packages are largely a matter of "pay for luck."[14]

Moreover, Piketty holds "no doubt" that growing income inequality contributed to the American financial turmoil in 2008, which resulted in severe recession and increased household debt (as the economy slowed and wages stagnated for those with low and medium incomes).[15] If income inequality continues to expand in the United States (and around the world), we should anticipate more periods of economic instability and expect that they will be increasingly severe and prolonged. The future course of the nation depends, in good measure, on what public policies and institutions are put in place to regulate the relationship between capital and labor. [16] Many Americans do not recognize where their interests lie; therefore, they accept inequality because of confusion about political morality—a political morality manipulated by Republicans who continue to advocate, despite all evidence to the contrary, for certain policies benefiting the wealthy that have never been statistically validated (cutting taxes to create jobs, for instance). Many lower- and middle-class Americans support tax cuts that do not plausibly benefit themselves or their children, even though these same folks find some kinds of inequality unfair and even dangerous. [17] That unreflective adoption of conservative political morality corresponds with the popularity of Milton Friedman and other Chicago School economists (including George Joseph Stigler) who stirred suspicion concerning the state's role in the economy, and in society more generally. They helped to create an intellectual climate that made the conservative revolution possible.

Other contributing factors to the reemergence of wealth inequality beginning in the 1980s include changes to political and electoral systems to protect and promote concentrated wealth, a judicial system that privileges high-income earners, the bolstering of property rights for the wealthy, and increased responsiveness to affluence by elected officials. The modern American campaign finance system facilitates contributions to politicians by businesses, and its creation during the mid-1970s coincides with the beginning of the era of high growth and rising inequality in which we find ourselves today. [18] A massive tax cut in 1981 lowered high-income tax rates considerably and inaugurated a prolonged trend of flattening in the tax code. As additional tax cuts followed, they emptied federal coffers and soon military spending far exceeded reductions to education and other public services. During the first six years of the 1980s, the "Gipper" increased the federal budget deficit by roughly $150 million per year. [19] A relatively extended period of (fairly unified) Republican ascendancy allowed the party to formulate and implement ideologically coherent policies. Democratic presidents have been unable or unwilling to overturn such policies, contributing to growing inequality more pronounced than in other leading democracies, and most concentrated at the very top of income distribution. [20]

In modern American politics, corporate interests and those of the wealthy are too frequently aligned, together producing tremendous sums to support political causes favoring their narrow interests (including low rates of taxation). Consequently, the American welfare state now stands out among rich democracies for its *low levels of public spending* (with the nation devoting only 14 percent of GDP to social spending programs compared to 26.5 percent in Western Europe)—*and a 36 percent minimum wage decline in real value between 1979 and 2006.*[21] What one scholar calls the "perverse openness" of corporate influence and money in American politics allows federal courts to frustrate progressive agendas by limiting the powers of the federal government to regulate economic activity or constrain influential interests.[22] Although not a new phenomenon, this flow of money from businesses and the wealthy into the political system skews outcomes. In recent years, a number of superrich individuals have run for political office partly using their own fortunes. Meg Whitman, former CEO of eBay, ponied up over $140 million in her campaign for the California governorship, and Michael Bloomberg spent $108 million during his run for a third term as mayor of New York City.[23] Donald Trump committed $65 million of his own money to winning the presidency in 2016.[24]

A string of legal decisions by the Supreme Court dating back to the nineteenth century eased the flow of more money into the political system. In 1886, *Santa Clara CO v. Southern Pacific Railroad* first established the legal precept that corporations were persons within the meaning of the Fourteenth Amendment. In 1977, *United States v. Martin Linen Supply Co* held that the Double Jeopardy Clause prohibited appellate review and retrial of corporate defendants.[25] In *Buckley v. Valeo* a year earlier, the court declared restrictions on campaign contributions violated the First Amendment's free speech guarantee but left open questions about whether the long-standing ban on corporate campaign contributions was constitutional.[26] In 2010, *Citizens United v. Federal Election Commission* reversed legislative efforts to keep corporate money from corrupting democracy in a ruling that gave "artificial entities" the same rights of "free speech" as living human beings.[27] In *Burwell v. Hobby Lobby*, the court determined in 2014 that closely held for-profit corporations (purporting to support religious principles that opposed offering contraception as mandated by the Affordable Care Act) count as "persons," and in recognizing the free exercise of rights by corporations, the ruling changed the way that we think about the moral and legal status of business enterprises.[28] Incorporation, which once provided limited liability to investors, now meant that like a real person, a corporation could buy and sell property, sue in court and be sued, and borrow money.

Given that legal provisions designated for living human beings (including free speech and religious liberty) now apply to corporations, it makes sense to extend that rationale and to "diagnose" corporations with antisocial characteristics and behaviors, much as a psychiatrist would diagnose patients. In the book and documentary film *The Corporation* (2004), Joel Bakan puts the modern American corporation on the psychiatrist's couch and compiles a checklist of symptoms evidenced by his patient: "insatiable greed, self-preoccupation, power lust, willingness to harm others without remorse, pursuit of profit at the expense of communities and the whole society."[29] When these and other antisocial characteristics and behaviors are culturally programmed, so that they cannot act differently, corporations become "sociopathic" or "psychopathic."[30] For instance, company law compels the "corporate patient" to externalize costs without regard for the harm it may cause to people, to communities, or to the natural environment, and in this sense corporations (such as Enron) act as the system requires: they maximize short-term profit and carry out unethical and socially destructive acts.[31] This sociopathic programming may currently enjoy the imprimatur of the law, but political scientist and cultural critic Michael Parenti calls it a "profit pathology," and its effects are clearly visible in contemporary American society.[32]

Because every expense that business entities unload onto the consumer benefits their bottom line, American corporations began to replace private pensions (once a hallmark of compensation with guaranteed payouts) around 1978 and to offload their retirement obligations onto their employees through defined-contribution 401(k) and IRA type plans. Many of these plans relied on worker contributions, and they proved riskier and less predictable.[33] As a result of that transference of retirement obligations onto workers, 48 percent of middle-income households held no retirement savings accounts in 2010, and the retirement savings of African American and Hispanic workers fell significantly behind those of whites.[34] Today, most 401(k) plans provide about half of what is needed for a comfortable retirement, and therefore millions of Americans are left with the loathsome "choices" of saving more, working longer, or living on less.[35] "Golden years" are becoming bleak and cold.

During the Great Recession of 2008, Bank of America, Goldman Sachs, J. P. Morgan Chase, Countrywide, Washington Mutual, and AIG—*all business entities programmed to maximize short-term profits*—engaged in "unethical, destructive behavior, whether predatory loans or issuing toxic financial instruments that they secretly bet would fail."[36] Fortunes were made through such duplicity, but the financial crisis that resulted hammered away at the middle class (already under duress and in decline for decades). Additional tax cuts for the wealthy, weakened unions, rising unemployment, and the deregulation of industry forced millions of middle-income people out of their homes and into bankruptcy; simultaneously, "free trade" agreements put middle-level workers in direct competition with lower-paid workers in emerging economies.[37] The middle-class share of the nation's total income (one indicator of social equality) fell from 53 percent in 1968 to 45 percent in 2012, and the collapse of the housing bubble during the Great Recession resulted in a spike in foreclosures and massive losses of equity.[38] During the limited recovery from 2009 to 2011, income for the top 1 percent grew by 11.2 percent, while that of the bottom 99 percent declined by 0.4 percent. In sum, by early 2014, the top 1 percent garnered 95 percent of all income growth in the wake of recession.[39]

Much like individuals stricken with sociopathy (or psychopathy—interchangeable terms with intertwining clinical histories, and both conditions listed as antisocial personality disorders in the *Diagnostic and Statistical Manual of Mental Disorders*), sociopathic institutions contribute to the creation of sick societies injurious to their citizenry. A pattern of corporate disregard for the rights of others, and callousness toward the social effects of a shareholder orientation, are etched indelibly into the bodies and minds of people across the nation. Poverty has a continuous cumulative effect on health over a lifetime, and about 15 percent of the American population was poor in 2010, or about 2.5 percent higher than before the Great Recession of 2008.[40] Americans living in and near poverty today have shorter life spans, work longer, and collect fewer benefits than their healthier and wealthier counterparts (who enjoy longer lives and collect more Social Security checks). Untenable levels of social inequality affect those living above the poverty line and in the middle class, as well. In 2012, nearly 49 million households experienced food insecurity or disruption of normal eating patterns due to insufficient resources, while more than 600,000 people suffered homelessness in January of that year alone.[41]

The United States also exhibits a pattern of poorer health from birth to old age than thirteen other advanced nations, despite spending the highest proportion of GDP on healthcare of any country. It ranks lowest in maternal mortality and deaths from noncommunicable diseases and highest in deaths from diabetes and cardiovascular and communicable diseases, and a recent report from the Institute of Medicine and the National Research Council shows that Americans under age fifty suffered poorer health and experienced shorter lives than peers in other developed countries, and they endured higher rates of heart and lung disease.[42] Low-income Americans enjoy less access to healthcare, which puts them at greater risk of mortality, and they are more likely to engage in unhealthy behaviors and to work in unhealthy environments. A discernible racial dimension to American poverty remains palpable as well when Hispanics and blacks are less often insured, despite being more likely to inhabit living quarters and workspaces that expose them to disease, injury, death, and disabilities.[43] A strong correlation also exists between wealth inequality and conspicuous health and social problems: a greater prevalence of mental illness, higher rates of drug and alcohol addiction, lower life expectancy and higher infant mortality, greater obesity, lower education performance for children, more teenage births, increased violence and homicide, higher imprisonment rates, and less social mobility.[44] Make no mistake, inequality is a profound social disease: it sickens and it kills.

In sociopathic societies, giant for-profit healthcare corporations like Hospital Corporation of America (HCA), and global pharmaceutical companies such as Merck, generate great wealth by utilizing patents and political lobbying to restrict access to essential generic medicines for epidemics (though they might have saved thousands of lives).[45] Why is the American public not in revolt against these and other profit indecencies, and how do such corporate leaders live with themselves? For answers, we look to the ideological bombardment that the American public received over decades, financed by moneyed interests to glorify private corporations and effectively cast a shadow of distrust over public and nonprofit ownership. Neoliberalism left virtually no aspect of American lives untouched after corporate takeovers of public utilities, public healthcare, public education, and public prisons. Harvard professor Paul Sweezy believes that we have moved from a competitive form of capitalism to "monopoly capitalism" run by "gigantic, oligopolistic global companies in league with corporate politicians" that deform lives, but which nevertheless is doomed by the multiple forms of sociopathy inherent in the monopoly system (including saturation advertising and the encouragement of unsustainable debt).[46] The rhetorical tropes of efficiency trotted out to justify the corporate takeover of healthcare delivery, for instance, hide sociopathic profit motives that have become the sole reason for their existence.

Michael Parenti describes a disconcerting experience at a medical center affiliated with Sutter Health—a "not-for-profit" hospital system in California. A few days after his abdominal surgery, nurses went on strike systemwide in protest of a corporate culture that demanded sacrifices from patients, as well as from those who provided their care, but still managed to pay its executives millions of dollars. As an enterprise ostensibly dedicated to the public good, Sutter Health pays no property taxes to California, or to any of the state's municipalities, and no corporate taxes to the federal government. Still, Sutter touts itself as a "price leader" in the industry for having "successfully cut costs and raised profits."[47] This dubious profit formula squeezes employees by eliminating essential positions, increases the workloads of remaining staff members, and creates a culture of fear that discourages dissent. At one Sutter affiliate, management slashed more than 350 positions, including some of those occupied by professionals in its skilled nursing facility. Such moves garnered Sutter Health scrutiny from unions, consumer groups, and insurers for its low-wage and high-price business strategy.[48]

Physicians at Sutter Health average about $185,000 per year, a tidy sum to most Americans, but generally considered appropriate given their years of training and costly medical school tuitions. By contrast, hospital executives—many managers and coordinators who probably could not heal anyone—bring home around $600,000 per year, plus perks. The chief executive at Aetna earned $977,000 in 2012—a modest sum really when compared with a total compensation package of $36 million (the bulk from stocks and options); the president of Barnabas Health earned a paltry $21.7 million the same year.[49] Only in sociopathic cultures do corporate leaders make so much more than the highly trained doctors and nurses who care for patients (and thereby fulfill the altruistic core missions of their institutions). As executive salaries in the healthcare industry grow, so do the costs of hospital care (at nearly four times the rate of inflation by some estimates), and medical insurance companies (often passing for "not-for-profit" enterprises) maximize their bottom lines by increasing premiums and withholding payments. The greatest profiteers in the industry are health maintenance organizations (HMOs) whose business model relies on charging customers steep monthly payments, underpaying staff members, and requiring doctors to see more patients. The Affordable Care Act intended to address those unconscionable practices, but hospitals still overcharge the poor and inflate billing with charges no one can "explain or defend."[50] Moreover, the Trump administration seems determined to slowly dismantle "Obamacare" after failing to repeal it in 2017.

As hospitals across the nation cut staff to boost bonuses for fat-cat executives, they add patients to nurses' workloads and dangerously compromise the quality of care that patients receive. Writing for *Slate*, clinical nurse Theresa Brown explains that people die when the number of patients under the care of nurses rises above an established safe maximum (which varies according to the sickness of their patients). Nurses "dispense medication; monitor IVs; dress wounds; translate between patients and physicians; respond to immediate needs for relief of pain or vomiting; and serve as a first alert system when a patient becomes dangerously unstable."[51] They stand among the most important people in the healthcare industry—their comparatively low pay for such important responsibilities notwithstanding. Corporate downsizing of staff turned medical errors into a leading cause of death nationally, and *for-profit hospitals make two to four times as many medical errors as not-for-profit institutions*. They also offer fewer examinations, release more patients prematurely, and employ fewer skilled staff and trained cleaners (resulting in dangerous hospital infections), and they tend to keep patient-staff ratios high, rely excessively on shift work, and fail to make follow-up inspections of procedures.[52] The homeless and the uninsured remain among the hardest hit by the conversion to privatized "free market" medical care, since they pay more than those with coverage.

For-profit prisons are an additional symptom of the profit pathology in American business that negatively impacts society and culture. Although the Thirteenth Amendment to the U.S. Constitution "abolished" slavery, it authorized "involuntary servitude" for prisoners as part of punishments for crimes. It thus enabled the continuation of racialized forced labor in the South. Many former slaves presumably freed by that amendment found themselves suddenly designated "vagrants," "loiterers," and "trespassers" as white southern elites, facing an urgent need for cheap labor, imprisoned former slaves for petty crimes and made them inmates. In this manner, they created the foundation for "lucrative, profit-driven, white-owned businesses."[53] Following the Civil War, a process known as convict leasing permitted the renting out of inmates to supply low-cost labor for coal mining, logging, turpentine production, railroad construction, and farmwork.[54] Beginning in the mid-1980s, for-profit imprisonment reappeared when mandatory sentencing disproportionately incarcerated black men, and it generated considerable returns for private prison owners and their shareholders.

For-profit prisons, located predominantly in the South, were filled with black men following the implementation of the "War on Drugs," which jailed hundreds of thousands of people for nonviolent drug and property offenses from the 1970s and 1980s onward. For-profit detention facilities, which accommodated that influx, made money from the labor of their inmates, as well as from "their bodily ability to generate per diem payments for their private keepers." By 2003, *nearly 37,000 out of every 100,000 black males aged twenty to twenty-four were in prison*, making the business of incarceration a mechanism for injustice and social stratification.[55] With only 5 percent of the world's population, the United States held almost a quarter of the globe's inmates (approximately 2.2 million) in 2012. Blacks constitute only 12 to 13 percent of the nation's population, but they make up over 40 percent of the prison population.[56] Currently, the incarceration rate for African American males is eight times higher than that of white males. In recognition of these faults, the Department of Justice announced in 2016 that it would phase out its use of private prisons, in part due to their higher rates of assault and more frequent uses of force than in federal facilities.[57] However, since the Department of Justice only has authority over federal prisons, that decision impacted only a fraction of people in jail, as the vast majority of prisoners remain in state facilities.[58] In February 2017, Attorney General Jeff Sessions issued guidance for scrapping the new Obama administration policy. A year later President Trump's "zero-tolerance" stance on illegal immigration pushed thousands of undocumented immigrants into for-profit detention centers run by private prison operators, who donated hundreds of thousands of dollars to the president's election campaign and to his inauguration.[59]

The private prison industry is built on a business model that treats inmates as commodities on which huge profits can be reaped by keeping imprisonment rates high, increasing the total size of the inmate population, and moving incarceration from government facilities to private corporations—a process euphemistically known as "privatization" (a keystone of neoliberal ideology). Businesses, such as Corrections Corporation of America, benefited enormously over the years as American internment rates exceeded those of any other advanced democracy. Corrections Corporation reported nearly $71 million in profits *during the first quarter of 2006*—and a staggering $1.3 billion for the year. Likewise, GEO Group, which manages correction facilities in twelve states (and in countries around the world), reported total profits of nearly $1.3 billion in 2010.[60] Obviously, when the overriding purpose of private enterprise becomes profit and capital accumulation, rather than protecting the interests of community stakeholders, the effects of that pathology become demonstrable in society: unsustainable income inequality; higher rates of poverty, hunger, and homelessness; the diminution of government and corporate responsibility; and escalating incarceration rates. However, we need not marvel at these and other undesirable social consequences of unrestrained greed, for "where money is the measure of all things," the Renaissance statesman Saint Thomas More observed, "justice and prosperity will be nearly impossible."[61]

The antisocial forces inherent in twenty-first-century American capitalism permit gross negligence in the stewardship of the environment, as well. Too many multinational firms treat the earth's life-sustaining resources (arable land, drinkable water, clean air) as commodities to be bought and sold, or used as primary ingredients for a variety of products, while giving little thought for the delicate balance of the biosphere—a shared human inheritance. The Deepwater Horizon oil spill in 2010 exemplifies the long-term costs of putting profit before people and the environment. Fourteen years before the explosion that led to the spill, chief executive John Browne claimed that BP, formerly British Petroleum, would take a leading role tackling global climate change. That pro-environmental propaganda diverted attention from a string of accidents leading up to the Horizon spill, but it was business as usual at BP. In March 2005, an explosion at a BP refinery in Texas that killed fifteen workers and injured nearly 180 others was blamed on "willful negligence of safety standards," for which BP paid $108 million in fines (or less than 2 percent of its $6 billion in profits from the first three months of 2010).[62] The following year, a leaking BP pipeline in Alaska resulted in the largest oil spill on land in that state's history.[63]

The blowout of the Deepwater Horizon, a giant oil rig in the Gulf of Mexico that drilled a mile below the surface, remains the worst environmental disaster in American history, and it was preventable. In March 2008, the Occupational Safety and Health Administration (OSHA) called BP out for having one of the worst safety records in the industry. At the Deepwater Horizon site, management overlooked questions concerning the integrity of the rig and exerted unreasonable pressure while drilling, thereby fracturing the rock and its well. Rather than ceasing to drill, "BP management compared safety to profit-maximization and made the decision to plug the fractures in an effort to maximize profit."[64] The plug held, for a time, but after countless emergency indications, natural gas leaked into the air. The ensuing explosion forced 5 million barrels of oil into the Gulf of Mexico over eighty-seven days, killed eleven people and injured seventeen more, and spoiled hundreds of miles of coastline.[65] A federal judge approved a $20 billion settlement against BP in 2016 for that calamity (including civil penalties), though the fines will be paid out over sixteen years.[66] Even in the face of such a heady amercement, modern corporate plunderers (like Tony Hayward, CEO of BP at the time of the Deepwater Horizon explosion) appear largely unconcerned with the looming ecological disaster associated with climate change, but then again, such people are often "more wedded to their wealth than to the Earth upon which they live, more concerned about the fate of their fortunes than the fate of humanity."[67]

Sensible regulation might curtail these and other ramifications of the myopic pursuit of profit, yet for most of the twenty-first century corporations have generally escaped regulative scrutiny through adept public relations in tandem with political and judicial complicity in advancing their profit-driven agendas. One such trick was the repeal of the Banking Act of 1933 (better known as Glass-Steagall) in 1999; Congress passed that legislation after the stock market crash of 1929 to prevent another financial catastrophe by separating investment banking from commercial banking. With that separation, American consumers gained access to safe and reliable financial institutions that left mergers, acquisitions, and derivatives to the investment banks. In the late 1990s, Wall Street banks, anxious to increase their profits, diluted the law with the assistance of Federal Reserve Chairman Alan Greenspan by reinterpreting legal language in a manner that created a loophole permitting "escalating expansion by commercial banks into underwriting securities and other investment banking operations by allowing them to do first 5 percent, then 10 percent, and finally 25 percent of their business in these higher-risk areas"[68]

Loosening of financial regulations like Glass-Steagall encouraged giant conglomerations to become "too big to fail," meaning their collapse would wreak havoc in the national economy. In the case of the reinterpretation of Glass-Steagall, the reintegration of investment banking with commercial banking meant that when Citigroup and other megabanks were struck by the financial earthquake of 2008, they did not possess adequate reserves to cover their losses. In the end, necessity demanded that taxpayers rescue banks to avoid the collapse of financial markets. In 2010, former Federal Reserve chair Paul Volcker advocated barring all regulated banks from proprietary trading on their own account in order to keep those financial institutions from putting the economic system at risk again.[69] Not implemented until 2015, five years later than planned due to years of political delay tactics and corporate litigation, it remains unclear how effectively the "Volcker Rule" will reign in risky speculative investing that does not benefit customers. With a business tycoon now as president, a tycoon who first appointed fellow magnates to high-ranking government posts, we easily envisage another wave of deregulation instead.

Whereas following World War II corporations invested a share of their profits into their communities through a variety of foundations, charitable giving programs, and community outreach initiatives, that sense of corporate social responsibility is largely absent in contemporary American business. Over twenty-five years, corporate giving as a percentage of profits declined from 2.3 percent to just 1.3 percent in 2001, and then to an estimated 0.8 percent in 2013—a regrettable trend attributable to increased global competitiveness, changes in corporate culture and the role of the CEO, and the way that dollars move from companies to nonprofits.[70] As a concern for the impact of business activities on local communities evaporated, internationalization permitted corporations to set rules for global markets that "virtually eliminate workers' bargaining power, while environmental and other standards have been ignored."[71] From the 1980s to 2000s, corporations used mergers and acquisitions to consolidate on a global scale (thus reducing job creation), and as free trade deals sent jobs overseas, technology-inflicted additional job losses, and worker wages stagnated with their purchasing power (due to inflation).[72]

In a single generation, the well-paid manufacturing jobs that swelled the ranks of the middle class following World War II disappeared—and the approximately 1.5 million manufacturing jobs that were spared paid just $12 per hour or less. To appreciate the extent of underemployment in the United States in 2017, imagine that nearly 25 million people earn less than $10.10 per hour, and 79 percent of the 3.5 million people who earn lower than the federal minimum wage (of $7.25 per hour) hold high school degrees, and over 40 percent of them completed a degree or have some higher education.[73] The creation of a new American social class, "the working poor," is a further repercussion of corporate malfeasance: less people spending money slows the economy. Publically traded fast-food corporations operate in an industry known to underpay workers and to trap them in a cycle of working poverty. Why offer a minimum hourly wage to workers, knowing the negative impact of earnings that do not reach subsistence levels? Because just seven fast-food corporations reaped $7.44 billion in profits in 2012 (and paid their executives handsomely with $52.7 million going to the highest paid and $7.7 billion distributed in dividends and buybacks).[74] Meanwhile, half of their frontline workers rely on at least one public assistance program just to make ends meet. Of the ten largest fast-food companies draining state and federal coffers, McDonald's tops the list with an estimated average cost to taxpayers of $11.2 billion in public assistance for its employees. Next to American fast-food corporations, Walmart does the most to keep low-income workers in poverty. The average Walmart worker earned less than $9 per hour in 2012, even though the company made $17 billion in profits alone.[75] The gouging of labor by corporations on this scale creates downward pressure on wages, and it passes the social costs of unethical business practices onto citizens who finance assistance programs for the working poor.

Central to Walmart's business model is achieving lower price points by purchasing cheap products from emerging nations and reducing costs through better logistics and improved prediction of markets. In one sustained effort at decreasing expenditures, Walmart pressured its American suppliers to move at least 25 percent of their production to China, and forced them to do so by pitting them against each other to constantly deliver lower prices. Most suppliers had little choice but to comply, since Walmart was vital to their businesses.[76] Walmart also pioneered the "move offshore or die" mentality that swept across the United States. Target, Costco, Best Buy—along with big manufacturers like Boeing and giant multinationals such as Hewlett-Packard, Cisco, and Apple—followed suit. Americans soon bought $1.9 trillion more in goods from China than we sold, and the nation lost 2.6 million jobs to the Middle Kingdom between 2001 to 2010.[77] In 2015, goods and services imported from China reached $497 billion, while exports totaled just $161 billion, meaning that the U.S. trade deficit with China hit $336 billion.[78] Some scholars estimate that before a period of recalibration that balances trade is complete, the United States could lose tens of millions of jobs, a bleak prospect that will force major changes in American industry and society, since it will affect how people earn their living, impact their wages, and undermine their job security.[79] The exploitation of workers in emerging nations by multinational corporations adds another dimension to this hardship, though one regrettably beyond the scope of this study.

As American corporations restructured to locate semi-skilled and skilled jobs abroad, outsourcing further bifurcated the labor force into better-paid and poorer-paid workers. The casualization of employment relations that followed led to a startling increase in the number of casual (or unsheltered) jobs and in part-time work, including in historically high-paying professions such as law. Casualization also weakened or altogether eliminated claims that employees made on the companies employing them, including for retirement benefits and healthcare, thus worsening their overall position in the labor market.[80] In advanced capitalist nations such as the United States, casualization creates unstable employment conditions, and too often when multinational corporations retool, restructure, and relocate overseas, they shed labor without providing alternative employment opportunities.[81] If corporate management aims only to maximize shareholder returns, and corporate social responsibility is a thing of the past, then the casualization of labor will pass as sound corporate policy.[82] When contingency becomes embedded in business culture—and is tolerated by American workers—it weaves its way into the social fabric and becomes harder to unwind. One wonders, for instance, if the majority of underpaid part-time ("adjunct") professors currently teaching on campuses across the nation will ever be allowed to cast off their contingency and join the (shrinking minority of) full-time tenurable faculty members.

Virtually all job growth in the slow recovery that followed the Great Recession of 2008 occurred in the number of temporary jobs. The United

States now has 2.7 million temporary workers—more than at any time in the nation's history.[83] With the prevalence of workplace contingency increasing, employees are less likely to have pensions, savings accounts, or healthcare coverage. Job insecurity also creates poisonous work atmospheres where bullying goes unchecked, fear runs rampant, executive decision making goes undebated, and management becomes dysfunctional. Sound familiar? Well, in the race to drive down wages, American employers violated "the trust and commitment of burnt-out employees who could make their companies smarter and more dynamic."[84] The same might be said for 1099 workers, "independent contractors," who along with other victims of labor casualization may soon become citizens of a nation of "surplus people," the human casualties of shortsighted corporate greed. In a more rational, humanitarian, and egalitarian economy, we "could employ all Americans who want to work in useful and necessary jobs."[85] Truly, as Charles Derber observes:

> This [situation] reflects something deeply irrational but central to U.S. capitalism. The core concern of corporate elites is profit, not jobs. And if more profits can be made in shifting production abroad, elites will take that path. Doing so brings massive short-term profits at the cost of jobs and domestic infrastructure, but it is profoundly irrational, even for elites in the long-term, because it will produce massive domestic deterioration and revolt. Nonetheless, it is the decision—one of short-term profit-seeking over long-term social health and full employment—that U.S. employers have made.[86]

Such irrational desire for short-term gain at any cost among business leaders is indicative of a deeply entrenched profit pathology with calamitous social consequences.

As American corporations blazed a trail in outsourcing workers, cutting benefits, and casualizing labor, corporations found new ways to manufacture desire for goods and services that promised happiness, but too often purchased misery. At the beginning of the twentieth century, metropolitan newspapers and popular magazines became substantial businesses that derived their chief revenues from advertisers. During the 1920s, the last great decade of undisputed newspaper supremacy in communicating news, advertising revenue rose to three times that from the sale of papers.[87] Alongside a process of turning news dailies into chains with readily detectable pro-business biases (such as those run by William Randolph Hearst), national magazines including *Time*, *Saturday Evening Post*, *Businessweek*, *Fortune*—together with their advertisers—essentially filtered the news through a structure of business organizations to keep public opinion in tune with business interests. New social norms emerged from that filtering, norms that mirrored how elite groups, fairly unified in morals and beliefs, saw their culture: middle to upper class, businesslike, religiously Judeo-Christian. "Objectivity" meant observing standards of expression, and anything deemed disparaging to those cultural ideals became "controversial."[88] The bourgeoning film industry (dominated by monopolistic companies such as Fox, Paramount, Metro-Goldwyn-Mayer, and Warner Brothers) provided another means to generate revenue from advertising and to indoctrinate the American public with business values.

Advertising reached a new level of maturity as a social institution following the Great Depression, one ranking with education or religion as an agency of social control (although it lacked social goals and responsibilities outside of the maintenance of profitable markets).[89] Starting in the 1930s, advertisers abandoned the notion of people as rational beings, and instead regarded human beings as essentially nonrational and emotional. Before too long, advertisers discovered that the social sciences, especially psychology, could supply effective methods of persuading readers with their advertisements and manipulating buying behavior. As technology progressed, that approach was extended to other media. The arrival of television in living rooms extended the reach of big business into the minds of ordinary Americans and contributed to the construction of a mass consumer culture, now emulated around the world (even in formerly communist countries like China and Russia). Advertising, high geographical mobility, leisure time, and mass communications centered American cultural values more uniformly around those supplied by the needs of business.[90]

From the mid-twentieth century onward, advertisers increasingly trained the child and conditioned the parent for the role of consumer by articulating a rationale of material values in the same way that organized religion outlined a rationalization for spiritual ones. For instance, with the help of child psychologists, corporations developed scientific breakdowns of different types of "nags" used by children to manipulate parents into buying certain products and business services.[91] Young children are particularly susceptible to media manipulation; the American Academy of Pediatrics acknowledges that children under eight years of age cannot developmentally understand the intent of advertisements and therefore accept their claims as true. This susceptibility makes them appealing targets for manipulation by sociopathic corporations willing to employ deception. Since children are tomorrow's consumers—and therefore the backbone of capitalism—the lack of ethics evident in such tactics has little pertinence to companies trying to move products and generate profits.[92]

American consumer culture now channels desire in ways that feed "an atmosphere of invidious distinction and cravings for immediate gratification" at odds with communal feeling, and so we shrink, as Herbert Marcuse has suggested, into "empty receptacles of desire," infinitely plastic and decentered, and infantilized by insatiable craving as a form of faux self-expression.[93] He describes these passive captives of "false needs" nurtured by consumer society as "one dimensional" people. Corporations did not cease fomenting a consumer culture syndrome when they fled the United States for cheaper manufacturing platforms overseas; average monthly charges on credit cards nearly quadrupled between the late 1970s and late 1990s. As wages declined, Americans borrowed more on credit, which meant one medical emergency or automotive breakdown potentially put millions of people at risk of slipping into the ranks of the working poor. They made less money for their work, but they were still encouraged to gratify every fancy in the marketplace with goods increasingly tied to identity and status.[94]

Advertisers understand that human beings have a strong bias towards misperceiving the world, often positively or optimistically (as exemplified in the myth of American exceptionalism), and they know that some suckers will not accept having been taken in, even when proof of their deception is provided.[95] Because people exhibit a need to hold on to established beliefs, the advertiser, like the confidence artist, ultimately sells hope that we will be happier, healthier, richer, more loved, better looking, younger, smarter, and a deeper and more fulfilled human being as a result of our purchases.[96] In this respect, advertising is a great con game wherein people are manipulated into purchasing behaviors to their financial and psychological detriment. Because Americans overconsume and conflate what they own with their identity, Jean Twenge calls us a "nation of phonies": phony rich people (with interest-only mortgages and piles of debt), phony beauty (a result of plastic surgery), phony celebrities (via reality television), phony student geniuses (from grade inflation), a phony national economy (with trillions of dollars in government debt), and phony friends (on social media).[97] Such a bogus mode of being has hollowed American culture.

In July 1979, President Jimmy Carter addressed the American public with the intention of speaking about the energy crisis strangling the nation as a consequence of disruptions in oil supplies following the Iranian Revolution. In what became known as the "malaise speech," Carter presciently asserted that the "true problems of our Nation" ran much deeper than "gasoline lines or energy shortages, deeper even than inflation or recession." Carter saw a crisis of confidence that struck at "the very heart and soul and spirit of our national will. We can see this crisis in the growing doubt about the meaning of our own lives and in the loss of a unity of purpose for our Nation," as well as in the "erosion of our confidence in the future," threatening to destroy the social and political framework of America.[98] Carter contends:

> In a nation that was proud of hard work, strong families, close-knit communities, and our faith in God, too many of us now tend to worship self-indulgence and consumption. Human identity is no longer defined by what one does, but by what one owns. But we've discovered that owning things and consuming things does not satisfy our longing for meaning. We've learned that piling up material goods cannot fill the emptiness of lives which have no confidence or purpose.[99]

Should they fail to grasp this essential point, Carter stressed that Americans could—in pursuit of a mistaken ideal of freedom (i.e., "the right to grasp for ourselves some advantage over others")—choose a road of self-interest leading to social fragmentation and conflict between narrow interests that are doomed to failure.

From the vantage point of 2019, one is struck by President Carter's assessment of the potential plummeting of American culture into an abyss of consumerism, and his understanding that human lives require more meaning than that purchased by the next thing we can afford (or not afford) to buy. Carter sensed that we might remain a society of one-dimensional people living shallow materialistic lives and should make ready for the social fissures of dissent that radical inequality breeds. Alternately, we might follow the traditions of our past, since "all the lessons of our heritage, all the promises of our future point to another path, the path of common purpose and the restoration of American values," which are tantamount to a "rebirth of the American spirit."[100] By rejecting the status quo that puts profits before the common good, and implementing sensible policies and laws that constrain sociopathic corporate behaviors (from wage slavery to tax evasion, environmental destruction to deceptive advertising), we ensure individual well-being, which means having all the things required for the good life, by rejecting narrow profit-taking motivation. What is required for the good life? Physical and psychological security, material sufficiency, education, and the ability to participate in civil society through democracy and the rule of law.[101]

As a result of consumerist indoctrination, which over generations urged Americans to invest their possessions with identity, memory, and emotion (to the detriment of their spiritual lives), breaking free of the pernicious influence of advertising will hardly be effortless. Human beings think in terms of stories that form the basis of thought, a feature of our minds that makes us all receptive to advertising and marketing. Our thoughts follow patterns similar to those of a conversation wherein "first one person (perhaps ourselves) speaks. Then naturally others make their point, to which we, or others, may respond."[102] In the ensuing dialogue, our minds may change point of view or find novel ways of interpreting information, but these internal narratives leave us open to deception and manipulation, because most advertising is essentially a grafting of its own stories onto the mental narratives running in our minds (that make us more likely to buy a product, service, or object of desire). Narrative also shapes political campaigns, as well as the sale of tobacco, junk bonds, and drugs.[103]

In one of the more notorious examples of that corporate deception, American tobacco companies spent a generation denying accumulating evidence that cigarette smoking is a major cause of lung cancer and other illnesses, and they engineered promotional campaigns and blocked "any legislation designed to curtail this insidious addiction."[104] When the public health consequences of smoking became clear, tobacco advertisements were subjected to regulation, and in 1970 Congress passed the Public Health Cigarette Smoking Act, which required warning labels on cigarette packaging and banned cigarette advertising from television and radio.[105] Despite those restrictions, tobacco marketing campaigns lured an estimated 6 million adolescents into experimenting with cigarettes between 1988 and 1997 using cartoon figures (such as Joe Camel).[106] Likewise, over the last thirty years, American corporations have marketed processed foods and beverages to young people with kid-friendly images (frequently appearing alongside claims of "natural" ingredients) and contributed to the doubling of obesity in children, and its tripling in adolescents.[107] According to the American Academy of Pediatrics, the physical, emotional, and social health implications of obesity include type 2 diabetes, asthma, high blood pressure and cholesterol, low self-esteem, negative body image, depression, and discrimination.[108] Clearly, our susceptibility to advertising narratives has contributed to shocking disruptions in our pursuit of health and happiness.

Nobel Laureates George Akerlof and Robert Shiller observe that democracy may be the best form of government known to mankind, but it does not protect us from the exercise of desire and its consequences.[109] Contrary to the promises of advertisers, consumer capitalism, characterized by an almost infinite variety of choices that cater to individual whims, often creates expectations that are difficult to fulfill and that bring regret.[110] Happily, not all consumer societies are the same: some are more efficient, while others, like our own, are endowed with more resources that we waste on a prodigal scale.[111] Given that reality, we could think more about how changes in lifestyle might lower the demand for products and resources to sustainable levels, for example by improving choice architecture—a framework of information, rules, and opinions from valued groups, so that freedom of choice is preserved for people, while encouraging new habits of consumption.[112] The current afflictions of American society reflect the emptiness of inner lives spent pursuing material desires and fleeting pleasures.

One year after delivering his "malaise speech," President Carter lost his bid for reelection to Freidman flagbearer Ronald Reagan. The celebration of greed that followed remains infamous, and the income and wealth inequality that surged from enacting neoliberal policies continues to rip through American culture nearly two decades into the twenty-first century. The working poor die sooner than their richer, healthier, and longer-living neighbors. Many victims of income inequality also suffer from chronic stress that causes secretion of the hormone cortisol in the bloodstream and results in damage to the brain and immune system over prolonged periods.[113] Piketty reminds us that the resurgence of inequality after 1980, on the heels of decades of income convergence, "is largely due to the political shifts of the past several decades, especially in regard to taxation and finance. The history of inequality is shaped by the way economic, social, and political actors view what is just and what is not, as well as by the relative power of those actors and the collective choices that result."[114]

Because there is no natural spontaneous process to prevent destabilizing inegalitarian forces from prevailing permanently,[115] we should ask if American society can survive even higher levels of inequity generated by capitalism. In posing that question, we recognize that our national myths of upward mobility no longer accord with fact, since self-reliance and hard work (sometimes in multiple low-paying jobs) no longer guarantee access to a living wage, healthcare, or dignity in retirement. One of the great tragedies of corporate greed, beyond its deleterious effects on society, is that money cannot buy happiness, a truth universally acknowledged—and almost universally ignored. Although money unquestionably offers a stay against financial anxiety, once basic needs are met, it does not produce additional happiness. Gains in happiness taper off once subsistence is reached, whereas material desires grow along with income but fail to result in greater levels of contentment.[116] The democratic populism that marked the 2016 presidential campaign, and the Occupy Movement that preceded it, augur well for a move away from the neoliberal agendas of Ronald Reagan and his Republican and Democratic successors, who have so poorly served the majority of Americans, despite their promises of freedom of choice and trickledown wealth from billionaire "job creators."

In this chapter, we traced the formation of a virulent form of American capitalism that took root in the 1980s, hiding in the tropes of individual and market freedom, but that shrunk the middle class and frayed social safety nets (using false narratives of "welfare moms" growing indolently rich on the dole). The wholesale purchase of the neoliberal sales pitch by American voters brought unwelcome consequences, including the jettisoning of corporate social responsibility, the casualization of labor, outsourcing and offshoring, a shrinking middle class, fast-food wages in professions that once provided a living wage, and the establishment of for-profit hospitals, prisons, and colleges. Meanwhile, a new class of "supermanagers" secured historically unprecedented compensation packages for themselves from corporations often engaged in antisocial behaviors (and sometimes run by psychopaths rewarded for layoffs and downsizing). The control of the American government is currently narrowly concentrated at the peak of the income scale, and the vast majority of people not belonging to the 1 percent (or 0.1 percent) have been virtually disenfranchised. For this reason, MIT professor emeritus Noam Chomsky believes that plutocracy has replaced American democracy, "if by that concept we mean political arrangements in which policy is significantly influenced by the public will," and he wonders if the nation "can survive really existing capitalism and the sharply attenuated democracy" that accompanies it.[117]

As we contemplate police brutality and its violent reprisals, and mass shootings by disaffected citizens and terrorist sympathizers, and we contrast our gated communities with urban blight, charter schools with public schools, and the virus of "affluenza" with the homelessness that is its reflection, we find a country more deeply divided than in the age of the robber barons. However, since the nation's founding, business occupied a uniquely privileged social position, from which it encouraged tolerance for high degrees of inequality in terms of wealth and power. Mark Twain, who coined the term "Gilded Age," once wisecracked: "Some men worship rank, some men worship heroes, some men worship power, some men worship God, and over these ideals they dispute and cannot unite, but they all worship money."[118] Perhaps this defect in human nature explains the American inclination to heroicize those who through business become rich and famous. In any case, with the depletion of neoliberalism as a viable economic and political theory, the ascension of a new American business hero is on the horizon, one who works with government to shape policies and regulations that make the nation increasingly prosperous, better educated, and more globally competitive.

NOTES

1. Jiddu Krishnamurti, *Total Freedom: The Essential Krishnamurti* (New York: Harper One, 1996), 315.

2. Derber, *Sociopathic Society*, 5.

3. Derber, *Sociopathic Society*, 4.

4. Piketty, *Capital in the Twenty-First Century*, 292–93.

5. David Harvey, *A Brief History of Neoliberalism* (Oxford: Oxford University Press, 2007), 2.

6. Phillip Brown, Hugh Lauder, and David Ashton, *The Global Auction: The Broken Promises of Education, Jobs, and Incomes* (Oxford: Oxford University Press, 2012), 4–5.

7. Ferrara, *Palace of Ashes*, 113.

8. Brown, Lauder, and Ashton, *The Global Auction*, 5.

9. Brown, Lauder, and Ashton, *The Global Auction*, 24.

10. Piketty, *Capital in the Twenty-First Century*, 302–03.

11. Piketty, *Capital in the Twenty-First Century*, 303.

12. Piketty, *Capital in the Twenty-First Century*, 303.

13. Piketty, *Capital in the Twenty-First Century*, 334.

14. Piketty, *Capital in the Twenty-First Century*, 335.

15. Piketty, *Capital in the Twenty-First Century*, 297.

16. Piketty, *Capital in the Twenty-First Century*, 358.

17. John Ferejohn, "Rising Inequality and American Politics," in *The New Gilded Age: The Critical Inequality Debates of Our Time*, ed. David Grusky and Tamar Kricheli-Katz (Stanford: Stanford University Press, 2012), 121.

18. Ferejohn, "Rising Inequality and American Politics," 123–24.

19. Ferrara, *Palace of Ashes*, 118.

20. Ferejohn, "Rising Inequality and American Politics," 129.

21. Manza, "Unequal Democracy in America," 134.

22. Manza, "Unequal Democracy in America," 141.

23. Manza, "Unequal Democracy in America," 143.

24. Jeremy W. Peters and Rachel Shorey, "Trump Spent Far Less than Clinton, but Paid His Companies Well," December 9, 2016, http://www.nytimes.com/2016/12/09/us/politics/campaign-spending-donald-trump-hillary-clinton.html

25. Richard S. Gruner, *Corporate Criminal Liability and Prevention* (New York: Law Journal Press, 2016), 5–44.

26. Thomas J. Baldino and Kyle L. Kreider, *U.S. Election Campaigns: A Documentary and Reference Guide* (Santa Barbara, CA: Greenwood, 2011), 140.

27. Bill Moyers, introduction to *Corporations Are Not People: Why They Have More Rights than You Do and What You Can Do About It* (San Francisco: Berrett-Koehler, 2012), xi.

28. Micah Schwartzman, Chad Flanders, and Zoë Robinson. *The Rise of Corporate Religious Liberty* (Oxford: Oxford University Press, 2016), xiv–xv.

29. Derber, *Sociopathic Society*, 5.

30. Derber, *Sociopathic Society*, 6.

31. Derber, *Sociopathic Society*, 5.

32. Michael Parenti, *Profit Pathology and Other Indecencies* (New York: Paradigm, 2015), 56.

33. Ronald P. Formisano, *Plutocracy in America: How Increasing Inequality Destroys the Middle Class and Exploits the Poor* (Baltimore: Johns Hopkins University Press, 2015), 70.

34. Formisano, *Plutocracy in America*, 72.

35. Smith, *Who Stole the American Dream?*, 184 & 188.

36. Derber, *Sociopathic Society*, 5–6.

37. Formisano, *Plutocracy in America*, 22.

38. Formisano, *Plutocracy in America*, 54.

39. Formisano, *Plutocracy in America*, 13–14.

40. Angus Deaton, *The Great Escape: Health, Wealth, and the Origins of Inequality* (Princeton, NJ: Princeton University Press, 2013), 180.

41. Formisano, *Plutocracy in America*, 109 & 112.

42. Formisano, *Plutocracy in America*, 104–5.

43. Formisano, *Plutocracy in America*, 112.

44. Formisano, *Plutocracy in America*, 118–19.

45. Derber, *Sociopathic Society*, 8.

46. Derber, *Sociopathic Society*, 15–17.

47. Parenti, *Profit Pathology and Other Indecencies*, 59.

48. Parenti, *Profit Pathology and Other Indecencies*, 59–60.

49. Parenti, *Profit Pathology and Other Indecencies*, 63.

50. Parenti, *Profit Pathology and Other Indecencies*, 60–61.

51. Theresa Brown, "Lightening Nurses' Loads," *Slate*, May 10, 2016, http://www.slate.com/articles/health_and_science/medical_examiner/2016/05/in_honor_of_nurses_week_let_s_take_action_to_reduce_how_many_patients_each.html

52. Parenti, *Profit Pathology and Other Indecencies*, 64.

53. Michael A. Hallett, *Private Prisons in America: A Critical Race Perspective* (Urbana: University of Illinois Press, 2006), 1–2.

54. Hallett, *Private Prisons in America*, 2.

55. Hallett, *Private Prisons in America*, 3–4.

56. Formisano, *Plutocracy in America*, 24.

57. Carrie Johnson, "Justice Department Will Phase Out Its Use of Private Prisons," *NPR*, August 18, 2016, http://www.npr.org/sections/thetwo-way/2016/08/18/490498158/justice-department-will-phase-out-its-use-of-private-prisons?sc=17&f=1001&utm_source=iosnewsapp&utm_medium=Email&utm_campaign=app

58. Ben Norton, "Incarceration Nation: U.S. Has Miles to Go in Ending Private Prisons, Legal Advocates Warn," *Salon*, September 7, 2016, http://www.salon.com/2016/09/07/incarceration-nation-the-u-s-has-miles-to-go-in-fixing-private-prisons-legal-advocates-warn/

59. Lauren Gill, "Trump Administration Giving Boost to Private Prison Campaign Donors, Leaked Memo Shows," *Newsweek*, January 30, 2018, http://www.newsweek.com/trump-private-prison-campaign-donors-leaked-memo-795681

60. Byron Eugene Price and John Charles Morris, *Prison Privatization: The Many Facets of a Controversial Industry, Volume 3* (Santa Barbara, CA: Praeger, 2012), 47–48.

61. Beaud, *A History of Capitalism*, 43.

62. Carl Safina, *A Sea in Flames: The Deepwater Horizon Oil Blowout* (New York: Crown, 2011), 60.

63. Mike Magner, *Poisoned Legacy: The Human Cost of BP's Rise to Power* (New York: St. Martin's, 2011), x–xi.

64. Joseph W. Weiss, *Business Ethics: A Stakeholder and Issues Management Approach* (San Francisco: Berrett-Koehler, 2014), 159–60.

65. Weiss, *Business Ethics*, 114–115.

66. Alan Neuhauser, "Judge Approves $20B Settlement in 2010 BP Oil Spill," *US News and World Report*, April 4, 2016, http://www.usnews.com/news/articles/2016-04-04/judge-approves-20b-settlement-in-2010-bp-deepwater-horizon-oil-spill

67. Parenti, *Profit Pathology and Other Indecencies*, 139.

68. Smith, *Who Stole the American Dream?*, 146–47.

69. Smith, *Who Stole the American Dream?*, 149–50.

70. Eugene R. Tempel and Timothy L. Seiler, *Achieving Excellence in Fundraising* (Hoboken, NJ: Wiley & Sons, 2016), 87.

71. Formisano, *Plutocracy in America*, 23.

72. Formisano, *Plutocracy in America*, 61.

73. Formisano, *Plutocracy in America*, 62 & 95.

74. Formisano, *Plutocracy in America*, 98.

75. Formisano, *Plutocracy in America*, 98.

76. Smith, *Who Stole the American Dream?*, 251–52.

77. Smith, *Who Stole the American Dream?*, 259.

78. https://ustr.gov/countries-regions/china-mongolia-taiwan/peoples-republic-china

79. Jagdish N. Bhagwati, Alan S. Blinder, and Benjamin M. Friedman, *Offshoring of American Jobs: What Response from U.S. Economic Policy?* (Cambridge, MA: MIT Press, 2009), 28.

80. Berch Berberoglu, *Globalization in the 21st Century: Labor, Capital, and the State on a World Scale* (New York: Palgrave Macmillan, 2010), 98–99.

81. Berberoglu, *Globalization in the 21st Century*, 99.

82. Otto Newman and Richard De Zoysa, *The American Dream in the Information Age* (New York: Palgrave Macmillan, 1999), 105–6.

83. Heffernan, *A Bigger Prize*, 269.

84. Heffernan, *A Bigger Prize*, 270.

85. Derber, *Sociopathic Society*, 78.

86. Derber, *Sociopathic Society*, 79.

87. Cochran, *Business in American Life*, 288.

88. Cochran, *Business in American Life*, 289.

89. Cochran, *Business in American Life*, 291.

90. Cochran, *Business in American Life*, 260.

91. Joel Bakan, *The Corporation: The Pathological Pursuit of Profit and Power* (New York: Free Press, 2004), 119–20.

92. Bakan, *The Corporation*, 121–22.

93. Fraser, *The Age of Acquiescence*, 303–5.

94. Fraser, *The Age of Acquiescence*, 307–9.

95. Konnikova, *The Confidence Game*, 201 & 307.

96. Konnikova, *The Confidence Game*, 321.

97. Heffernan, *A Bigger Prize*, 243–44.

98. Michael Nelson, *Guide to the Presidency and the Executive Branch*, 5th ed. (Los Angeles: Sage, 2013), 1891.

99. Nelson, *Guide to the Presidency and the Executive Branch*, 1892.

100. Nelson, *Guide to the Presidency and the Executive Branch*, 1892.

101. Deaton, *The Great Escape*, 24.

102. Akerlof and Shiller, *Phishing for Phools*, 41 & 45.

103. Akerlof and Shiller, *Phishing for Phools*, 46.

104. Peter Corning, *The Fair Society: The Science of Human Nature and the Pursuit of Social Justice* (Chicago: University of Chicago Press, 2011), 123.

105. Christopher J. Ferguson, *Media Psychology 101* (New York: Springer, 2016), 61.

106. Gayle Brewer, *Media Psychology* (New York: Palgrave, 2011), 78.

107. Mary M. Doyle Roche, "Children, Virtue Ethics, and Consumer Culture" in *Virtue and the Moral Life: Theological and Philosophical Perspectives*, ed. William Werpehowski and Kathryn Getek Soltis (Lanham, MD: Lexington Books, 2014), 89.

108. Doyle Roche, "Children, Virtue Ethics, and Consumer Culture," 88.

109. Akerlof and Shiller, *Phishing for Phools*, 82.

110. Alejo José G. Sison, *Happiness and Virtue Ethics in Business: The Ultimate Value Proposition* (Cambridge: Cambridge University Press, 2014), 88–89.

111. Frank Trentmann, *Empire of Things: How We Became a World of Consumers, from the Fifteenth Century to the Twenty-First* (New York: Harper, 2016), 684.

112. Trentmann, *Empire of Things*, 688.

113. Sison, *Happiness and Virtue Ethics in Business*, 48.

114. Piketty, *Capital in the Twenty-First Century*, 20.

115. Piketty, *Capital in the Twenty-First Century*, 21.

116. Sison, *Happiness and Virtue Ethics in Business*, 57 & 63.

117. Noam Chomsky, *Because We Say So* (San Francisco: City Lights, 2015), 94.

118. Bob Hostetler, *American Idols: The Worship of the American Dream* (Nashville, TN: Broadman & Holman, 2006), 190.

Conclusion

Moral Capital and the New Business Hero

The commons, from which the conception of the common good derives, were open collective spaces established out of an ideal notion of land stewardship that predates the development of individual and national property rights. The traditional European view of the commons as belonging to the entire community was an acknowledgment of the plentitude of God, as well as a practical way of managing common-pool resources using collective forms of organization.[1] As a theory of private property emerged from the fifteenth to eighteenth centuries, the enclosure movements that were their expression put an end to the commons as communal and semi-autonomous spaces by using the law to reutilize and reimagine them.[2] Today, land is divided into parcels, seas have boundaries, airspace comes under national jurisdiction, and human beings will be soon advancing property claims in our solar system and in the wider universe (should our species not annihilate itself first). We might revisit the medieval ideal of the commons, that is, the common good, or social arrangements conducive to ordinary people's rights and welfare, and the fulfillment of their just aspirations.[3]

Renewed emphasis on the common good might also impel us to find novel ways to cultivate human development in its richest diversity and to discover social arrangements that respect individual rights and protect social welfare.[4] The American "religion of capitalism," as it exists today, calls on us to embark on a ceaseless hunt for pleasure and acquisition, and it sanctifies a "maniacal quest for wealth at the expense of others that turns human beings into beasts of prey."[5] For this reason, the Christian Book of Revelation defines the single-minded drive for profit as service to the "beast."[6] That demonic impulse compels the corporate hustlers of our time—who are the

123

direct descendants of the whalers and sealers who plundered the seas, the gold speculators and railroad magnates who stole Native American lands, the "pioneers" who wiped out buffalo herds, and the oil and mineral tycoons who despoiled natural resources at home and abroad.

In light of that historical record, capitalism and democracy as they exist may ultimately be incompatible—at least as long as predatory, state-supported, capitalist institutions dedicated in principle to private gain, power, and dominion (and to the disenfranchisement of the majority of the American population) persist with that orientation.[7] Consider, for instance, attempts by corporations to hide the causes and effects of global warming, which undermine our prospects of surviving that looming catastrophe.[8] The necessity for a new direction seems more urgent than ever given the violence and divisiveness that the profit pathology has wrought in the United States and around the world. For these reasons, in this chapter, we consult voices from the past and present that promote management values and practices that strengthen social bonds and improve life for everyone—not just the privileged few. Our acceptance of capitalism need not mean "economic freedom always has a priority over competing conceptions of the collection and distribution of social goods, or of other responsibilities owed to employees, customers, society, and the environment."[9] Society charters corporations and permits them to conduct business only within contractually imposed limits, which could be revised to curb the excesses of American capitalism and reacquaint business with notions of corporate social responsibility.

As it stands, American culture encourages us to think more about our careers and the acquisition of goods than the cultivation of our inner lives. Our Calvinist and Puritan heritage bestows an overly pragmatic mindset that frowns upon unprofitable and "unproductive" activities, while our modern consumer culture encourages self-interest and the pursuit of pleasure and insatiable craving for the next novelty.[10] Contemporary American culture "teaches us to promote and advertise ourselves and to master the skills required for success," but it "gives little encouragement to humility, sympathy, and honest self-confrontation, which are necessary for building character."[11] The consumer marketplace "encourages us to live by a utilitarian calculus, to satisfy our desires and lose sight of the moral stakes involved in everyday decisions."[12] Conservative commentator David Brooks argues in *The Road to Character* (2015) that the competition to succeed and to win admiration is now so fierce and engrossing that self-examination is nearly impossible. Introspection can infuse life with purpose and lead to the cultivation of humility and learning. These traits are evident in "Adam II," Brook's ideal model of a psychological evolution out of the trap of narcissistic self-esteem, of "selfies," and of status updates on social media that mark the low waters of our shallow consumer culture.[13]

The development of character through contemplation and self-examination that Brooks proposes is no frivolous pursuit, for from it springs a host of positive social ramifications. As the influential psychologist Abraham Maslow wisely observed: "Sick people are made by a sick culture; healthy people are made possible by a healthy culture. But it is just as true that sick individuals make their culture more sick and that healthy individuals make their culture more healthy. Improving individual health is one approach to making a better world."[14] Healthy people are naturally motivated by growth possibilities, and once their basic needs for safety, belongingness, love, respect, and self-esteem are met, healthy individuals become self-actualized, meaning that they realize their potentials, capacities, and talents (often as a mission call, vocation, fate, or destiny), and they naturally attain a fuller knowledge and acceptance of their intrinsic nature through an "unceasing trend toward unity, integration, or synergy."[15] Self-actualizers possess superior perceptions of reality and exhibit more spontaneity, heightened problem centering, autonomy and resistance to enculturation, and detachment and desire for privacy, as well as an unusual acceptance of self, others, and nature.[16] They exhibit more democratic personality structures, experience heightened creativity, identify more with the human species, and enjoy a higher frequency of peak experiences (transcendental moments of expanded perception or insight) than those unable to realize self-actualization.[17] In other words, the psychological life of the individual is "lived out differently when he is deficiency-need-gratification-bent," versus when he is growth dominated, growth motivated, and self-actualizing.[18]

Self-actualized people adopt a "non-valuing, non-judging, non-interfering, non-condemning attitude towards others," and they cultivate a "choiceless awareness" that permits more insightful perception.[19] Self-actualizers turn boredom and restlessness into an impetus for growth, and when they reach peak experiences, values of justice, goodness, simplicity, truth, beauty and self-sufficiency emerge in their personalities. Self-actualized people are "most often compassionate and understanding and yet also more capable of righteous indignation than the average person," meaning that they "give vent to their justified indignation and disapproval more wholeheartedly and with less uncertainty than do average people."[20] For these reasons, we see how a society composed of more self-actualizers would comprehensively transform business, law, government, education, and healthcare delivery. The fact that there exists "*a kind of dynamic parallelism or isomorphism here between the inner and the outer*" means for Maslow that as a person becomes closer to his own Being or perfection for any reason, she tends to see strength and power in the world (just as depression makes the world appear less good).[21] This observation aligns Maslow with many of the world's mystical traditions, which honor the fundamentally nondual relationship between self and world.

The Hindu expression "*Tat tvam asi*" (Thou are that) from the *Chandogya Upanishad* states that relationship most explicitly.[22]

When the individual and the world move toward perfection, they become more like one another—in other words, each makes the other possible.[23] Contrariwise, when artificial needs replace authentic ones and people move away from self-actualization, then advertising, shopping, branding, and easy credit turn citizens into bored passive consumers trapped in a spend-work-consume cycle that leaves them unhappy, lonely, mentally unstable, and deeply in debt.[24] Although Maslow locates the sources of growth and humanness essentially within the person and not society, he acknowledges that cultures can either be growth fostering or growth inhibiting, and that human beings "need a framework of values, a philosophy of life, a religion or religion-surrogate to live by and understand by, in about the same sense that he needs sunlight, calcium, or love" to prevent feelings of valuelessness fostering apathy, amorality, hopelessness, and cynicism (which manifest themselves somatically, as well).[25] Having given up the possibility of improving the human species by individual psychotherapy sessions as a quantitative impossibility, Maslow championed the proper management of the work lives of human beings as a means to improve them and the world.[26]

To explore the role of work in creating a better society, Maslow studied management "as a sort of Visiting Fellow at a Non-Linear Systems, Inc. plant in Del Mar, California," where he formulated a progressive theory of "eupsychian" management that made possible higher forms of social and interpersonal organization.[27] He envisioned the "eupsychian" society that "would be generated by 1,000 self-actualizing people on some sheltered island where they would not be interfered with" and from whose experience could be extrapolated the "higher" forms of interpersonal and social organization possible in principle.[28] Whereas the term "utopian" carries connotations of something unrealizable, "eupsychian" (combining the Greek roots *eu* meaning good and *psyche* denoting mind) implies "*only real possibility and improvability* rather than certainty, prophesy, inevitability, necessary progress, perfectibility, or confident predictions of the future. I am quite aware of the possibility," asserts Maslow, "that all mankind may be wiped out. But it is also possible that it *won't* be wiped out. Thinking about the future and even trying to bring it about is, therefore still a good idea," he reasons.[29] The dominant role of business in American culture inspired Maslow to take up questions of management and leadership, and his conclusions challenge neoliberal policies and agendas currently ascendant in countries around the world (including the United States, Australia, South Africa, and Great Britain).

Maslow's path toward personal growth encourages the development of the individual through the community, the group, the team, and the workplace in the enlightened enterprise. All human beings prefer meaningful work to meaningless work, for "if work is meaningless, then life comes close to being meaningless."[30] Work should be psychotherapeutic and "psycho-gogic" (mentally stimulating), and for that to happen regressive forces that prompt individuals and organizations away from health and growth (including scarcity of goods, threats to basic need gratifications, loss or separation leading to bereavement, bad communications, suspicion, and dishonesty and lying) must be eliminated since they create toxic work environments.[31] Maslow sought to avoid any organizational situation where human dignity was overlooked, for how could "any human being help but be insulted by being treated as an interchangeable part, as simply a cog in a machine?" Truly, the only "human, reasonable, intelligible way to respond to this kind of profound cutting off of half of one's growth possibilities," argues Maslow, is by "getting angry or resentful or struggling to get out of the situation" in which one is "being exploited or dominated or treated in an undignified way."[32] We recall the repetitive and dehumanizing work on Henry Ford's assembly lines at the River Rouge factory, which even the $5 Day could not make meaningful and self-actualizing.

Under unenlightened leadership, Maslow discovered that an organization is "split up, more disassociated, less bound together, less tied together, less integrative," and its leaders tend to neurotically and compulsively need power and to use it for "overcoming, overpowering, hurting people," or for "their own selfish gratifications, conscious and unconscious, neurotic as well as healthy."[33] Unenlightened managers with considerable authority often act in ways that disregard convention, morals, and their impact on others—and power is also a strong predictor of sexual harassment because it disinhibits aggression.[34] The best managers, on the other hand, "increase the health of the workers whom they manage" (through gratification of basic needs as well as meta-needs for goodness, justice, and law), because they are "psychologically healthier people than poor managers."[35] While true that the healthier workers are to start with, the more they benefit from eupsychian management, a certain kind of democratic manager turns a profit for the firm, while making everyone in it happier and healthier by ushering them toward a holistic social synergy that recognizes mutual interdependence ("what is good for others is good for me").[36] It is "easy enough to increase profits and production and to make a good balance sheet by putting on pressure in the short run, using up reserves and strength and throwing away long-term investments, and so on," argues Maslow, as if anticipating the Jack Welchs and Al Dunlaps of the 1980s and 1990s. Enlightened managers have a "citizen's responsibility, their eupsychian responsibility" to teach a single truth: "That everything in the world is related to everything else and everybody in the world is related to everybody else and everybody now living is related to everybody who is going to live in the future, and in this way we all influence one another, and we might as well know this scientifically."[37]

These synergetic (and mutually beneficial) relationships that Maslow highlights insure that whatever improves one part of the society at any point also tends to improve the rest of society, just as "whatever tends to improve the whole human being tends to improve all other human beings."[38] In the eupsychian ("healthward") society, emphasis is placed on creating the social conditions that lead to health, and on encouraging the social synergisms that are ameliorative and push society toward values of wholeness, simplicity, goodness, beauty, effortlessness, playfulness, and truth. We develop the ability to do what needs doing and to foster, protect, and enhance these values.[39] We create a better world by countering injustice, unfairness, and dishonesty wherever we find it. As Plato noted in the *Republic*, the best person to give power to in an organization is the person who does not want it. The one who seeks for power, Maslow asserts, "is just exactly likely to be the one who shouldn't have it, because he neurotically and compulsively needs power" and is apt to use it "very badly; that is, use it for overcoming, overpowering, hurting people."[40]

In American business, antagonisms traditionally arise from class differences between upper and lower managers, as well as in other groups in the organization where strong/weak, superior/inferior, dominant/subordinate variables persist.[41] Ultimately, though, no business enterprise or society can be truly efficient unless superior people are freely chosen and elected to run it by other people. For any culture to work, it must possess the ability to admire, to follow, and to choose the most efficient leader, as well as the capacity to detect factual superiority.[42] When it can do so, a minimum amount of antagonism and hostility exists towards superiors elected to lead. Healthy people "have no need for power over other people; they don't enjoy it, they don't want it, and they will use it only when there is some factual need in the situation for it."[43] Growing out of pathology and into health takes away "all the necessities for power over other people," thus automatically changing the whole philosophy of management and leadership in positive ways, even absent any conscious effort to do so.[44] Under eupsychian management, corporate policy satisfies higher needs in the work environment (in a nonmonetary way) by creating work situations that intrinsically bring about higher needs realization conducive to self-actualization and therefore to better performance.[45] Our current system does not allow accounting for gains made under enlightened policy in terms of "value" on balance sheets, and so redefining profit would necessarily involve redefining what is meant by "cost" and "price."

Chapter 4 highlighted a significantly higher rate of pathology among American corporate leaders than in the general population, and it pointed out that in the current political environment, business leaders increasingly nominate themselves and finance their own campaigns. Those realities suggest the presence of psychological and social factors of regression in American society. To become healthy, business organizations require a steady supply of fairly well-matured and well-educated personalities, and thus Maslow proposed a tax against enterprises that eroded the effects of political democracy and those that make their people "more paranoid, more hostile, more nasty, more malevolent, more destructive, etc."[46] Simply put, when business organizations commit sabotage against society, they should be made to pay for it. Constructing a culture that encourages people to develop in ways that promote the goodness and health of society is the primary challenge facing the United States in this century, but it will be met more easily now that we understand that unhealthy individuals create unhealthful societies, whereas mentally healthy, self-actualized people make good societies that promote the well-being of the citizenry.

Maslow concedes that his vision for eupsychian business may be idealistic, but he recognizes the possibility for gradual change resulting from the simultaneous effort of institutions and subinstitutions in society, and he appreciates the need for hard work and commitment to bring it about.[47] His acknowledgment of the synergistic nature of our social relations to one another and the environment suggests that spiritual—not consumer—values advance self-realization and bring society closer to ideals of justice. Should our species survive centuries of pillaging the earth's resources, practices that have marred the capitalist experiment since its inception, the day will come when our ruinous environmental practices will seem uninformed and primitive. Like the enlightened salesmen who understands that dishonesty destroys business, Maslow's approach to making a better society, wherein people may live more complete and meaningful lives, is a practical necessity in the twenty-first century.

Peter Drucker recognized the possibility for business to acquire moral capital through changes in management and a rededication to social responsibility. Drucker, regarded by many as the founder of modern management, explained that at around 300 to 1,000 employees, businesses needed management because a variety of tasks had to be performed with cooperation, synchronization, and communication. "Management is *tasks*. Management is a *discipline*," but management "is also *people*."[48] A manager sets objectives, organizes, motivates and communicates, measures, and develops people, including himself or herself. Whether one "develops subordinates in the right direction, helps them to grow and become bigger and richer persons, will directly determine whether he or she will develop, will grow or wither, become richer or impoverished, improve or deteriorate."[49] The best managers command respect and demand exacting work of themselves and others; they consider what is right (and not who is right) and value integrity over intelligence. The manager who lacks these qualities of character, Drucker declares, "no matter how likeable, helpful, amiable, no matter, even, how competent or brilliant—is a menace who is unfit to be a manager."[50] Indeed, the "one qualification the manager cannot acquire but must bring to the task" is character.[51]

Management, for Drucker, is a liberal art: "liberal" because it deals with the fundamentals of knowledge, wisdom, and leadership, and an "art" because of its practice and application. Good management draws on the "knowledge and insights of the humanities and social sciences—on psychology and philosophy, on economics and history, on ethics as well as the physical sciences."[52] Because management and managers fulfill important social functions embedded in governmental and political systems (and in values, customs, and beliefs) that shape culture and society, management can never be a "value-free" science.[53] Drucker conjectured that management might someday become the discipline and practice through which the humanities might "again acquire recognition, impact, and relevance."[54] While that return of prestige to the liberal arts has yet to materialize, in his view the "profit motive and its offspring, maximization of profits," are fundamentally "irrelevant to the function of a business, the purpose of a business, and the job of managing a business. In fact, the concept is worse than irrelevant: it does harm."[55] The true measure of an enterprise and its management rests in satisfied customers, healed patients, and learned students—and not in the quality of its output or "bottom line" alone.[56] Because management has a vested self-interest in a healthy society, its first job is to anticipate its social impact—coldly and realistically—and ask itself: "Is what we do right, in the best interest of the customer and society?" If not, then "it is the responsibility of the company to educate the customer and society so that the negative impact can be eliminated." For any society to prosper, it must have engines of capital formation, but Drucker also understands that a "healthy business, a healthy university, a healthy hospital cannot exist in a sick society."[57]

As long as management thinks in terms of the maximization of shareholder wealth, it will fail to make rational decisions with respect to its social responsibilities, and it will be unable to explain those decisions to others inside and outside of business.[58] It behooves business to work to secure the right kind of regulation and not avoid it altogether. Drucker held management accountable for the performance of their institutions, and for the welfare of the community as a whole through a "commitment, conviction, and dedication to the common good" by business leaders.[59] The reasons for adopting such an altruistic stance are not moral so much as practical, because businesses that knowingly do harm to society end up endangering their own long-term survival. To be legitimate, management must be held accountable for its actions. In adopting such a position, Drucker stands at odds with Milton Friedman, who sought to loosen corporations from all interests save those of shareholders. Friedman's appeals for economic freedom and self-interest may have won out so far, but Drucker's legacy includes an ongoing concern with social responsibility and corporate flourishing in contemporary business ethics.

The application of the word "management" to the governing organ of an institution or business enterprise is an American innovation, and if today's corporate managers are to commit to business integrity (as it is being taught in undergraduate and graduate programs), then they must be persuaded their commitment will not undermine personal or organizational success—but actually contribute to it. Unfortunately, a preponderance of short-term bottom-line thinking in contemporary business continues to pose a challenge to those who correctly link profitability and ethics.[60] That situation may be changing, observe ethicists Ronald Green and Aine Donovan, as a result of a dramatic increase in the level of corporate misconduct over the last three decades:

> From CEOs and CFOs to mid-level managers, the 1980s mantra "greed is good" seemed to have been an accepted rule of thumb. Two or three years of federal prison and the mandatory fine of several million dollars often left convicted business leaders still wealthy beyond the average person's wildest dreams. The risk, it seemed, was worth the reward, but with the increasingly negative image that business was gaining came the call for the introduction of ethics training in the workplace and in the curriculum of business schools.[61]

The fact that business students cheat more than any other group out of all academic disciplines may point toward a need for ethics training at the tertiary level, particularly since ethical problems often start in school and are carried into the corporate environment.[62] Some of those who advocate for "stockholder thinking" nevertheless believe that corporate responsibility requires more from business leaders than maximizing shareholder satisfaction, and comprehensive "moral thinking" by corporations means embracing a fiduciary responsibility to stockholders while maintaining broader obligations to stakeholders, for example by managing "the organization with attention paid to its qualified or conditional responsibilities to advance human dignity and a just community."[63] The creation of wealth is a critical value by which businesses should be measured, but it is one among many.

As Maslow and Drucker show, and contemporary business ethics affirm, nothing but limited conceptions of profit keeps businesses from becoming value-creating institutions managed to promote the interests of all stakeholders. Providing meaningful work and a living wage are pertinent business values, and those who manage with organizational integrity foremost in mind can remain realistic about human nature, while understanding that uprightness is achieved by assuming that people will do the right thing.[64] Establishing a good moral climate in the workplace insures compliance with substantive and widely held moral principles, including fairness, avoidance of bias, and the inclusion of employee voices in the governing rules of the organization.[65] Similarly, when a considerable number of journalists and business ethicists believe executive compensation is so high that it challenges social norms of fairness, we must understand that corporate leaders are "being rewarded unfairly at the expense of the rest of the employees and perhaps also at the expense of stockholders."[66] If a CEO sees her organization as a means to personal enrichment, instead of as a cooperative enterprise involving everyone in the organization, then she might feel entitled to outsized rewards. Following such faulty logic explains why "people in higher income brackets are much more likely than those with lower incomes to say that individuals get rich primarily because they work hard," rather than on account of factors such as "luck or being in the right place at the right time."[67] Critics note that compensation committees composed primarily of other CEOs set executive remuneration and that many of their members suffer from "cognitive bias toward overvaluing their personal contributions and of blaming their shortcoming on either others or impersonal forces beyond their control."[68] Greed, a character flaw, affects the moral climate of an organization and of society more broadly.

Milton Friedman correctly predicted a return to the cold calculus of the marketplace, and he argued accordingly that the sole social responsibility of a business was to deploy its resources and engage in activities designed to increase its profits—so long as it operated openly, freely, and without deception or fraud.[69] Some who heeded Friedman's call for a renewed focus on revenue, and who advocated for freer markets and less government regulation, conveniently ignored the economist's caveat about observing transparency, avoiding trickery, and adhering to the "rules of the game." As a result of that omission, Wall Street executives garnered outrageous salaries and scandalous perks, and business tycoons, chasing bottom-line efficiency, embodied the vaunted success symbols of American society. In my estimation, the election of Donald Trump, a crude narcissist and remorseless property speculator, to the highest office in the land heralds the beginning of a cultural shift away from the uninhibited avarice that has characterized American business culture from the 1980s onward. A new business hero is taking shape, and this leader resists greed and egoic self-aggrandizement for the sake of the common good. In place of the psychopathic job slashers of the late twentieth century, the very best CEOs of the next generation, we may hope, will put the short-term and long-term interests of their companies, and of human beings, before mere profit.

Ray Anderson, the founding chairman of Interface Inc., foreshadows that kind of enlightened leadership. In his book on profits, people, and purpose in business, Anderson writes that global enterprise and industry must radically change their ways just to survive. We need to transition away from "an old and dangerously dysfunctional model to a far better one that will operate in harmony and balance with nature—thrive in a carbon-constrained world, and put down the threats of global climate disruption, species extinction, resource depletion, and environmental degradation."[70] The old business model of pillage worked when the earth was mistakenly thought a repository of endless resources, but today that "take-make-waste" business economy deserves to be relegated to the steam age. Anderson boldly calls for "nothing short of a vast, ethically driven, redesign of our industrial system—a new industrial revolution that corrects the many things the first one got wrong."[71] The old view holds that businesses exist to make a profit, when in fact their leaders must find a higher purpose than the bottom line. What CEO, the late author asks, "expects to stand before her or his Maker someday and talk about share-holder value? Or market share? Or the clever manipulation of a gullible public?"[72]

Anderson's vision for business may sound hopelessly naïve to some, but that assumption would be mistaken. After growing his company into a world leader in modular carpeting over twenty years (with more than a billion dollars in sales annually), before his death in 2011 Anderson set Interface on a course to become the first enterprise in history to achieve true sustainability (with a goal of zero environmental impact by 2020)—while increasing profits. That audacious plan meant shutting down Interface smokestacks, closing effluent pipes, making carpets from recyclable materials, eliminating landfill scrap, and taking nothing from the earth not easily renewed.[73] Those sagacious moves gave Interface a competitive edge by proving a powerful marketplace differentiator. Costs went down as profits rose, because a strong environmental ethic has no equal for attracting and motivating good people.[74] In addition to his many other accolades, *Time* magazine called Ray Anderson a "Hero of the Environment," *US News* hailed him as "America's Greenest CEO," and *Fortune* twice named Interface among the "100 Best Companies to Work For."[75] Anderson's use of religious language to describe his journey to discovering the interconnectedness of life is compelling. It includes an "epiphany," an experience derived from reading Paul Hawken's *The Ecology of Commerce* (1993), and "confessions" of ecological mistakes. Hawken repeatedly calls for a "higher purpose" in business than profit. Members of groups such as Social Venture Network (established in the 1980s) share a similar vision, and they support innovative entrepreneurs and business leaders who contribute to the well-being of their employees, their customers, their investors, their communities, and the environment.[76]

The dearth of just work—I invoke John Ruskin here—and an increase of labor contingency (that is labor on demand) are alarming causes for great concern; as technology in the workplace continues to displace jobs, we face an employment crisis of potentially unparalleled proportions. Advances in computer engineering such as self-driving vehicles (able to operate nonstop and more safely than human beings) will bring tremendous efficiency gains, but they will put millions of people out of work in the coming decades. Given the current economic environment, financial rewards for technological innovation will most likely be concentrated in a few hands, thus only exacerbating income and wealth inequality. Highly skilled professionals will also find themselves suddenly obsolete as technology develops exponentially more quickly than our conscience. Robotic surgery, for instance, will supplant surgeons in the operating room and perform more procedures with fewer errors, and trained medical staff will lose jobs to automated laboratories, android patient attendants, and robotic cleaning crews. In a just society, the financial rewards for the development of laborsaving technologies would be more evenly distributed, for example through universal basic income programs that provide a basic standard of living at sustenance levels. Such moves would also grant citizens more time to raise children and enjoy life, and massive retraining projects could prepare them to contribute meaningfully to society in different capacities.

As it stands, shortsighted business practices and a lack of government support will relegate many people to the ranks of the underemployed or working poor, and as more Americans sink into poverty, they pull national prosperity down with them. Human beings are more sensitive to loss than to gain, and happiness is not "found" so much as synthesized out of feelings, life satisfaction, and conformity to the normative ideal of the good life.[77] The unemployed report much lower levels of happiness than their employed counterparts, and jobless people suffer higher incidences of depression, anxiety disorders, loss of self-esteem, strained personal relationships, addiction, suicide, and mortality due to poor general health.[78] That is to say, work uplifts the spirit, and the creation of just work is the entrepreneur's most important contribution to social welfare and the common good. Just work aligns our aptitudes and talents with tasks or jobs that society needs performed, and it engages our interests, purposes, and most distinctive capacities.[79] Whether pleasant or unpleasant, useful or destructive, just work prompts deeper reflection regarding the meaning of life. For this reason, providing self-actualizing and meaningful work, which leads to personal growth and social amelioration, should be the first priority of good businesspeople and sensible policy makers.

Choosing how one will work invites the construction of a framework of values that makes sense of the demands and rewards of workaday life, and as a result one's labors are more ably conceived in an interpretive context that provides meaning.[80] Without such a structure, "a job is just a job." It might offer self-support and the means to meet other obligations (including those of family dependents), but just work is a calling and source of fulfillment and devotion facilitated by managers dedicated to social responsibility. How people work together to satisfy their present desires affects the aspirations they have later on, and what kinds of people they will become, observes the philosopher John Rawls.[81] These and other positive outcomes of just work suggest that leaders of business enterprises and social institutions do well to make decisions with some view of human good in mind—and to design their organizations to realize it. More than freedom of occupational choice, just work involves "equality of opportunity, and fair distribution of resources" in an economic system that "molds as it also constrains and directs" individual choice, and secures self-respect for citizens and protects individual rights.[82]

A just society observes the core values of equality and freedom, and it ensures nondiscrimination in the distribution of jobs, keeps careers open to talented individuals, and allows everyone a fair opportunity to compete for positions. In such a health-oriented culture, people retain the right to quit and change jobs as they please, and all forms of physical coercion in the workplace are banished. Regardless of the work that one performs, a guaranteed income of the highest sustainable level allows citizens of the ideal state to concentrate their energies on raising families, caring for the sick and elderly, and pursuing constructive hobbies and interests. In any society, ideal or actual, the question of what to do with those unwilling to work, who have little compunction about freeloading off those preferring labor as a lifestyle or expression of personal responsibility, poses a real dilemma (since it seems to violate the principle of social reciprocity).[83] Reimagining the nature of work, therefore, presents significant challenges, but we know the alternative: ongoing layoffs, continuing downsizing, outsourcing to low-wage areas, loss of job security, wage stagnation, and poorer working conditions in the United States and around the world.

While escaping work altogether may remain a far goal for some, just and self-actualizing work is achievable when business enterprises and social institutions operate in synchrony with the common good in view. Only a few jobs will prove a perfect fit for each of us; nonetheless, we can address work conditions in creative and sensible ways that do not undercut productivity—for example, by restructuring repetitive and physically arduous or dangerous work in ways that render it more suitable to human capacities and energies.[84] Sharing or rotating jobs that do not carry internal rewards might guard against a human tendency to render people who perform the worst work socially invisible, and limiting such jobs to shorter workweeks, allowing flexible schedules, and instituting clear regulations on overtime offer promising opportunities for moving toward just work. Because no job should consume one's entire life, tempering the value of work "protects against the abuse of that value in the name of practices that are exploitative, an abuse to which the [Protestant] work ethic is particularly prone."[85] Quakers, like other Protestant groups, stressed the importance of cultivating a direct relationship with God, and they made work a form of pious worship and an occasion to serve the Lord not for profit, but for perfection. In this manner, all their labor—whether it involved great craftsmanship or the drudgery of everyday chores—was consecrated.[86] Until the shared benefits of labor-saving technologies mean that we can all work less, and more meaningfully, we might follow the Quaker example and recognize that happiness does not depend on what we have, or what we do—as much as who we become.

In flow, or the psychology of optimal experience, we find a formulation of the value of work that recognizes people are happiest when they become completely involved, focused, or immersed in an activity—a state of mind reflected in expressions such as being "in the zone," "in the groove," or "in the pocket."[87] Flow describes attention to a task so complete that nothing else matters to the individual—not food, time, or the self. In a state of flow, every action, movement, and thought follows inevitably from the previous one, like playing jazz, so that one's entire being is engaged in the activity and every skill is used to the utmost. As the ego falls away, the activity becomes intrinsically (rather than extrinsically) rewarding, bringing with it self-forgetting and a sense of ecstatic nonduality. Experienced in many different domains of life, one enters flow at work with the development of the ability to direct attention or mental energy toward activities at which one excels. Recent interest in mindfulness in the workplace (for its physiological and psychological benefits) offers the potential of using flow psychology to render work more meaningful and engaging, and flow can also be integrated into management practices for greater social impact.[88] At its best, flow fosters growth in skill and ability and adds richness to consciousness and personality, thus spurring one towards self-actualization.

Psychologist Mihaly Csikszentmihalyi, who named the psychological concept of flow, recognizes that for much of history, "the great majority of people who lived at the periphery of 'civilized' societies had to give up any hope of enjoying life in order to make the dreams of the few who had found a way of exploiting them come true."[89] Unlocking the potential of flow inside and outside of the modern workplace provides a unique opportunity for the development of autotelic personalities (in which curiosity, persistence, and humanity emerge), thereby making possible the enjoyment of otherwise daunting working conditions. Redesigning jobs to incorporate flow activities (as much as possible) improves quality of life through work by training people to hone their skills, to recognize opportunities for action, and to set reachable goals that contribute to optimal experience.[90] Jobs become autotelic (having a self-contained goal or purpose) when they resemble games that provide variety, appropriate and flexible challenges, clear goals, and immediate feedback, which make work more enjoyable regardless of the worker's level of development.[91]

By contrast, passive entertainment depletes energy that people could use to focus on complex goals, but which gets squandered instead "on patterns of simulation that only mimic reality."[92] Such "consumer-citizens" are passive observers who often accept national politics as another form of reality television entertainment. Chronically restless, unsatisfied, anxiety ridden, and in a state of arrested psychological development, these people cycle through endless rounds of consumption—not for spiritual awakening but for fleeting sensations that satiate one discontent only to seed another.[93] To construct a postconsumerist and postdesire culture, we cast off political systems rooted in capital accumulation that rely upon a psychology of delayed gratification, as well as those based on mass consumption, oriented toward instant gratification, and sustained by "a psychology of arrested adolescence and moral indifference."[94] The lures of consumer culture infiltrate "the lowest depths of proletarian life" and translate material goods into a kind of "psychic balm" that promises personal liberation and reinvention, but actually only makes tolerable a state of permanent wage labor and declining social mobility.[95]

By revising roles for corporate leadership, shifting managerial attitudes away from profit, changing the moral climate of business, emphasizing corporate social responsibility and sustainability, and creating just work that facilitates flow, the self and society are positively transformed. When a young man asked Thomas Carlyle how to make the world better, the Scottish philosopher jeered: "Reform yourself. That way there will be one less rascal in the world."[96] Of course, we should encourage re-use, cradle-to-cradle product design, recycling, and greater fuel efficiency as positive contributions to a better world, but those efforts do little to curb the appetites of "consumer-citizens" for material goods. For this reason, changes in lifestyle and in the workplace, which boost psychological health and lower demand for products and resources, are fundamental to effecting enduring change. If neoliberals continue to frame public debate in terms of freedom of choice, markets, and the sovereign consumer unopposed, then positive forms of "liberal paternalism" that nudge people (and corporations) toward more sustainable behaviors will fall short of the sweeping cultural transformation that happens when those ideas become embedded in social norms and expectations.[97] To that end, Americans might take more active roles in social movements that encourage cities and states to provide material infrastructure and promote higher standards of living for everyone—and support those movements that foster an appreciation of the pleasures that derive from deeper and longer-lasting connections to fewer things.[98]

Because American civic-based, civil society movements date back at least to the colonists' refusal to import British goods in the 1760s and 1770s (most famously at the Boston "Tea Party"), activism might be regarded as a moral obligation of citizenship. During the nineteenth century, slave-produced goods were shunned by conscientious buyers around the nation, and in the twentieth century many movements for racial and social justice effectively used boycotts to foster social reformation. From roughly 1890 to 1940, agrarian populism, good-government progressivism, and New Deal experimentalism emerged out of a more expansive view of the role of government, and even in our own era of small government, ethical consumerism and investment are part of "shopping for a better world."[99] Positively stated, the power of civil society movements underscore that we are not locked into a neoliberal future, as civil rights legislation, the formation of Medicare, and the creation of the Environmental Protection Agency demonstrate. On the other hand, since there is nothing inherent in twenty-first-century economies that requires them to become fairer or more egalitarian,[100] Americans must decide if increasing income inequality since the 1980s is acceptable—and if not, what mix of institutional reforms should be directed at countering it. The United States remains a country of egalitarian promise, a land of opportunity for millions of immigrants from humble backgrounds, observes Thomas Piketty, but it is also a nation of extremely brutal inequality, especially in regards to race.[101]

We began this study by noting the transformative potential of capitalism and illustrating how in each epoch it has been a creative and destructive social, political, and economic force. At the moment, capitalism functions simultaneously on a local, regional, national, and worldwide scale with a hierarchical system that "covers the five continents, a world market, multinational groups, and international indebtedness."[102] Capitalism is a factor for unification and standardization, for better transportation, faster communication, and easier exchange, but it also accentuates inequalities, differences, and disparities that bring proletarianization, urbanization, a wage payment system, and "unification of consumption objects with productive processes and ways of living."[103] Through greater control of scientific research and its applications, huge corporations have markedly multiplied their creative and destructive potential. For the first time in human history decisions affecting the species and life on earth are being made by business enterprises with enormous financial, technical, and industrial resources at their disposal.[104] The survival of the human species and the ecological balance of the planet are imperiled. Before it is too late, the exploitative excesses of our model of capitalism must be restrained.

The new global economy (globalization) brought immense hopes regarding the eradication of poverty, particularly in emerging nations, but it also fostered massive inequality (highlighted by the fact that some people are now as rich as countries).[105] In an ideal world, a progressive global tax on capital—not on income—would restore equilibrium to the dynamics of wealth accumulation. Perhaps short of that unrealistic expectation in the current political and social environment, taxes (regional, national, or continental) might be essayed. In Piketty's view, a progressive global tax on capital would expose wealth to democratic scrutiny, a necessary condition for effective regulation of the banking system and international capital flows, and it would "promote the general interest over private interests while preserving economic openness and the forces of competition."[106] A progressive tax would also help children to gain equal access to education (regardless of their parents' income) and insure healthcare for everyone, while eliminating poverty in the elderly through public pensions. Forms of welfare benefits such as these are subjected to intense interrogation in Europe and the United States, where they are conflated with people "living on the dole," when in actuality the sums involved in providing such safety nets constitute a very small part of state social spending.[107]

Since the anxieties of globalization weigh heavily on the least skilled workers in wealthy countries, a globally progressive tax system would permit everyone to benefit from internationalization.[108] It would integrate taxes on income, inheritance, and capital for all taxpayers, and reach a compromise between incentive logic (favoring a tax on capital stock) and insurance logic (favoring a tax on revenue resulting from capital) for business.[109] As for the historical antecedents of progressive taxation, during the twentieth century, the United States innovated the confiscatory tax on excessive incomes and fortunes, and it was the first nation to attempt raising tax rates above 70 percent, initially on income between 1919 and 1922 and then on estates from the years 1937 to 1939.[110] The top American income tax rate rose to 79 percent in 1937, and the Victory Tax Act of 1942 raised it further to 88 percent, before it peaked out at 94 percent in 1944 (due to various surtaxes). All told, "over the period 1932–1980, nearly half a century, the top federal income tax rate in the United States averaged 81 percent," compared with around 37 percent during the Obama administration.[111] According to estimates by Piketty and his colleagues, the optimal top tax rate in developed countries is probably above 80 percent on incomes over $500,000 or $1 million a year, which would "drastically reduce remuneration at this level but without reducing the productivity of the US economy, so that pay would rise at lower levels." Taxes would have to approach 50 to 60 percent on incomes above $200,000 for the country to invest more in education and healthcare while reducing the federal deficit. All of these social policies remain "well within the reach of the United States."[112]

In addition to progressive taxation, we should not neglect the importance of government investment in industry and infrastructure as a means of boosting economic growth. Hedrick Smith cites the Erie Canal, the transcontinental railroad, the moon landing, and the Internet as historical examples of government spending that benefited the private sector.[113] Moreover, the partnerships required by large infrastructure projects spur domestic job creation, help regenerate manufacturing, and expand exports. For this reason, London School of Economics professor Anthony Atkinson champions technological innovation and public policies that encourage the employability of workers in humane jobs, and he places responsibility on governments for targeting and reducing unemployment and guaranteeing work to all who seek it. Atkinson envisions a national pay policy that includes a living minimum wage and a capital endowment (minimum inheritance) paid to all American citizens in adulthood.[114] The reduction of economic inequality that would follow should facilitate equal access to opportunity—a key feature of modern democratic societies. Lower levels of poverty and inequality challenge improvement of social problems such as sickness and crime, and they are more compatible with democracy and in line with widely held conceptions of the good society.[115]

Corporate tax havens offer another opportunity for meaningful financial reform. When Steve Jobs died in 2011, the world mourned him as a brilliant entrepreneur and designer, yet Apple under his leadership excelled at avoiding billions of dollars in federal taxes, along with taxes in California and more than twenty other states. Nonetheless, Jobs's net worth was estimated at $8 billion at the time of his death (highlighting a pattern of lavishly compensated executives examined in previous chapters).[116] Many Americans resent vast accumulations of wealth at the expense of the public good, which corporate taxes are supposed to support in return for access to national markets and infrastructure (without which the exchange of goods would become impossible). Tax havens, like those used successfully by Apple to avoid paying federal and state taxes, should be closed. Imagine that by 2016 the largest fifty American companies stashed away more than a trillion dollars in foreign tax havens, thereby evading an estimated $111 billion in federal taxes *per year*.[117] The insurgent populist bid by Bernie Sanders in 2016 was propelled by a long-simmering public discontent concerning current levels of income and wealth inequality, and it augurs well for the formation of new social movements to counter pro-business initiatives emanating from the Trump White House.

Education reform must stand at the center of attempts to jolt the United States out of its neoliberal rut, and no effort should be spared to equip workers with the skills that they need to succeed in an age of intense global competition for human resources (which drives down wages for professional and nonprofessional workers). In higher education, the United States continues to fall behind other leading nations in STEM fields, as well as in support for humanities disciplines. Science and the humanities remain vital to national competitiveness as countries around the world develop their own "world-class" universities. In our knowledge-driven global economy, expertise in science and technology is crucial, but "unless there is a steep change in education combined with quality job opportunities that enable students to utilize their technical knowledge, more of the jobs in knowledge-intensive fields will migrate to Asia regardless of cost differences."[118] I wrote *Palace of Ashes* (2015) to address the crisis in American higher education and direct readers to that volume for a more in-depth treatment of the topic. Suffice it to say, state and federal funding of higher education propelled more equally shared prosperity following World War II, a positive trend that endured until the Reagan presidency.

Increased wage inequality in the United States is due in part to a failure to invest sufficiently in higher education, and if that tendency continues, social mobility will decline further as income increasingly determines access to higher learning.[119] Already, too many Americans fail to receive necessary training due to the high cost of tuition, even though educational investment reduces inequality, raises productivity, and makes the country more globally competitive.[120] Those now attending American institutions of higher learning graduate with historically unprecedented levels of student indebtedness, a consequence of extremely high tuitions and fees used to pay for administrative bloat, excessive executive compensation, and campus beautification initiatives. The adjunctification of the faculty and the failure to pay part-time faculty members a living wage, a travesty of social justice taking place on campuses across the country, is another symptom of the casualization of labor that begs redress.

From its inception, American culture has proven highly accommodating to business and commercial enterprise, and at various times it made merchants, entrepreneurs, and tycoons cultural icons and accorded them positions of considerable social stature. In the desire for profit, however, lurks the pale face of avarice that esteems the accumulation of capital above the dignity of human life. The history of American forced labor and slavery testifies to the worst excesses of the mercantile impulse embedded in capitalism. When American business culture actively promotes Friedman-like values of shareholder interest above others, then those in enterprise are given lease to see the world in terms of self-serving aspirations of acquisition at any cost, and from such a base, we get payday loans and easy credit at exorbitant interest rates to exploit the poor, dubious financial products designed to prey on the elderly, the dumping of harmful chemicals into the environment, and junk-bond schemes that generate wealth by defrauding investors. These and other sociopathic business practices have devastating consequences on millions of people left behind by self-interested business leaders and politicians who continue to support neoliberal policies as fewer citizens share in the nation's wealth.

Finally, despite the mad dash for more, there are things (as everyone realizes) that money cannot buy. While intense concentrations of capital generate poverty and shrink the middle class, beyond a certain point (about $70,000 per year in 2013), additional income does almost nothing to improve happiness (though those with more money report having better lives). Material riches offer scant protection from anxiety, fear, sorrow, illness, or death, for instance, nor are they "required to experience the happiness and enjoyment of everyday life."[121] Throughout most of human history, there was "no inequality, at least within groups of people who lived together and knew each other. Inequality is one of the 'gifts' of civilization."[122] The consequences of inequality are readily apparent in the United States, where life expectancy that once ranked in the middle among wealthy nations is now second to the bottom, and Japan—which was last in 1950—now ranks first. African Americans and Hispanics continue to endure the highest levels of poverty, meaning they do not have enough to fully participate in society, their families and children are not able to live lives in which people do not have choose between buying groceries or pharmaceuticals, and they are not able to meet the social standards of decency.[123]

Social and economic inequality tell us something important about the sense of justice in a country, as do the tangible consequences of wealth inequity: poor health, falling educational achievement, higher crime rates, increased obesity, weaker friendships, and greater violence.[124] Nobel Prize–winning economist Joseph Stiglitz finds it intriguing that relatively poor Mauritius, a small island nation off the east coast of Africa, manages to provide free healthcare and higher education for all its citizens, along with free transportation for its youth and elderly, "when the United States seemingly says it can't afford them." In fact, we can provide these services to all Americans, according to Stiglitz, and investments in them would make our country stronger, but it remains "a matter of *choice*, a reflection of priorities—priorities set by a political process where disproportionate weight is given to the interests and views of the top."[125] If we are paying attention, investment in people pays dividends, as Mauritius demonstrates.

To transform the United States from an impersonal society into the "more perfect union," which has always been a part of the nation's promise, political and business leaders need to reconsider what constitutes a good society, rather than crafting pro-business legislation that disenfranchises competing interests. Those of us in fields of endeavor outside of business or politics should educate ourselves and others about the root causes of income and wealth inequality and its unraveling effect on the social fabric of the nation. We should demand better healthcare than that delivered by massive corporations like Columbia HCA; buy products made by socially responsible companies; insist on better state and federal funding for higher education by being active politically; vote for populist agendas; and join labor unions and campaigns for a living wage.[126] Since single-class movements tend to reproduce existing forms of oppression (even as they work for change), interclass alliances remain essential to democracy. Interacting in meaningful ways with people holding different political and economic views builds a sense of common destiny and community, and prevents the phenomenon of individuals advancing their own narrow interests through advocacy.[127]

Skeptics and cynics will counter that people are fundamentally selfish, and that the violence, pollution, warmongering, profiteering, and so-called "development" that is warming the planet are simply proof of that unfortunate truth about human nature. While true that the propensity for selfishness at the core of the mercantile mind (and perhaps rooted in human nature) is locatable to some degree in all cultures, a particularly virulent form of merchantry took shape in the West, which justified closing the commons and making land, sea, and even the very air into property to be owned, bought, sold, and used along with human resources. This mental affliction, which Hernán Cortés erroneously believed could be cured with gold, now threatens our survival and perhaps that of the planet. Yet, when we recognize the root of social discord and strife in our own minds, we make a leap out of conditioned consciousness toward a better world. We are creatures wondrously endowed with free will and the ability to live in the here-now with extraordinary clarity and receptivity, and selfishness and greed are states of consciousness that may be transformed in a variety of ways (from contemplative prayer, seated meditation, and fasting to peak experiences and psychedelic trips in clinical settings). Within each of us "lies the existential mystery of *being*," and only by remaining unconscious of that reality do we stay "trapped within an ego-driven wasteland of conflict, strife, and fear," which only seems ordinary because we have been "brainwashed into a state of suspended disbelief where a shocking amount of hate, dishonesty, ignorance, and greed are viewed as normal and sane."[128] In these dark times, we can no longer afford to remain blind.

NOTES

1. Lucy Finchett-Maddock, *Protest, Property and the Commons: Performances of Law and Resistance* (New York: Routledge, 2016), 127.

2. Finchett-Maddock, *Protest, Property and the Commons*, 119.

3. Chomsky, *Because We Say So*, 145.

4. Chomsky, *Because We Say So*, 145.

5. Chris Hedges, *Wages of Rebellion: The Moral Imperative of Revolt* (New York: Nation Books, 2015), 42.

6. Hedges, *Wages of Rebellion*, 42–43.

7. Chomsky, *Because We Say So*, 94 & 148.

8. Chomsky, *Because We Say So*, 97.

9. George G. Brenkert and Tom L. Beauchamp, *The Oxford Handbook of Business Ethics* (Oxford: Oxford University Press, 2010), 7.

10. Sison, *Happiness and Virtue Ethics in Business*, 98.

11. David Brooks, *The Road to Character* (New York: Random House, 2015), xiii.

12. Brooks, *The Road to Character*, xiii.

13. Brooks, *The Road to Character*, xi–xii.

14. Abraham Maslow, *Toward a Psychology of Being* (New York: Van Nostrand Reinhold, 1968), 6.

15. Maslow, *Toward a Psychology of Being*, 25.

16. Maslow, *Toward a Psychology of Being*, 26.

17. Maslow, *Toward a Psychology of Being*, 26.

18. Maslow, *Toward a Psychology of Being*, 27.

19. Maslow, *Toward a Psychology of Being*, 40.

20. Maslow, *Toward a Psychology of Being*, 122.

21. Maslow, *Toward a Psychology of Being*, 122.

22. Kim Knott, *Hinduism: A Very Short Introduction* (Oxford: Oxford University Press, 2016), 28.

23. Maslow, *Toward a Psychology of Being*, 95.
24. Trentmann, *Empire of Things*, 5.
25. Maslow, *Toward a Psychology of Being*, 206 & 211.
26. Abraham Maslow, *Maslow on Management* (New York: Wiley and Sons, 1998), 1–2.
27. Maslow, *Maslow on Management*, xxi.
28. Maslow, *Maslow on Management*, xxii–xxiii.
29. Maslow, *Maslow on Management*, xxiii.
30. Maslow, *Maslow on Management*, 39.
31. Maslow, *Maslow on Management*, 53.
32. Maslow, *Maslow on Management*, 62.
33. Maslow, *Maslow on Management*, 155 & 259.
34. Heffernan, *A Bigger Prize*, 97.
35. Maslow, *Maslow on Management*, 94–95.
36. Maslow, *Maslow on Management*, 95–96.
37. Maslow, *Maslow on Management*, 143.
38. Maslow, *Maslow on Management*, 125.
39. Maslow, *Maslow on Management*, 156.
40. Maslow, *Maslow on Management*, 155.
41. Maslow, *Maslow on Management*, 184.
42. Maslow, *Maslow on Management*, 182.
43. Maslow, *Maslow on Management*, 185.
44. Maslow, *Maslow on Management*, 185.
45. Maslow, *Maslow on Management*, 239.
46. Maslow, *Maslow on Management*, 75.
47. Maslow, *Maslow on Management*, 279–83.
48. Peter F. Drucker, *Management: Revised Edition* (New York: HarperCollins, 2008), 3–4.
49. Drucker, *Management*, 9.
50. Drucker, *Management*, 10.
51. Drucker, *Management*, 10.
52. Drucker, *Management*, 25.
53. Drucker, *Management*, 12.
54. Drucker, *Management*, 25.
55. Drucker, *Management*, 213.
56. Drucker, *Management*, 24.
57. Drucker, *Management*, 213–14.
58. Drucker, *Management*, 218.
59. Drucker, *Management*, 230.
60. Ronald M. Green and Aine Donovan, "The Methods of Business Ethics," in *The Oxford Handbook of Business Ethics*, ed. George G. Brenkert and Tom L. Beauchamp (Oxford: Oxford University Press, 2010), 33.
61. Green and Donovan, "The Methods of Business Ethics," 37.
62. Green and Donovan, "The Methods of Business Ethics," 37.
63. Kenneth E. Goodpaster, "Corporate Responsibility and Its Constituents," in *The Oxford Handbook of Business Ethics*, ed. George G. Brenkert and Tom L. Beauchamp (Oxford: Oxford University Press, 2010), 150–51.
64. Norman E. Bowie, "Organizational Integrity and Moral Climates," in *The Oxford Handbook of Business Ethics*, ed. George G. Brenkert and Tom L. Beauchamp (Oxford: Oxford University Press, 2010), 703.
65. Bowie, "Organizational Integrity and Moral Climates," 708–9.
66. Bowie, "Organizational Integrity and Moral Climates," 707.
67. Robert H. Frank, "Why Luck Matters More than You Might Think," *Atlantic*, May 2016, http://www.theatlantic.com/magazine/archive/2016/05/why-luck-matters-more-than-you-might-think/476394/
68. Bowie, "Organizational Integrity and Moral Climates," 707.
69. Friedman, *Capitalism and Freedom*, 133.

70. Ray C. Anderson and Robin White, *Confessions of a Radical Industrialist: Profits, People, Purpose—Doing Business by Respecting the Earth* (New York: St. Martin's, 2009), xiii.

71. Anderson and White, *Confessions of a Radical Industrialist*, 5.

72. Anderson and White, *Confessions of a Radical Industrialist*, 269.

73. Anderson and White, *Confessions of a Radical Industrialist*, 2.

74. Anderson and White, *Confessions of a Radical Industrialist*, 5.

75. Ray C. Anderson, *Business Lessons from a Radical Industrialist* (New York: St. Martin's Griffin, 2011), xi.

76. http://svn.org/who-we-are/about-svn

77. Sison, *Happiness and Virtue Ethics in Business*, 135.

78. Sison, *Happiness and Virtue Ethics in Business*, 155.

79. Russell Muirhead, *Just Work* (Cambridge: Cambridge University Press, 2004), 1–2.

80. Muirhead, *Just Work*, 6–7.

81. Muirhead, *Just Work*, 14.

82. Muirhead, *Just Work*, 14.

83. Muirhead, *Just Work*, 16–17.

84. Muirhead, *Just Work*, 171,

85. Muirhead, *Just Work*, 175–76.

86. David Yount, *How the Quakers Invented America* (Lanham, MD: Rowman & Littlefield, 2007), 10.

87. Sison, *Happiness and Virtue Ethics in Business*, 124.

88. Sison, *Happiness and Virtue Ethics in Business*, 126–27.

89. Mihaly Csikszentimihalyi, *Flow: The Psychology of Optimal Experience* (New York: Harper & Row, 1990), 144.

90. Csikszentimihalyi, *Flow*, 157.

91. Csikszentimihalyi, *Flow*, 152.

92. Csikszentimihalyi, *Flow*, 163.

93. Fraser, *The Age of Acquiescence*, 315 & 322.

94. Fraser, *The Age of Acquiescence*, 315.

95. Fraser, *The Age of Acquiescence*, 309–10.

96. Csikszentimihalyi, *Flow*, 191.

97. Trentmann, *Empire of Things*, 688.

98. Trentmann, *Empire of Things*, 688–89.

99. Akerlof and Shiller, *Phishing for Phools*, 140 & 151.

100. Brown, Lauder, and Ashton, *The Global Auction*, 125 & 148.

101. Piketty, *Capital in the Twenty-First Century*, 161.

102. Beaud, *A History of Capitalism*, 259.

103. Beaud, *A History of Capitalism*, 259.

104. Beaud, *A History of Capitalism*, 310.

105. Piketty, *Capital in the Twenty-First Century*, 471

106. Piketty, *Capital in the Twenty-First Century*, 471.

107. Piketty, *Capital in the Twenty-First Century*, 477–79.

108. Piketty, *Capital in the Twenty-First Century*, 497.

109. Piketty, *Capital in the Twenty-First Century*, 527.

110. Piketty, *Capital in the Twenty-First Century*, 505.

111. Piketty, *Capital in the Twenty-First Century*, 507.

112. Piketty, *Capital in the Twenty-First Century*, 513.

113. Smith, *Who Stole the American Dream?*, 383.

114. Anthony B. Atkinson, *Inequality: What Can Be Done?* (Cambridge: Harvard University Press, 2015), 237–38.

115. Atkinson, *Inequality*, 301.

116. Formisano, *Plutocracy in America*, 179–80.

117. Alexia Fernández Campbell, "The Cost of Corporate Tax Avoidance," *Atlantic*, April 14, 2016, http://www.theatlantic.com/business/archive/2016/04/corporate-tax-avoidance/478293/

118. Brown, Lauder, and Ashton, *The Global Auction*, 155.

119. Piketty, *Capital in the Twenty-First Century*, 485.

120. Piketty, *Capital in the Twenty-First Century*, 485.

121. Deaton, *The Great Escape*, 53–55.

122. Deaton, *The Great* Escape, 78.

123. Deaton, *The Great* Escape, 184.

124. Heffernan, *A Bigger Prize*, 112.

125. Joseph E. Stiglitz, *The Great Divide: Unequal Societies and What We Can Do About Them* (New York: Norton & Company, 2015), 310.

126. Derber, *Sociopathic Society*, 286–90.

127. Fred Rose, *Coalitions across the Class Divide: Lessons from the Labor, Peace, and Environmental Movements* (Ithaca, NY: Cornell University Press, 2000), 7 & 11.

128. Adyashanti, *The Way of Liberation: A Practical Guide to Spiritual Enlightenment* (Campbell, CA: Open Gate Sangha, 2012), 10.

Bibliography

Adyashanti. *The Way of Liberation: A Practical Guide to Spiritual Enlightenment*. Campbell, CA: Open Gate Sangha.

Akerlof, George A., and Robert J. Shiller. *Phishing for Phools: The Economics of Manipulation and Deception*. Princeton, NJ: Princeton University Press, 2015.

Alvarez, Alex. *Native America and the Question of Genocide*. Lanham, MD: Rowman & Littlefield, 2016.

Anderson, Ray C. *Business Lessons from a Radical Industrialist*. New York: St. Martin's Griffin, 2011.

Anderson, Ray C., and Robin White. *Confessions of a Radical Industrialist: Profits, People, Purpose—Doing Business by Respecting the Earth*. New York: St. Martin's, 2009.

Atkinson, Anthony B. *Inequality: What Can Be Done?* Cambridge: Harvard University Press, 2015.

Babiak, Paul, and Robert D. Hare. *Snakes in Suits: When Psychopaths Go to Work*. New York: HarperCollins, 2006.

Bakan, Joel. *The Corporation: The Pathological Pursuit of Profit and Power*. New York: Free Press, 2004.

Baldino, Thomas J., and Kyle L. Kreider. *U.S. Election Campaigns: A Documentary and Reference Guide*. Santa Barbara, CA: Greenwood, 2011.

Beaud, Michel. *A History of Capitalism: 1500–2000*. New York: Monthly Review Press, 2002.

Belfort, Jordan. *Wolf of Wall Street*. New York: Bantam, 2007.

Berberoglu, Berch. *Globalization in the 21st Century: Labor, Capital, and the State on a World Scale*. New York: Palgrave Macmillan, 2010.

Bevington, David, ed. *The Complete Works of Shakespeare*. New York: HarperCollins, 1992.

Bhagwati, Jagdish N., Alan S. Blinder, and Benjamin M. Friedman. *Offshoring of American Jobs: What Response from U.S. Economic Policy?* Cambridge, MA: MIT Press, 2009.

The Bible: Authorized King James Version. Oxford: Oxford University Press, 2008.

Blackford, Mansel G. *A History of Small Business in America*. Chapel Hill, NC: University of North Carolina Press, 2003.

Blake, William. "Milton: A Poem." In *The Complete Poetry and Prose of William Blake*, ed. David Erdman. Princeton, NJ: Princeton University Press, 1991.

Bowie, Norman E. "Organizational Integrity and Moral Climates." In *The Oxford Handbook of Business Ethics*, ed. George G. Brenkert and Tom L. Beauchamp, 701–24. Oxford: Oxford University Press, 2010.

Brading, A. *Miners and Merchants in Bourbon Mexico 1763–1810*. Cambridge: Cambridge University Press, 1971.

Bremer, Francis J., and Tom Webster. *Puritans and Puritanism in Europe and America, Volume One.* Santa Barbara, CA: ABC-CLIO, 2005.

Brenkert, George G., and Tom L. Beauchamp. *The Oxford Handbook of Business Ethics.* Oxford: Oxford University Press, 2010.

Brewer, Gayle. *Media Psychology.* New York: Palgrave, 2011.

Brinkley, Douglas. *Wheels for the World: Henry Ford, His Company, and a Century of Progress.* New York: Viking, 2003.

Brooks, David. *The Road to Character.* New York: Random House.

Brown, Meredith Mason. *Frontiersman: Daniel Boone and the Making of America.* Baton Rouge: University of Louisiana Press, 2008.

Brown, Phillip, Hugh Lauder, and David Ashton. *The Global Auction: The Broken Promises of Education, Jobs, and Incomes.* Oxford: Oxford University Press, 2012.

Carnegie, Andrew. *The Gospel of Wealth and Other Timely Essays.* Eastford, CT: Martino Fine Books, 2010.

Chaucer, Geoffrey. *The Canterbury Tales by Geoffrey Chaucer.* New York: Houghton Mifflin, 2000.

Chernow, Ron. *Titan: The Life of John D. Rockefeller, Sr.* New York: Random House, 1998.

Chomsky, Noam. *Because We Say So.* San Francisco: City Lights, 2015.

Cochran, Thomas C. *Business in American Life: A History.* New York: McGraw-Hill, 1972.

Conrad, Joseph. *Heart of Darkness.* New York: St. Martin's, 1989.

Cooke, D.J., Adelle E. Forth, and Robert D. Hare. *Psychopathy: Theory, Research and Implications for Society.* New York: Springer Science, 1997.

Cooper, Helen. *Oxford Guides to Chaucer: The Canterbury Tales.* Oxford: Oxford University Press, 1996.

Corning, Peter. *The Fair Society: The Science of Human Nature and the Pursuit of Social Justice.* Chicago: University of Chicago Press, 2011.

Csikszentimihalyi, Mihaly. *Flow: The Psychology of Optimal Experience.* New York: Harper & Row, 1990.

Csikszentmihalyi, Mihaly. *Good Business: Leadership, Flow, and the Making of Meaning.* New York: Viking, 2003.

Deaton, Angus. *The Great Escape: Health, Wealth, and the Origins of Inequality.* Princeton: Princeton University Press, 2013.

Derber, Charles. *Sociopathic Society: A People's Sociology of the United States.* New York: Routledge, 2013.

Drucker, Peter F. *Management: Revised Edition.* New York: HarperCollins, 2008.

Durant, Will. *The Age of Faith: A History of Medieval Civilization—Christian, Islamic, and Judaic—from Constantine to Dante: A.D. 325–1300.* New York: Simon and Schuster, 1950.

Eby, Clare Virginia. *Dreiser and Veblen: Saboteurs of the Status Quo.* Columbia MO: University of Missouri Press, 1998.

Egerton, Clement, ed. *The Golden Lotus: Volume Four.* New York: Routledge, 1959.

Ellis, Bret Easton. *American Psycho.* New York: Vintage, 2010.

Ferejohn, John. "Rising Inequality and American Politics." In *The New Gilded Age: The Critical Inequality Debates of Our Time,* ed. David Grusky and Tamar Kricheli-Katz, 115–30. Stanford, CA: Stanford University Press, 2012.

Ferguson, Christopher J. *Media Psychology 101.* New York: Springer, 2016.

Ferrara, Mark S. *Barack Obama and the Rhetoric of Hope.* Jefferson, NC: McFarland, 2013.

Ferrara, Mark S. *Palace of Ashes: China and the Decline of American Higher Education.* Baltimore: Johns Hopkins University Press, 2015.

Finchett-Maddock, Lucy. *Protest, Property and the Commons: Performances of Law and Resistance.* New York: Routledge, 2016.

Fishwick, Marshall William. *The Hero, American Style.* New York: D. McKay Co., 1969.

Formisano, Ronald P. *Plutocracy in America: How Increasing Inequality Destroys the Middle Class and Exploits the Poor.* Baltimore: Johns Hopkins University Press, 2015.

Franklin, Benjamin. *The Autobiography and Other Writings.* New York: New American Library, 1961.

Fraser, Steve. *The Age of Acquiescence: The Life and Death of American Resistance to Organized Wealth and Power*. New York: Little, Brown, and Company, 2015.

Friedman, Milton. *Capitalism and Freedom*. Chicago: University of Chicago Press, 1962.

Geisst, Charles R. *Beggar Thy Neighbor: A History of Usury and Debt*. Philadelphia: University of Pennsylvania Press, 2013.

Giraldez, Arturo. *The Age of Trade: The Manila Galleons and the Dawn of the Global Economy*. Lanham, MD: Rowman & Littlefield, 2015.

Goodpaster, Kenneth E. "Corporate Responsibility and Its Constituents." In *The Oxford Handbook of Business Ethics*, ed. George G. Brenkert and Tom L. Beauchamp, 126–60. Oxford: Oxford University Press, 2010.

Gordon, John Steele. *The Business of America*. New York: Walker & Co, 2001.

Grassby, Richard. *The Business Community of Seventeenth-Century England*. Cambridge: Cambridge University Press, 1995.

Green, Ronald M., and Aine Donovan. "The Methods of Business Ethics." In *The Oxford Handbook of Business Ethics*, ed. George G. Brenkert and Tom L. Beauchamp, 21–45. Oxford: Oxford University Press, 2010.

Greenwood, Andrea, and Mark W. Harris. *An Introduction to the Unitarian and Universalist Traditions*. Cambridge: Cambridge University Press, 2011.

Gregg, Dorthy. "John Stevens: General Entrepreneur." In *Men in Business: Essays in the History of Entrepreneurship*, ed. William Miller, 120–152. Cambridge: Harvard University Press, 1952.

Grizzard, Frank, and D. Boyd Smith. *Jamestown Colony: A Political, Social, and Cultural History*. Santa Barbara, CA: ABC-CLIO, 2007.

Gruner, Richard S. *Corporate Criminal Liability and Prevention*. New York: Law Journal Press, 2016.

Hagstrom, Robert G. *The Warren Buffett Way*. Hoboken, NJ: John Wiley & Sons, 2005.

Hall, Stuart. "The Question of Cultural Identity." In *Modernity and Its Futures: Understanding Modern Societies*, ed. Stuart Hall, David Held, and Tony McGrew, 273–325. Cambridge, UK: Polity Press, 2003.

Hallett, Michael A. *Private Prisons in America: A Critical Race Perspective*. Urbana, IL: University of Illinois Press, 2006.

Handlin, Oscar. "The Development of the Corporation." In *The Corporation: A Theological Inquiry*, edited by Michael Novak and John W. Cooper, 1–16. Washington, DC: AEI Press, 1981.

Harvey, David. *A Brief History of Neoliberalism*. Oxford: Oxford University Press, 2007.

Hedges, Chris. *Wages of Rebellion: The Moral Imperative of Revolt*. New York: Nation Books, 2015.

Heffernan, Margaret. *A Bigger Prize: How We Can Do Better than the Competition*. Philadelphia: PublicAffairs, 2014.

Herman, Arthur. *Freedom's Forge: How American Business Produced Victory in World War II*. New York: Random House, 2012.

Holton, Woody. *Abigail Adams: A Life*. New York: Atria, 2010.

Hostetler, Bob. *American Idols: The Worship of the American Dream*. Nashville, TN: Broadman & Holman, 2006.

Hunt, Edwin S., and James Murray. *A History of Business in Medieval Europe, 1200–1550*. Cambridge: Cambridge University Press, 1999.

Isaacson, Walter. *The Innovators: How a Group of Hackers, Geniuses, and Geeks Created the Digital Revolution*. New York: Simon & Schuster, 2014.

Jackson, Kenneth T. *Crabgrass Frontier: The Suburbanization of the United States*. Oxford: Oxford University Press, 1985.

Knott, Kim. *Hinduism: A Very Short Introduction*. Oxford: Oxford University Press, 2016.

Konnikova, Maria. *The Confidence Game: Why We Fall for It . . . Every Time*. New York: Viking, 2016.

Krishnamurti, Jiddu. *Total Freedom: The Essential Krishnamurti*. New York: HarperOne, 1996.

Krooss, Herman E., and Charles Gilbert. *American Business History*. New York: Prentice-Hall, 1972.

Kupperman, Karen Ordahl. *The Jamestown Project*. Cambridge, MA: Belknap, 2007.

Kupperman, Karen Ordahl. *Providence Island, 1630–1641: The Other Puritan Colony*. Cambridge: Cambridge University Press, 1993.

Kwolek-Folland, Angel. *Incorporating Women: A History of Women and Business in the United States*. New York: Palgrave Macmillan, 2002.

Lane, Wheaton J. *Commodore Vanderbilt: An Epic of the Steam Age*. New York: Alfred Knopf, 1942.

Lawson, Russell M. *The Sea Mark: Captain John Smith's Voyage to New England*. Hanover, MA: University Press of New England, 2005.

Lightfoot, Kent G. *Indians, Missionaries, and Merchants: The Legacy of Colonial Encounters on the California Frontiers*. Berkeley: University of California Press, 2005.

Lloyd, Gordon. *The Two Faces of Liberalism: How the Hoover-Roosevelt Debate Shapes the Twenty-First Century*. New York: M&M Scrivener, 2006.

Lowe, Janet. *Jack Welch Speaks: Wit and Wisdom from the World's Greatest Business Leader*. Hoboken, NJ: John Wiley & Sons, 2006.

Magner, Mike. *Poisoned Legacy: The Human Cost of BP's Rise to Power*. New York: St. Martin's, 2011.

Manza, Jeff. "Unequal Democracy in America." In *The New Gilded Age: The Critical Inequality Debates of Our Time*, ed. David Grusky and Tamar Kricheli-Katz, 131–60. Stanford, CA: Stanford University Press, 2012.

Maslow, Abraham. *Toward a Psychology of Being*. New York: Van Nostrand Reinhold, 1968.

Means, Howard. *Money and Power: The History of Business*. New York: John Wiley & Sons, 2001.

Muirhead, Russell. *Just Work*. Cambridge: Cambridge University Press, 2004.

Nasaw, David. *Andrew Carnegie*. New York, Penguin, 2006.

Nelson, Michael. *Guide to the Presidency and the Executive Branch*, 5th ed. Los Angeles: Sage, 2013.

Newman, Otto, and Richard De Zoysa. *The American Dream in the Information Age*. New York: Palgrave Macmillan, 1999.

Olk, Paul. "Lessons from U.S. History for the 21st Century Corporation: The Changing Structure of Organizations and Role of Managers." In *Good Business: Exercising Effective and Ethical Leadership*, ed. James O'Toole and Don Mayer, 72–83. New York: Routledge, 2010.

Ornstein, Allan. *Class Counts: Education, Inequality, and the Shrinking Middle Class*. Lanham, MD: Rowman & Littlefield, 2006.

Parenti, Michael. *Profit Pathology and Other Indecencies*. New York: Paradigm, 2015.

Piketty, Thomas. *Capital in the Twenty-First Century*. Cambridge, MA: Belknap, 2014.

Price, Byron Eugene, and John Charles Morris. *Prison Privatization: The Many Facets of a Controversial Industry, Volume 3*. Santa Barbara, CA: Praeger, 2012.

Riddle, John M. *A History of the Middle Ages, 300–1500*. Lanham, MD: Rowman & Littlefield, 2016.

Robertson, James Oliver. *American Myth, American Reality*. New York: Hill & Wang, 1980.

Robinson, James M., ed. *Nag Hammadi Library in English*. Leiden, Netherlands: Brill, 1990.

Roche, Mary Doyle. "Children, Virtue Ethics, and Consumer Culture." In *Virtue and the Moral Life: Theological and Philosophical Perspectives*, ed. William Werpehowski and Kathryn Getek Soltis, 77–94. Lanham, MD: Lexington Books, 2014.

Rose, Fred. *Coalitions across the Class Divide: Lessons from the Labor, Peace, and Environmental Movements*. Ithaca, NY: Cornell University Press, 2000.

Rosner, Brian S. *Greed as Idolatry: The Origin and Meaning of a Pauline Metaphor*. Grand Rapids, MI: Eerdmans, 2007.

Roy, David Tod, ed., *The Plum in the Golden Vase or, Chin P'ing Mei: The Gathering*. Princeton, NJ: Princeton University Press, 1993.

Roy, David Tod, ed., *The Plum in the Golden Vase or, Chin P'ing Mei: The Rivals*. Princeton, NJ: Princeton University Press, 1993.

Saikaku, Ihara. *The Life of an Amorous Woman and Other Writings*. New York: New Directions, 1969.

Safina, Carl. *A Sea in Flames: The Deepwater Horizon Oil Blowout*. New York: Crown, 2011.

Samuel, Lawrence R. *The American Middle Class: A Cultural History*. New York: Routledge, 2014.

Sawyer, John E. "Entrepreneur and Social Order." In *Men in Business: Essays in the History of Entrepreneurship*, ed. William Miller, 7–22. Cambridge: Harvard University Press, 1952.

Schwartzman, Micah, Chad Flanders, and Zoë Robinson. *The Rise of Corporate Religious Liberty*. Oxford: Oxford University Press, 2016.

Shammas, Carole. "The Revolutionary Impact of European Demand for Tropical Goods." In *The Early Modern Atlantic Economy*, ed. John J. McCusker and Kenneth Morgan, 163–85. Cambridge: Cambridge University Press, 2001.

Sison, Alejo José G. *Happiness and Virtue Ethics in Business: The Ultimate Value Proposition*. Cambridge: Cambridge University Press, 2014.

Slack, Charles. *Hetty: The Genius and Madness of America's First Female Tycoon*. New York: Harper Perennial, 2005.

Smith, Hedrick. *Who Stole the American Dream?* New York: Random House, 2013.

Stevenson, Laura Caroline. *Praise and Paradox: Merchants and Craftsmen in Elizabethan Popular Literature*. Cambridge: Cambridge University Press, 2002.

Stiglitz, Joseph E. *The Great Divide: Unequal Societies and What We Can Do About Them*. New York: Norton & Company, 2015.

Stiles, T. J. *The First Tycoon: The Epic Life of Cornelius Vanderbilt*. New York: Alfred A. Knopf, 2009.

Stovall, Floyd. *American Idealism*. New York: Kennikat, 1943.

Tempel, Eugene R., and Timothy L. Seiler. *Achieving Excellence in Fundraising*. Hoboken, NJ: Wiley & Sons, 2016.

Trentmann, Frank. *Empire of Things: How We Became a World of Consumers, from the Fifteenth Century to the Twenty-First*. New York: Harper, 2016.

Tolle, Eckhart. *The Power of Now*. Vancouver, BC: Namaste, 2004.

Van Cleve, John Walter. *The Merchant in German Literature of the Enlightenment*. Chapel Hill: University of North Carolina Press, 1986.

Veblen, Thorstein. *The Higher Learning in America: A Memorandum on the Conduct of Universities by Business Men*. Baltimore: Johns Hopkins University Press, 2015.

Veblen, Thorstein. *The Theory of Business Enterprise*. New York: Augustus M. Kelley, 1965.

Villette, Michel, and Catherine Vuillermot. *From Predators to Icons: Exposing the Myth of the Business Hero*. Ithaca, NY: ILR Press, 2009.

Wallach, Janet. *The Richest Woman in America: Hetty Green in the Gilded Age*. New York: Doubleday, 2012.

Watts, Steven. *The People's Tycoon: Henry Ford and the American Century*. New York: Knopf, 2005.

Weiss, Joseph W. *Business Ethics: A Stakeholder and Issues Management Approach*. San Francisco: Berrett-Koehler, 2014.

Wiesner-Hanks, Merry E. *Early Modern Europe, 1450–1789*. Cambridge: Cambridge University Press, 2006.

Williams, Eric. *Capitalism and Slavery*. Chapel Hill: University of North Carolina Press, 1994.

Wood, Gordon S. *The Americanization of Benjamin Franklin*. New York: Penguin, 2005.

Wyllie, Irvin G. *The Self-Made Man in America: The Myth of Rags to Riches*. New Brunswick: Rutgers University Press, 1954.

Yount, David. *How the Quakers Invented America*. Lanham, MD: Rowman & Littlefield, 2007.

Index

About the Author

Mark S. Ferrara is the author of several books including *Palace of Ashes* (2015) and *Sacred Bliss* (2016). An associate professor of English at State University of New York, Ferrara has taught for universities in South Korea, in China, and on a Fulbright Scholarship in Turkey. His work has been reviewed in publications such as the *Washington Post, China Daily,* and *Inside Higher Education.*